RAILWAY STATIONS
OF THE
NORTH EAST

RAILWAY STATIONS
OF THE
NORTH EAST

K. HOOLE

DAVID & CHARLES
Newton Abbot   London   North Pomfret (VT)

British Library Cataloguing in Publication Data

Hoole, K.
  Railway stations of the North East.
  1. Railways—England, Northern—Stations
  —History
  I. Title
  385'.314'09428   TF302.G7
  ISBN 0-7153-8527-5

Typeset by Typesetters (Birmingham) Ltd,
Smethwick, West Midlands,
and printed in Great Britain
by Redwood Burn Limited, Trowbridge, Wilts
for David & Charles (Publishers) Limited
Brunel House Newton Abbot Devon

Published in the United States of America
by David & Charles Inc
North Pomfret Vermont 05053 USA

CONTENTS

To my late wife, Jennifer,
who assisted with much of this work

PREFACE

'There is nothing in a railway which demands such serious attention as the stations, both as to their numbers, position, and the mode of constructing them. The number and situation will of course be mainly determined by the nature and extent of the surrounding population; and the first step should be to get a good map of all the places within the sphere of the railway, and to mark upon it the population of each place from the last parliamentary census: bearing in mind that taking, for the present, railway travelling to be twice as fast at half the cost of coach travelling, that a very wide portion of the country will receive the benefit of a long line.

There is no doubt but that the greater the number of stations, the more the travelling will increase; for it has always been hitherto found that the quick and cheap transit by a railway has not only increased the already existing traffic, but has actually created it where no traces could be found of it before. The nature of the produce, and the state of trade should also be taken into account in determining both the number and the situation of the stations.

The minor stations along the line may be divided into two classes. The first might consist of merely one room, serving for office and waiting-room, where nothing but passengers and small parcels are sent either up or down. Such stations would do for small villages or points where only a limited traffic is expected. We do not, however, recommend these, although they are used on several railways. The other class should be a house containing an office, waiting-room in common, or which is better, one for each class of passengers, ladies' waiting-room, and two rooms for the inspector of police to reside in, a small office for the police, and a porters' room. To this would have to be added, if water was required to be pumped, a steam engine, and the requisite room for the engineer, a locomotive engine house when necessary, and a covered space for holding spare carriages, trucks, horseboxes, &c, together with the requisite sheds, and an office for the goods department.

The entrance to the station should be protected from the weather, so that when carriages drive up, the passengers can alight under shelter, and there should be a platform next the railway, about the same height as the carriage floors, so that the passengers can walk into the railway carriages without having to climb up the steps. Arrangements should be made, for the passengers who are going into the carriages to go all in upon one side, and those going out should get out from the other side; for which purpose the entrance should be on one side of the railway, and the exit on the other side. A light roof should be thrown over both lines of rails and their stages; in fact, the passengers should be entirely under cover from the time of leaving the vehicles which bring them to the station, till the time the train takes them away. This occasions very little expense, and is a great addition both to health and comfort.

For such a station two clerks would be required, one for passengers, parcels, and private carriages, the other for goods. An inspector, and about four policemen, with porters, according to the extent of the traffic, would probably be sufficient; the whole should be well lighted up with gas, if it can be conveniently got; and it would much conduce to the comfort of the passengers, particularly ladies, if a decent female attended in the waiting-room, and had for sale pastry, biscuits, or sandwiches, with lemonade and ginger beer.'

P. A. Lecount in RAILWAYS, published in 1839

1

INTRODUCTION

The last North Eastern Railway public timetable was issued on 2 October 1922 and listed 629 stations owned, or partly owned, by the company, although at 16 of these stations (on the Axholme Joint, the Methley Joint, and the South Yorkshire Joint lines) the NER did not actually provide any of the regular passenger services. On the other two jointly owned lines – the Otley & Ilkley (four stations) and the Swinton & Knottingley (six stations) – the NER shared the workings with the Midland, although over the Swinton & Knottingley at that time there was only one NER working in each direction each day – and that in the middle of the night on the Newcastle–Bristol mail and vice versa. An odd feature of one of the Swinton & Knottingley stations – Ferrybridge – was that it was not actually situated on the Joint line, but north of the junction with the Burton Salmon–Knottingley line and thus just in NER territory. This was due to the fact that there was no suitable site south of the junction and the NER agreed to make some of its land available. The Great Central exercised running powers over the S&K.

The NER also had a share in six jointly owned stations:

Hawes and Holbeck	Joint with MR
Leeds (New) and Tebay	Joint with LNWR
Normanton	Joint with LYR and MR
Penrith	Joint with CK&P and LNWR

Thus there were 597 wholly owned NER stations at Grouping (of which 20 had just been acquired with the Hull & Barnsley Railway), although at some stations other companies paid a rental for use of the NER station. In addition there were numerous market day, private, racecourse, works, staff and excursion stations or platforms, not to mention the many stations which had become redundant over the years but which continued in railway service although not for public passenger trains.

Smallest in size were the short wooden platforms erected for staff use and not advertised in the public timetable; they were usually situated at some remote location where railway employees were required to live or work, such as the marshalling yard at Gascoigne Wood, near Selby. At another location, Joan Croft, on the main line between Selby and Doncaster, similar platforms were erected for the convenience of platelayers' and crossing keepers' families wishing to visit Doncaster on Saturdays for their week-end shopping. Largest were the stations at Newcastle with 15 platforms, closely followed by York and Hull, each with 14 platforms, although York eventually had 16.

By far the most numerous were the main line and branch line wayside stations serving a village or a market town, with an up and a down platform to handle passenger and parcels traffic, a goods yard, warehouse, and coal cells to handle the freight and mineral traffic. Some of the minor branches warranted only a single line, but even then most stations had a house for the stationmaster and his family, usually with the offices in the same building, and a goods yard. In NER days each station had its own stationmaster but economies forced the LNER to put two or three adjacent stations under one stationmaster. Unlike other concerns in a similar situation it was easy for the stationmaster to join the branch train to visit the other stations under his control, and to return the same way, and he had the benefit of an internal telegraph and telephone system, even if it was rather primitive. Now, an area manager is responsible for numerous stations and he often has to visit his outlying stations and signalboxes by car or van as there is no suitable train service!

The staff at the wayside stations had to be able to turn their hand to any task, such as loading grain or potatoes in sacks in the goods yard, or loading cases of eggs, crates of rabbits (dead), or milk in 17-gallon churns at the passenger platform. Farmhands delivering the milk to the station were supposed to take it in turns to help load the milk, but swinging the heavy cans into the van required a skill which the railwayman alone was capable of acquiring through long practice, probably spilling the contents once or twice before becoming really proficient! Assistance also had to be given to the farmers' wives travelling to market with their baskets of butter, cheese, eggs, live and dead poultry etc, each passenger being allowed 60lb free of charge.

The porter at a wayside country station could have done with a course in domestic science as, depending on the stationmaster and his wife, he could be called upon to assist on wash-day, clean the windows, do the shopping, spring clean the carpets by beating them,

The station erected at Tynemouth when the Newcastle to North Shields line was extended eastwards in 1847. The passenger traffic was transferred to a new Tynemouth station when a new line along the coast was opened in 1882. (*W. Fawcett*)

or dig the garden. If he was lucky he might receive a shilling or so from the stationmaster. At the larger stations the porters had a number of duties to perform, but they always found time to meet the more important trains, positioning themselves along the platform opposite the coaches from which the most generous passengers were likely to alight, with a good tip in view.

The grade of porter-signalman meant a couple of shillings a week above the porter rate, an amount not to be sneezed at, but it often meant a reduction in staff in the never ending search for economy. However, in town or main line signalboxes which were open continuously three men would be employed on round-the-clock shifts, possibly with the help of a booking-lad or a lamp-lad. I heard recently of a lamp-lad at a main line box who was cleaning the spectacles on a semaphore signal when the signalman pulled off for an express, trapping the lad's hand. The signal was near the cabin but the signalman, on hearing the boy's cries, refused to put the signal back to danger to release his hand because he had received 'train entering section' from the box in the rear. Fortunately the stationmaster had heard what was happening and he instructed the signalman to restore the signal to danger even though it meant putting it to danger 'in the driver's face'.

At some stations the arrival of a train was looked upon as a social occasion, with the local inhabitants turning out to see who was arriving and who was departing. Scarborough station was 'infested with groups of idle youths, whose general appearance, habits and language cannot but be highly objectionable to the public. Parties of these youths who, either having no employment, or too idle to seek any, spend their time in such rude pastimes as are agreeable to their habits, an odd one or two earning a penny or two in aiding a foot-passenger with his effects', and that was in the 1890s!

North Eastern stations relied mainly on coal-gas and oil for lighting, although York had an electric power station from the 1890s, supplying arc lamps placed at strategic locations. This early power station was built outside the west wall of the station, but it was later replaced by a larger and more up-to-date installation on Leeman Road, which supplied the station, hotel, offices and yards.

At Hull the York & North Midland Railway signed an agreement in 1846 to purchase 'good pure gas' from the British Gas Light Co, but the NER commissioned a number of gasworks of its own at such locations as Alnmouth, Arthington, Castle Eden, Eaglescliffe, Ferryhill, Milford Junction, Pickering, Shildon, Thirsk, York etc. These coal-gas installations were often small, producing enough gas to supply the needs of the station and its ancillary buildings, but at some locations the signal lamps were also lit by gas. At larger installations, such as Shildon, gas was supplied to local inhabitants. Some of the gasworks were sold by the NER and developed by a local company formed to supply the town with gas; at other stations the NER closed its own works and went over to the local supply or, as an economy move, closed its works and relied on oil lamps. Many stations continued to be lit by gas until well into BR days; York, for instance, did not go 'all electric' until 1957 and Scarborough not until 1970.

Coaches were lit by oil-gas manufactured in NER works at Darlington, Hull, Leeds, Newcastle and York and gas mains with hydrants were laid between the tracks so that the gas tanks on the

0 1 2   5   10 feet

The Blyth & Tyne building at Backworth faced on to the road which crossed the line at the east end of Backworth station. Passenger facilities were later provided in a wooden building erected on the widened overbridge and on the platforms. The station was closed in 1977 ready for alterations necessary for the introduction of the Metro service. (*W. Fawcett*)

coaches could be filled as they were standing at the platforms. The gas had a distinctive smell easily discernible when entering the main stations! At out-stations where coaches needed to have their gas tanks filled this was done from rail tank wagons filled at the oil-gasworks.

Horse-drawn coaches and buses providing free transport for the patrons bound for local hotels were a feature at many NER stations, and although touting was prohibited it was practised by the hotel porters who met the trains. After World War I some hotels used their own motor buses to meet trains, but the improvement in public transport and the availability of taxis put a stop to them. Mention of hotel porters reminds me of the NER Station Hotel porters who carried luggage between the hotel and train for departing guests; they

13

were always very smart and resplendent in bright red coats to distinguish them from the station porters. I heard recently of a titled lady who marched a uniformed man into a stationmaster's office, complaining bitterly that he would not, or could not, give her information about the train she intended to catch. The stationmaster had to point out that the man was a GPO postman and not a railway employee!

The stationmasters at the top stations wore striped trousers, morning coat and top hat and these persisted well into LNER days. Some wore these clothes only on special occasions, but as a schoolboy I was always awed by the portly figure of Mr R. Ritchie, the stationmaster at Hull (Paragon) who always appeared so attired.

Some NER constituents were fortunate in being able to employ architects of note to design their stations, and later the NER's own staff architects produced some notable and functional stations, many of which are still in use. The most notable private architects were G. T. Andrews, who worked for the York & North Midland Railway, and Benjamin Green who received commissions from the Newcastle & Carlisle, and the York, Newcastle & Berwick companies. Without a doubt the most prolific designer of stations in the north east was George Townsend Andrews of York, who provided impressive stations from Hull in the south to Gateshead in the north, as well as many wayside stations, crossing-keepers' cottages, goods sheds, etc, with engine sheds and water tanks included for good measure.

Andrews is perhaps best remembered for the market town stations he designed for George Hudson and the York & North Midland Railway, with an overall roof to protect the passengers from the weather. After more than a century of use most of these roofs have had to be demolished, but Malton remains intact (although slightly modified from the original design) and it is the best example remaining in use.

In the very early days of railways there were recognised stopping places for the trains but few stations as such. Local hostelries and inns were used for shelter at some locations, but as passenger traffic developed in the 1840s better facilities were provided and purpose-built stations started to appear, such as York (1841), Darlington North Road (1842), Scarborough (1845), Whitby (1847), and Hull Paragon (1848). After 30 years some were found to be inadequate and a new generation of NER stations started to appear, such as Middlesbrough (1877), York (1877), Sunderland (1879), Alnwick

(1887), Darlington (1887), and Stockton (1893). However, where the existing station was capable of being enlarged it was not necessary to provide a completely new station and consequently some of the 1840-period stations have survived and are still handling trains. Examples are Scarborough (1845), Whitby (1847), Northallerton (1841), and even Newcastle Central (1850).

The NER had its own architect from its formation and holders of the post between 1854 and 1922 were:

Thos. Prosser	1854–1874
Benjamin Burleigh	1874–1876
Wm. Peachey	1876–1877
Wm. Bell	1877–1914
A. Pollard	1915–1922
Stephen Wilkinson	1922

William Bell, who was in charge when the second phase of station building was at its height, was also responsible for many other buildings required by an expanding railway system. By the time he became the NER architect he had been in the department for 20 years, and thus put in a total of 57 years with the company.

At Grouping very few NER branches were distinguished by having buildings to a uniform design along their length. This was because many of the branch lines were built in two or three stages, such as the Wearhead and Wensleydale branches, both constructed at three different periods. Most noticeable of the older lines with similar buildings were the Newcastle & Carlisle, with its small but handsome station houses, and the Newcastle & Berwick, which went to the other extreme and provided large and imposing edifices.

At a later date NER standard designs were favoured for some branches, such as the stepped gables of the 1860s on the Lanchester Valley and Pateley Bridge branches, and on the final section of the Esk Valley line west of Grosmont. The early 1880s saw a design featuring a two storey house built parallel to the track, flanked on each side by a projecting single storey building at right angles to the track, all built in brick. The Seamer-Pickering (1882) and Whitby-Loftus (1883) lines received this type of building and the same design was used for replacement or new stations on older lines.

A good example of standardisation appeared on the Alnwick-Coldstream line opened in 1887, where Bell provided a fine series of stations to the same basic design but differing in size according to the expected traffic requirements. Around the turn of the century

15

increased use was made of wood; existing open fronted waiting sheds were enclosed by fitting a wood and glass frontage, and some extensive waiting accommodation was provided in wooden structures with a glazed front, slated roof and brick chimney, good examples being at Ferriby and Middleton-in-Teesdale. Eventually stations were built completely of wood – buildings and platforms – such as the three stations between Selby and Goole.

The NER prepared a summary of the year's receipts and traffics at each station and issued a copy to the stationmaster so that he could judge the performance of his station, for after all he was the company's representative in the village or town. He was responsible for the running of his station and for getting traffic to be forwarded by rail. He also had to know how to load wagons so that the load did not move during its journey, how to couple and uncouple wagons and coaches – some with buck-eye couplers – the availability of the many types of tickets, rules and regulations, particularly those affecting block signalling and single line working introduced in the event of a major or minor mishap. His 'perks' were the occasional gift from grateful farmers – perhaps a chicken or a rabbit for Sunday dinner (never lunch!) – or a sack of potatoes, and there was always his coal business which brought in extra pounds. For his house he paid a rent of a few shillings a week, and if he was prepared to remain at a station for some time the company would increase the number of bedrooms to accommodate his growing family.

The NER also issued a small volume listing the villages served by each station, together with their population, and produced statistics showing the average number of journeys per head. Where a village was served by two stations the population was divided and estimated as a certain percentage using one station and the balance the other. This volume listed villages and hamlets up to twelve miles away from a station where there was no alternative NER or 'foreign' station, such as the moorland settlements north-west of Pateley Bridge, although this was exceptional and most villages were within three miles of a station.

The NER had no great suburban traffic and consequently few suburban stations. Botanic Gardens, Stepney and Wilmington at Hull were within the city boundary but the greatest local traffic was from Hessle, Ferriby and Brough in one direction, and Cottingham and Beverley in another, both warranting a regular interval service throughout the day from 1929. From outside the city there were

16

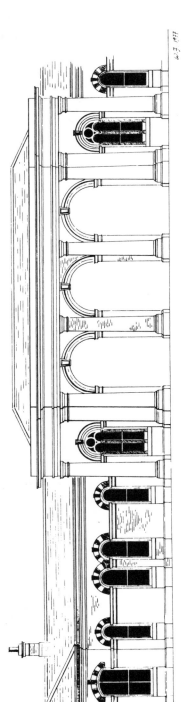

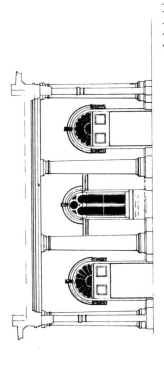

The frontage of Saltburn station, opened in 1861 and probably designed by William Peachey; fifteen years later he became the NER Architect. Although the station is still open trains no longer use the original building, which is currently being restored by a private developer. It is a Grade II listed building. (*W. Fawcett*)

season ticket holders from Withernsea, Hornsea and Bridlington. At Leeds, Cross Gates and Headingley were two sources of revenue but here it was the Harrogate traffic that was the most important, with influential passengers who quickly complained if the service was not to their liking.

The only real suburban service was in the Newcastle area, where the NER electrified the North Tyneside loop in 1904 to counteract the loss of passengers to the electric trams. In addition to developing the traffic in the inner areas such as Jesmond and Gosforth, the clean and speedy electric services to the coast developed the coastal area, with busy stations at Tynemouth, Cullercoats, Whitley Bay and Monkseaton. The line to South Shields was electrified in 1938 but now both north and south Tyneside areas are now served by the Tyneside Metro system.

The number of stations in Yorkshire, Durham and Northumberland formerly served by the NER is now down to 119, but this includes seven former Joint stations (Leeds, Burley-in-Wharfedale, Ben Rhydding, and Ilkley on the Otley & Ilkley Joint, and Pontefract (Baghill), Moorthorpe and Bolton-on-Dearne on the Swinton & Knottingley Joint). Also included are stations built more recently to serve housing developments, such as Newton Aycliffe and Gypsy Lane, and to serve such industrial developments as Allens West, British Steel Redcar, and Teesside Airport.

Although station closures were brought into prominence in 1963 by Dr Beeching they have been in progress for well over a century as lines developed and new stations were built. The LNER closed a number of North Eastern Area branches in the 1930s, some quite lengthy, such as the Alnwick–Coldstream, and the closure of most of the intermediate stations between York and Scarborough illustrated what was to follow. World War II postponed the fateful day for a number of stations, but as things got back to normal and traffic decreased to its pre-war level further cuts were necessary; in 1964, the year following the publication of Dr Beeching's notable 'Reshaping of British Railways' report, 68 stations on 12 North Eastern Region branches were closed to passengers. Since then the closures have been at a slower rate but at the time of writing some lines are living on borrowed time, notably the Hull–Scarborough and Middlesbrough–Whitby services, between them accounting for 26 stations which could disappear from the timetable, but it remains to be seen what effect the 1983 Serpell Report will have.

It is only comparatively recently that attention has been given to the history, design, and role of stations. For too long attention has been focused on locomotives and how Driver A made up two minutes on the journey between X and Y. Why not look afresh at your local station and ponder why it was built where it is (or was), how and why it developed, flourished and declined, the reason for its particular design, its traffics and flow of passengers, the staffing arrangements over the years, and the many other details that concern a station? I am sure you will find it of interest.

2

FEATURES
OF THE NORTH EASTERN

A feature of North Eastern stations was the extensive use of chocolate and cream coloured enamelled signs and nameboards, introduced about 1901, to provide directions to such places as BOOKING OFFICE, LADIES, PARCELS, TELEGRAPH, GOODS OFFICE etc. In October 1901 instructions were issued to stationmasters to see that the new signs were properly washed! At the larger North Eastern stations, and at some stations off the NER – Kings Cross for instance – an attractive tile map of the NER system was affixed to a convenient wall. This was made up of 64 square tiles for the lines, eight half tiles for the title, and 46 for the border, and appear to have been introduced in 1902. A common query regarding these maps is 'Why do they show a line from Beverley into the flat lands of Holderness?' This is because at the time the maps were made the NER was considering taking over the powers of the proposed standard gauge North Holderness Light Railway; however, the scheme fell through and the company introduced its first motor buses over a similar route in September 1903. The service was included in the 1922 timetable, listing the villages served by the buses, but they can hardly be included as North Eastern stations!

Another familiar sight at NER stations was the brass model of Stephenson's *Rocket* locomotive, mounted in a glass case and with the wheels revolving if a penny was inserted. The receipts originally went to the Railway Orphanage at Derby but now go to the Railway Servants' Orphanage at Crewe. The first two were installed at York and Scarborough in October 1891 and one or two remain. That at Bridlington was converted to electric operation in 1980 by a local driver and at the present 2p a time the takings can amount to £175 a year. Penny-in-the-slot weighing machines were installed at many NER stations from 1886, with the owners paying a rent of £10 a year for the first machine and £5 each for additional machines, although at

Leeds the rates were £20 and £10 respectively. Takings could amount to £60 a year per machine in the pre-1914 period.

Scent-spray machines were installed at Leeds in 1888, at a rental of £25 a year for three sites, but they proved unsatisfactory to the NER which, in the following year, gave the owners three months' notice to remove them.

At the larger stations a weighing machine was usually placed somewhere near the booking office, with the weigh-table level with the platform; the steelyard was sometimes protected by a wooden case. This was in the charge of a porter whose job it was to weigh and charge for excess luggage. Nearby would be a supply of luggage labels, colour coded for the different railways, the labels for NER stations having black lettering on white paper. They appear to have been introduced as early as 1865. The labels were kept in specially made wooden racks measuring 4ft high by 2ft 9in wide, divided into 195 small compartments, each holding a wad of labels for one destination. The racks were probably made in one of the NER's works and they cost £2.3s (£2.15) each in 1910. In more recent times the racks have been the targets for collectors as invariably old labels could be found in the bottom of the compartments and the labels themselves have now become collectors' items.

In 1905 the NER standardised its ¼, ½, ¾ and mile posts; they were made of cast iron and were required under an Act of Parliament passed in 1845. At the same time the company introduced a matching Distance Point or Datum Post, usually known as a DP post, which

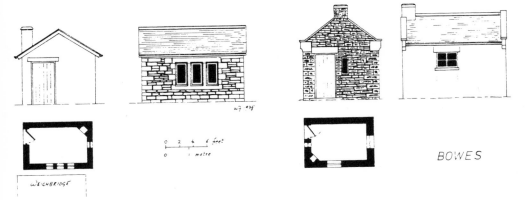

Most NER stations had a weigh house, or weigh cabin, at the entrance to the goods yard. This is the non-standard version at Bowes. (*W. Fawcett*)

had to be set up at the centre of the station buildings at intermediate stations, and at the buffer stops at terminal stations. They remain at virtually every station which is still open but York is a notable exception, where it has been missing for some years. As the Act states that 'No tolls shall be demanded or taken by the Company for the use of the railway during any time at which the boards hereinbefore directed to be exhibited shall not be exhibited' then perhaps the LNER and BR have been collecting fares illegally for the last 40 years? This would be a worthwhile exercise for A. P. Herbert's character Albert Haddock!

Before the larger stations became 'closed', ie: with ticket barriers manned by ticket collectors, tickets were often collected at ticket platforms situated just outside the station proper, where trains stopped for a few minutes for this to be done. These ticket platforms consisted merely of a wooden walkway for the staff as they moved from compartment to compartment, and there was no exit for passengers. 'Closed' stations meant the introduction of platform tickets and receipts at 1d a time could bring in more than £1000 a year at the largest stations.

In 1895 the NER introduced a Best Kept Wayside Gardens competition, with the system divided into four areas and with 15 cash prizes for each area. For the top five prizewinning stations the stationmaster received £4, with a further £2 to be divided equally amongst the staff. In 1907 the arrangements were changed to include all stations in one competition, with the top ten stations receiving a Special Class prize of £10 each 'to be divided amongst the staff at the discretion of the stationmaster'. This scheme was perpetuated by the LNER and by BR and attractive certificates were awarded to all prizewinning stations; they were often framed and hung in the waiting room, and have since become another collectors' item.

Another feature of the North Eastern was its hotels, which usually adjoined the station, although the Grand Hotel at West Hartlepool was an exception; they were at one time the best hotels in the area they served, although recently some have been criticised because of their age. For example the Royal Station Hotel at Hull was opened in 1851, the Zetland Hotel at Saltburn in 1863, and the Royal Station Hotel at York in 1878. The Zetland was sold some years ago and the other four were sold in 1983 under the Conservative Government's privatisation plans.

In LNER days the North Eastern Area engineer, John Miller (a

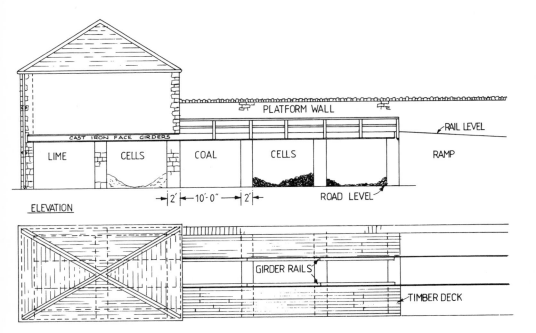

LIME CELLS COAL CELLS RAMP

PLATFORM WALL

RAIL LEVEL

CAST IRON FACE GIRDERS

ROAD LEVEL

ELEVATION

←2'←—10'-0"—→2'←

GIRDER RAILS

TIMBER DECK

PLAN

Typical NER coal cells and lime cells, with covering to the lime depot. The number of cells varied from station to station depending on the traffic. (*J. F. Addyman*)

Great Eastern man) tidied up many stations and provided concrete edging and large tubs for borders and flower displays. The tubs can still be found at long-closed stations, but the edging is much more difficult to locate as it is usually buried under weeds etc.

The NER issued some striking posters tempting passengers to visit 'The Breezy and Bracing Yorkshire Coast', 'Historic York', 'North Eastern England; The Land of Lore and Legend', or 'The Roman Wall; The Most Interesting District in Britain' but the finest posters appeared in the LNER period, from the brushes of such artists as Frank Mason, Doris and Anna Zinkeisen, Austin Cooper, Frank Newbould, Fred Taylor, Frank Brangwyn and many others. They brightened up many a drab booking hall, with their really blue skies, calm seas, sandy beaches and a bathing belle or two! Unfortunately posters were short-lived and one year's crop soon disappeared to make way for the next so that they were not fully appreciated at the time. Some fine posters were produced for BR, notably those by Terence Cuneo, concentrating more on the operation of the railway than its scenic beauties and his fine book 'The Mouse and His Maker' tells of the lengths he went to in order to get the picture exactly right. Now, alas, any posters or notices that do appear on a station are soon defaced and, in fact, many stations (particularly those that are unstaffed) do not even have details of the train service because of the attention of local vandals.

The North Eastern standardised many of its items of equipment, such as luggage barrows and platform seats, and actually issued a bound volume containing diagrams of the various types of standard (and non-standard) barrows and trolleys. Seats varied according to the class of station, the most common being one made up of three cast iron legs moulded to represent tree branches. At Scarborough, to accommodate waiting passengers, a continuous wooden seat 285ft long was built along the base of a retaining wall on Platform 1. In the 1970s this seat received little attention and it was allowed to deteriorate but now it is being repaired and repainted, but it could be a long time before there are sufficient behinds to cover its 285ft!

Clocks are synonymous with stations and the NER favoured those made by Potts of Leeds, especially for the larger stations. Many were illuminated, at first by gas but now by electricity, and many have been converted to electric operation, doing away with the need for the weekly wind. At wayside stations the clock mechanism was in the office and indicated the time on a clock face on the platform as well as in the office.

Often to be found in the vicinity of the booking office was the Telegraph Board giving details of the running of trains and their punctuality or otherwise. The blackboard was lettered in white and the details were chalked up for the information of staff and passengers. Now at some stations the same information is provided on TV screens placed adjacent to the destination indicators and at other convenient locations.

Railway stations housed bookstalls from an early date and although at one time some NER bookstalls were let to a local retailer they were eventually the monopoly of W. H. Smith & Son Ltd, with stalls at large and small stations, the latter including such stations at Beverley, Driffield, Malton, Pickering etc. Many of the smaller stalls were closed in the 1950s and 1960s but at some intermediate sized stations the stalls were taken over by the local manager as a private venture. On former Stockton & Darlington stations the Darlington firm of E. D. Walker operated the bookstalls.

Roller blind destination indicators were provided at the larger stations and the style of the wooden cases suggests that they were made in the NER's own works. At ticket barriers destination boards were suspended from a cast iron archway and the board was changed as required using a specially made tool to raise it high enough to hang on the hooks provided. When not in use the boards were stored in a purpose built cabinet.

On station platforms smaller boards were slotted end-on into holders mounted on a post so that the free end of the board pointed in the direction of the relevant train. Regular trains carried destination boards in two brackets mounted under the eaves on each side of the coach (usually those with a brake-van portion) but in 1907 there was a short lived change when the brackets were mounted on the roof just above the guttering. At terminal stations a porter was employed on reversing the boards; he would drop a window in the side away from the platform, put out an arm, reverse the board, withdraw his arm and shut the window in a movement perfected by years of experience! Another duty was the changing of the towels and the replenishment of the soap in lavatory compartments. The porter concerned carried the clean towels over his arm, the dirty towels in the same hand, leaving the other hand free to open the doors. Presumably he carried the tablets of soap in his uniform pocket.

Roof tanks serving lavatory compartments were filled from a cylindrical tank on wheels, with a hand pump fitted on one side. The hose from the tank was coupled to a fixed pipe on the coach and the water pumped up into the tank until it overflowed. These tanks were once a familiar sight and I recently came across one tucked away in a little used part of Scarborough station.

Gas was the universal form of lighting for stations and offices, but wayside stations relied on individual oil lamps at the top of wooden (later concrete) posts along the platform. The front panel of the lampcase included a small frame into which a separate glass bearing the name of the station could be inserted. Platforms were usually numbered at all except the smallest stations.

The North Eastern adopted a standard colour scheme of reddish brown and buff for its buildings, notably on wooden waiting sheds and toilets, which graced most station platforms. The LNER favoured light stone (BSS 61) or deep cream (BSS 53), and light Brunswick green (BSS 25) or deep Brunswick green (BSS 27) according to its Schedule of Colours issued in 1937. Station nameboards were black with white lettering. The NER affixed signalbox nameboards (using a small chocolate and cream enamelled sign) on the front of the cabin, making it virtually impossible for it to be read from a moving train on an adjacent line; the LNER used much larger black and white nameboards affixed at each end of the box, making the names far more readable. Lineside objects such as trespass notices etc were black and white, usually white lettering on a black background, but occasionally found with black lettering on a white background.

British Railways has used various colours, perhaps the most notable as far as the north east is concerned being the time when NE Region stations signs, timetable covers and notepaper headings all sported the same colour – tangerine! Now we have yellow mileposts and the face of the most important clock on York station is blue, making it impossible to read at a distance, whereas with the original black and white face it could be read from most parts of the station. Why such an unnecessary change?

Until 1932 consumable supplies for stations were distributed by the Stores Train, which toured the North Eastern Area. It usually consisted of three bogie vans, two of which carried such items as matches, brushes and shovels, ink, paper clips, sponge cloths etc, and the third, with built-in tanks, carried paraffin and oil. One of the vehicles had accommodation for the guard-cum-stores-issuer, who lived on the train when it was working far from its home base at Gateshead. The Stores train appears to have been introduced at an early date as a photograph exists of one on its travels in the 1870s.

At first stores were issued on demand as the train called at each station, but to save time this was altered so that each station sent in its stores requisition before the train set off from the Stores Department headquarters at Gateshead. Then it was merely a case of handing out the requisitioned items at each stop. Like many other companies the NER found it necessary to mark the items it supplied for internal use, either by affixing a small brass plate lettered NER, or embossing the same initials on the object. Even copper roof nails and pen nibs were so marked.

In the 1930s stations in the more scenic parts of the three north-eastern counties often housed two or three camping coaches, available to families for a week at a reasonable charge. They were introduced in 1933 using hurriedly converted ex-Great Northern

(opposite)⎯⎯⎯⎯⎯⎯⎯⎯⎯⎯⎯⎯⎯⎯⎯⎯⎯⎯⎯⎯⎯⎯⎯⎯⎯⎯⎯⎯⎯⎯⎯⎯⎯⎯⎯
The closure notice for internal circulation advising the demise of Eston station. (*K. Hoole Collection*)

LONDON & NORTH EASTERN RAILWAY
(NORTH EASTERN AREA)

PASSENGER MANAGER'S OFFICE .

CIRCULAR P.M.10/1929.

YORK. 5th March. 1929.

CLOSING OF ESTON STATION FOR PASSENGER TRAIN TRAFFIC.

Eston Station will be closed for passenger and parcels etc. traffic on and after Monday the 11th. instant.

The Company have entered into an arrangement with the Redwing Safety Services, Ltd. for a service of road motor omnibuses to run between Middlesbrough and Eston at the following times:-

WEEKDAYS.

Middlesbrough to Eston.	Eston to Middlesbrough.
8-40 am.	7-35 am.
9-10 am.	8- 5 am.
and every half hour to	and every half hour to
11-40 pm.	11- 5 pm.
12-10 am.	

SUNDAYS.

9-40 am.	9- 5 am.
and then same as above.	and then same as above.

Through tickets must be issued as at present to Eston and passengers advised that they can join the road service referred to at Middlesbrough Station, for Eston.

Parcels, etc. traffic and Passengers' Luggage, including P.L.A., C.L. and D.L. will also be conveyed by the road service between Middlesbrough and Eston and through booking of this traffic must also be continued.

Horse Box traffic now shewn to be dealt with at Eston Station will, in future, be dealt with at Middlesbrough and must be booked to the latter station.

All correspondence with regard to parcels, etc. traffic for Eston must be addressed to the Parcels Agent at Middlesbrough.

J. T. NAISBY,
Passenger Manager.

P.F.67,100
P.G.352/1.

six-wheel coaches in LNER teak livery. Later a standard green and cream colour scheme was adopted and after World War II bogie coaches with more and improved accommodation were available. The local stationmaster and his staff assisted the holidaymakers in the coaches under their control, supplying paraffin and making arrangements with a local farmer to supply milk, butter and eggs.

Stations and signalboxes maintained Occurrence Books, covering the happenings over the years. The strangest entry I have come across in one of these books read 'This branch was opened for traffic on 1 September 1862. Thos. Sadler was the first stationmaster and as twisted a specimen as you would find'.

It is a fact of life today that disused stations soon fall prey to vandals, and some so-called railway enthusiasts. However, in some parts of the north-east even some stations which are still open are a disgrace to BR and the local community. Neglect by BR in the face of mindless vandalism has led to stations which are filthy and unkempt and not fit for passengers to use. Waiting rooms and toilets have to be boarded up because of wanton damage; the roof – where there is one – leaks, and the station is a slum.

Now the best kept stations are those which are stations no longer! Over the last 20 years numerous stations have been sold by BR and in private hands they have been restored, renovated, repaired, improved and modernised, usually with care but occasionally with unhappy results. Some of them are now changing hands for the second or third time, at prices many times those realised when they were sold by BR. Consequently many of the smaller stations look set to remain in use for many years yet, but with no rails, no trains, and no passengers.

3

THE LARGEST STATIONS

Using the number of platforms as a criterion the North Eastern's three largest stations were Newcastle, with 15 platforms, and York and Hull each with 14 followed, surprisingly, by Scarborough with nine. Scarborough is the oldest, with much of the station dating from 1845, closely followed by Hull (1848) and Newcastle (1850); York, opened in 1877, replaced a station dating from 1841. All four are still in use although each has lost platforms as traffic has decreased.

Scarborough station, situated on a prime cross-roads site in the centre of the resort, was built during the Hudson era and designed by G. T. Andrews. It originally consisted of a train shed with the arrival platform on the north side and the departure platform on the south, with carriage sidings in between reached by means of turnplates at the inner and outer ends of the platforms. The train shed remains but now accommodates three platforms with No 3, much widened, on the site of the original arrival platform. Extensions outside the train shed provided two long platforms for excursion traffic (Nos 1 and 2) and on the south side, again outside the original train shed, four short platforms for local traffic (Nos 6, 7, 8, and 9). At the time of writing there is a plan to abandon these short platforms, to demolish the buildings, and to build a 'non-food superstore' on the site; an application for planning permission has been submitted to Scarborough Borough Council in the name of British Rail and the developer.

Although the 1845 station offices remain in use on the north side of the train shed (adjoining platform 3) accommodating the booking office, waiting rooms, stationmaster's office, etc, their external appearance facing the main thoroughfare has been greatly altered by the erection in 1884 of a fine clock tower and two large pavilions housing toilets!

The frontage has more recently been changed by the provision of shops, enquiry office and refreshment room, the latter displaced from its former location on Platform 3 by the British Rail Staff Association club rooms, which also occupy the one time small station hotel premises. The station forecourt was for many years surrounded by heavy cast iron railings, but these have been removed and replaced by dwarf walls containing flower beds. From 1906 the forecourt was the starting point for numerous summer half-day and day tours by NER motor charabancs and these were well photographed before they ceased in 1914 with the outbreak of World War I and the commandeering of many NER motor vehicles. Following the war the tours were operated by a private concern, eventually passing into the hands of United Automobile Services, which still runs the tours.

The seasonal nature of the traffic at Scarborough has long prevented the modernisation or renewal of the station, the argument being that it would be uneconomic to spend a large amount of money to provide facilities which would be used only in the short summer season and stand idle for the remainder of the year. In 1951 a scheme was announced whereby all the signalling in the area would be operated electrically, but this did not come about and it was only many years later that colour light signals were introduced piecemeal, leading to the closure of two of the four boxes controlling the main line into Scarborough (Gasworks and Washbeck) and the removal of the large gantries of lower quadrant semaphore signals dating back to NER days.

In 1934 an additional platform was built to accommodate Whitby line trains during the summer months, when the reversal necessary to get them into and out of the platforms on the south side of the station proved extremely inconvenient. The new platform, No 1A, was at the outer end of No 1 platform and could accommodate five coaches and an engine, the advantage being that the engines of trains bound for Whitby could propel the coaches out of the platform, before reversing to proceed through Falsgrave tunnel. Board of Trade regulations prevented trains being propelled out of the main platforms and from these the engine had to haul its train out of the station and then run round before setting off for Whitby. The closure of the Whitby line in 1965 made Platform 1A redundant and the track serving it has now been lifted.

Also gone is the extensive roof which covered the large cab rank adjacent to Platform 1, and the platform awnings which protected passengers boarding coaches outside the train shed; some of the awnings were brought down by heavy snowfalls and simply not replaced. The station changed from gas lighting to electric lighting in 1970 and the tower clock – the most used public clock in Scarborough

– also had its mechanism changed to do away with the weekly winding session performed by a member of the station staff.

Scarborough station, being a terminus, was difficult to work as in steam days every arriving train had to have its coaches taken to the carriage sidings by one of the local pilot engines, or propelled out by the train engine. Often the pilot engine had to remove the coaches to allow the train engine to go to the shed, and then propel them back into the platform; the pilot then had to be got out of the way so that another engine could couple on to the coaches to work the train away. At busy times, with return excursions and ordinary trains leaving every five or six minutes, it was a severe test of railway operating.

However, things were eased in 1908 with the building of a separate station for excursion traffic; this was variously known as Washbeck Excursion Station and Londesborough Road Station. It was situated just outside the 1845 station, on the north side of the line, but it had only two platforms – one bay and one through; the through platform allowed arriving trains to be unloaded and the empty coaches to be sent through Falsgrave tunnel to the carriage sidings at Northstead, where coaling, watering and turning facilities were available for the locomotives. In the evening returning excursions could be run into the through platform, quickly loaded with home-going excursionists, and despatched between trains from the 1845 station.

The last train left the excursion station on 24 August 1963, although it was not officially closed until 1966; since then part of the station has been occupied by a local grocery and bakery concern but it is still recognisable from trains entering Scarborough, with the insignificant entrance in Londesborough Road closed but virtually unchanged.

If the planned superstore gets the go-ahead at the 1845 station this will mean the demolition of the original York & North Midland goods shed, which has housed passenger traffic since the goods traffic was moved to a new goods station at Gallows Close at the turn of the century. This will leave platforms 3, 4 and 5 in the original train shed, and platforms 1 and 2 (the one-time excursion platforms) on the north-west outside the train shed.

When opened in 1845 the sole service was to and from York, joined in 1847 by the service to Hull, in 1882 by the service to Pickering, and in 1885 by the service to Whitby. The popularity of Scarborough as a holiday resort eventually led to the introduction of through trains or through coaches to and from such centres as London, Liverpool and Glasgow and although these ran chiefly during the summer months there was, before 1914, a good all-year-round service, particularly on the Scarborough-York-Leeds route. The Pickering line was closed in 1950 and the Whitby line in 1965, leaving the York and Hull services, with no access to the north except via York. Thus a rail journey from Scarborough to Whitby would now require a circular route via York, Darlington, Middlesbrough and Grosmont – 134 miles compared with 23½ miles before 1965!

The original station at Hull, opened in 1840 by the Hull & Selby Railway, was in the dock area near the River Humber and it soon became obvious that a station was required in the developing centre of the town, which was moving away from the river. By inserting connections between the Hull & Selby, the Bridlington branch (opened 1846), and the lines into the new station, it was possible to build a more spacious and more convenient centrally situated station which could accommodate both services. From 1 July 1845 the Hull & Selby was leased by the York-based York & North Midland Railway and thus came under the control of George Hudson; consequently the design of the new station was entrusted to G. T. Andrews and a tender of £51,500 for the erection of the building was accepted on 1 March 1847. The resulting station had an imposing frontage along its south side, containing the usual station offices etc, with a train shed behind, and it was opened on 8 May 1848; it was complemented by an adjoining hotel, opened in 1851, again to a design by G. T. Andrews.

As the industries and population of Hull increased, the station became too small to handle the traffic satisfactorily and in December 1902 tenders totalling £75,098 were accepted for 'alterations and additions' to the station. This involved rebuilding the old platforms and adding new, and demolishing the Andrews roof and replacing it with a new roof over old and new platforms. The new portion of the station was brought into use on 12 December 1904. The number of full-length platforms under the new roof was nine (Nos 1 to 9), with a short platform (No 10) on the south side; four further platforms on the south side, outside the overall roof and without protection of any kind, were intended for excursion traffic. At the same time a spacious booking hall was provided, moving the main entrance to the east (Paragon Square) end of the station and leaving the Andrews entrance tucked away in a backwater behind the buildings facing on to Anlaby Road. During demolition of the old roof part of it collapsed and, according to a contemporary report, 'eight workmen were more or less seriously injured after being thrown 30ft on to the line below'.

Old and New: (*above*) The last large station to be built by the North Eastern Railway was Hull Paragon, which has recently undergone extensive renovation, giving the station a new lease of life. Across the platforms there is a large circulating area, covered by two roof spans at right-angles to the five spans over the platforms. This is a 1953 view, with Coronation decorations in place. (*British Rail*); (*below*) The Metro station at Gateshead brings a change of style to the stations of Tyneside. (*Tyne & Wear PTE*)

North Road Station, Darlington: (*above*) British Rail allowed many stations to fall into a parlous state of neglect and disrepair, extremely off-putting to actual and intending passengers. This view illustrates Darlington North Road in 1973. (*N. E. Stead*); (*below*) North Road was fortunate in that it was taken under the wing of the North Road Museum Historical Trust and Darlington Borough Council, and under the supervision of a consultant architect it was sympathetically restored and carefully renovated for the Stockton & Darlington Railway 150th anniversary celebrations. (*Author's collection*)

Toilets, refreshment rooms, barber's shop etc were erected at the buffer-stop end of each pair of platform lines (2/3, 4/5, 6/7, 8/9), with ticket barriers between the buildings controlling the entrances to the pairs of platforms (1/2, 3/4, 5/6, 7/8). Although access between platforms was possible inside the barriers it was not encouraged and there were gates to prevent it; however, with the movement of staff between platforms they were often left open and closed only when a train arrived.

The Royal Station Hotel, at which Queen Victoria stayed in 1854, was extended at various times, the most extensive rebuilding and modernisation being carried out by the LNER between 1933 and 1935, making it the premier hotel in the city.

The City of Kingston-upon-Hull had a most enthusiastic Director of Museums in T. Sheppard; in co-operation with the LNER he set up a small railway museum on the station and this was opened by the City's Lord Mayor on 24 February 1933. On display were documents, photographs and models from the city's collection and the Hull & Barnsley Railway was well represented; access was from the station concourse and it was suggested that passengers waiting for trains could spend the time looking round the museum. Unfortunately it was destroyed during one of the numerous bombing attacks on Hull in World War II.

In 1929 regular interval services were introduced to Brough, Beverley, Withernsea and Hornsea, with the off-peak trains worked by Sentinel steam railcars. The basic services to Brough and Beverley were every 30 minutes at 15 and 45 minutes past the hour, with some additional Brough services provided by Selby and Goole trains, and some additional Beverley services by York and Bridlington trains. Withernsea trains ran at 40 minutes past the hour and Hornsea trains at 50 minutes past.

Hull had a number of through portions to Kings Cross, via Doncaster, and notable cross-country services to Liverpool via Doncaster, Sheffield and the GCR route, via Goole and Wakefield and the LYR route, and via Selby and Leeds and the LNWR route. Three trains left Hull for Liverpool in the space of 17 minutes – 8.55am (via GCR), 9.00am (via LNWR) and 9.12am (via LYR), all arriving in Liverpool between 12.27pm and 12.40pm, but at different stations. At some periods the trains via Sheffield and via Leeds carried restaurant cars, but the Sheffield train was reduced to a buffet car in the 1930s. Another service provided with a restaurant car was the

Newcastle–York–Hull train at 12.10pm from Newcastle, and the return working leaving Hull at 4.47pm (later 5.00pm); this train was made up of ex North Eastern corridor stock throughout.

The Kings Cross service eventually warranted Pullman facilities and from 1937 a Hull portion of the Yorkshire Pullman was joined to the main train at Doncaster. Now High Speed Trains run between Hull and Kings Cross and in May 1983 an HST power car was ceremonially named *City of Kingston upon Hull*. In 1960 the Hull–Liverpool service was concentrated on the former LNWR route via Leeds and Huddersfield, using specially built Trans-Pennine dmu sets built at Swindon, which for a time included a buffet car.

From 1924 Hull Paragon was host to the former Hull & Barnsley Cudworth trains diverted from the out-of-the-way Cannon Street station in Hull. These were cut back to Hull-South Howden in 1932 and ceased completely in 1955. The Hull to Hornsea and Withernsea services were withdrawn in 1964, and that to Market Weighton and York in 1965, leaving Hull to be served by three routes – to Doncaster (and beyond), to Leeds (and beyond) and to Scarborough.

Locomotives from other companies could be seen in Paragon station on various through services; for instance the Midland Railway worked a service into Hull from Sheffield, but this ceased in 1889; the LNWR worked in from Leeds between 1893 and 1915, and the Lancashire & Yorkshire commenced working passenger trains into Hull in 1900. The latter service survived the NER and LNER period and only ceased when taken over by diesel railcars in 1958; by then, of course, true L&Y locomotives had disappeared. Most of the NER, LNER and BR steam locomotives based at Hull and working out of Paragon station came from Botanic Gardens depot, the passenger engine shed, but some workings were taken by engines from Dairycoates shed, the freight engine depot. Now only Botanic Gardens diesel depot remains.

And what of Paragon station in the HST era? The extensive concourse remains, without a seat of any sort as I found to my sorrow the last time I was waiting for a train. But the most striking feature is the restored booking hall, part of a costly renovation programme carried out by British Rail between 1979 and 1981. Great care has been taken with the painting scheme for the booking hall, with its tiled walls and mosaic floor, making a most attractive introduction to what is the North Eastern's final major station.

Of the platforms under the roof No 1 has been removed to make way for a car park, and platforms 2 and 3 have been shortened, leaving

Nos 4–9 for the regular traffic. The gantries of NER semaphore signals protecting the exit from each platform disappeared in 1938 when Paragon box (at the end of platforms 1 and 2) and Park Street box (on the west side of Park Street overbridge) were replaced by a new electrically operated box also on the west side of Park Street bridge. The two displaced boxes had been converted from manual to electro-pneumatic operation in 1904/5.

The exterior of the station has also changed; the handsome cab shelter with its seven bays facing on to Paragon Square was reduced to six bays in 1935 to allow extensions to the hotel, but the clock tower was retained by moving it from the original south-east corner to the new corner. However, all this was swept away for the building of a new office block, Paragon House, in 1960; when completed in 1962 it accommodated the BR Hull Division offices but in 1970 the work was taken over by the Doncaster office and the accommodation at Paragon House became redundant.

Newcastle Central, the North Eastern's busiest station, was opened by Queen Victoria on 29 August 1850; it was designed by John Dobson but economy measures prevented the erection of the colonnade and portico of his original design and it was not until 1862 that a tender for a much reduced portico was accepted at £5428. This was the price the NER had to pay to get Newcastle Corporation to withdraw its opposition to the Newcastle & Carlisle/NER amalgamation, conditional upon the completion of the portico by 31 December 1863. The station has been extended on a number of occasions, the most extensive scheme being the addition of platforms 9 and 10 on the south side and platforms 1, 2 and 3 at the east end in 1893–5.

It must be remembered that although main line trains are travelling north-south the station itself is parallel to the River Tyne and thus roughly east-west. Trains for the north leave from the east end and for the south from the west end, although because of the triangular junctions at the south end of the High Level and King Edward bridges it is also possible for trains for the south to leave from the east end. No matter from which end they leave trains for the south can be routed via the Team Valley or coast lines.

Until 1894 the platforms were numbered in a haphazard way because of the piecemeal development of the station; thus in addition to platforms numbered conventionally from 1 to 9 there were platforms designated A1, A4, A5, B and C! The renumbering to 1–15 was part of the extension plan when platforms 1, 2 and 3 were fitted in at the east end to deal solely with local traffic, warranting a separate booking office and circulating area opened on 16 April 1894. These platforms came into their own when the North Tyneside system was electrified ten years later.

The extensions of the 1890s brought into being the famous 'largest railway crossing in the world' at the east end of the station, where the tracks into the station from the north end of the High Level Bridge crossed those into the station from Manors and the north. At first the lines off the High Level Bridge gave access to the parcels loading dock and all platforms at the east end of the station but on electrification access to the dock and platforms 1 and 2 was withdrawn, cutting out nine diamond crossings and restricting access to platforms 1 and 2 to trains from the Manors direction. The extensions on the south side added two through platforms, but even now Newcastle has only three through platforms as various schemes to join up bays at east and west ends have never materialised.

A station the size of Newcastle, with heavy main line and local traffic, requires a safe and efficient signalling system and an all-electric signalbox was opened in 1959. This replaced a life-expired electro-pneumatic system authorised in January 1906 at £52,600 for three boxes (east end, west end and King Edward Bridge) but this figure was increased by £36,100 with the addition to the scheme of Manors, Forth and Greensfield boxes, all three controlling the access to Central station from north, west and south respectively. When completed in 1910 the NER engineer was asked to explain the total cost of £140,572, overspending by £51,872!

The box at the east end (Newcastle No 1) was an overtrack structure with 259 levers, operating on the Westinghouse electro-pneumatic system, and this replaced a conventional box on the north side of the line, which had 244 levers. However, a National Railway Museum photograph reveals that there was an even earlier overtrack box controlling the lines at the east end. As at York there was a signalbox in the centre of the station (Newcastle No 2), and No 3 was at the west end, in the junction of the King Edward Bridge and Carlisle lines.

Until the introduction of electric trams in the Newcastle and Gateshead conurbation the North Eastern had a monopoly of local traffic but this decreased rapidly with the coming of the trams; even the electrification of the lines to Monkseaton and Whitley Bay merely allowed the NER to hold its own. Stations in the immediate Newcastle area accounted for the following figures:

PASSENGERS BOOKED

Station	1901	1911	Station	1901	1911
Bensham	153,353	69,998	Manors	989,781	565,231
Byker	100,401	28,741	Scotswood	226,677	117,431
Dunston	–	44,780	St Anthonys	32,428	11,283
Elswick	406,800	133,780	St Peters	112,636	37,111
Gateshead	915,592	775,946	Walker	172,563	37,247
Heaton	1,151,158	519,350	Walker Gate	116,487	56,278
Low Fell	36,084	26,703	West Jesmond	353,021	112,440

Newcastle Central has now virtually no interest in suburban and outer suburban traffic as it has all been handed over to the Tyne & Wear PTE to operate as its Metro system. The conversion to Metro was completed on the north bank of the Tyne in 1983 but the South Tyneside line to South Shields, due for completion in the autumn of 1983, was not ready until 1984.

The NER electric service from Newcastle Central commenced on 1 July 1904 but as at that time there was no connection between the Tynemouth line and the former Blyth & Tyne line at Manors a completely circular service could not be operated. Even when a connection between the two routes to the coast was opened on 1 January 1909 it was not until 1 March 1917 that a Central to Central service commenced, which continued until the withdrawal of electric working by British Rail; the last electric trains ran on 17 June 1967 and the workings were taken over by diesel multiple units.

The North Eastern also considered electrifying the lines on the south side of the Tyne but this was not carried out until the LNER introduced electric services between Newcastle Central and South Shields on 14 March 1938. This service had only half the life of the North Tyneside lines and electric traction to South Shields was abandoned on 7 January 1963; here too the service was taken over by DMUs.

And what of the station itself? It was described in an early account as 'one of those chef d'oeuvres of art on which the eye delights to linger' and it certainly was – and still is – an imposing station. Inside the station two sculptured medallions on the north wall feature Queen Victoria and the Prince Consort and carry the date 28th September 1849, but this was the date of opening of the High Level Bridge and for a year trains were handled at an earlier station near Manors, necessitating a reversal at the north end of the High Level. The actual opening date of the station is usually quoted as 30 August 1850 but this applies only to the York, Newcastle & Berwick trains using the east end and it was not completely opened until 1 January 1851 when the Newcastle & Carlisle trains commenced running into the west end of the station. However, the two halves of the station were separated by a barrier and had their separate entrances, each half having its own stationmaster and staff. Although the North Eastern was formed in 1854 it was 1862 before the Newcastle & Carlisle was absorbed and the station came under the control of the one company. At that time the east end accommodated four platforms and the west end only two, much of the space on the south side being taken up by sidings. Extensions in 1871 provided an island platform on the south side of the existing platforms, but at first the two faces were not 'through' platforms; this was replaced by another island platform, even further south, in the 1893–5 extensions already mentioned. This involved adding two spans to the roof, that on the south side being straight and housing platform 10 and four through sidings, with the other span being straight on its south side and curved on its north side, housing platforms 8 and 9 and two 'centre roads', which were not used for running purposes.

With the coming of the King Edward Bridge in 1906 it was possible to lead the four tracks into the existing west end layout with practically no alterations, giving the great advantage that at last the station could accommodate East Coast trains without the need for reversal.

On the south side of the station there were at one time three small engine sheds, but these appear to have been removed about 1890/1 to make way for the new platforms. As part of the same scheme the existing small turntable was replaced by a 50ft diameter turntable from Cowans, Sheldon, and a massive water tank holding 104,000 gallons was constructed; this appears in the background of many photographs taken in LNER and BR days at the west end of Central station. The turntable was removed in November 1926 and found a new home, cut down to 45ft, at Stanhope, in Weardale.

In the centre of the station the tracks are spanned by a footbridge giving access to platforms 9 and 10; this is unusual for the north east in having a ramp approach on the north side, and ramp and stepped approaches on the south side.

Between 1896 and 1945 an old colliery engine built at the nearby works of Robert Stephenson & Co stood at the east end of the island platform 9 and 10; previously it had stood in the open at the north end of the High Level Bridge. In 1945 it was removed to the Science Museum on the Town Moor.

In 1911 the staff at Newcastle Central consisted of the stationmaster, G. H. Saxby, a night stationmaster, ten assistant stationmasters, and some 700 assorted grades. In 1924 the staff had increased to 730, under the control of the stationmaster, T. C. Humphrey and three assistant stationmasters. The number of trains varied from year to year, from season to season, and from day to day, but at one time the station was handling some 750 trains a day, the busiest day of the week being Saturdays, especially those on which the miners in the surrounding pit communities were paid. Sunshine also played a large part in the amount of traffic as a fine sunny and hot Bank Holiday meant that most of the population of Gateshead and Newcastle made for the cooling breezes on the coast and the railway facilities were stretched to their limit. As a result of experience gained alternative timetables were drawn up and brought into use according to the weather!

Anyone arriving at Newcastle from the south for the first time cannot fail to be impressed by the view as the train emerges from the environs of Gateshead and crosses the magnificent King Edward Bridge, with views of sister bridges spanning the Tyne gorge to right and left. Westwards is the newly completed Redheugh Bridge (road), and eastwards is the recent Queen Elizabeth Bridge (Metro), followed by the 1849 High Level Bridge (road and rail), and beyond that the Tyne Bridge (road) opened in 1928. At a lower level is the Swing Bridge (road) of 1876, which replaced the nine-arch stone bridge built a century earlier. Then the view is gone as the train swings round to enter Central station at the west end.

Countless photographs have been taken of the east end of the station, where the ancient Castle stands in the junction between the lines to the north and those over the High Level Bridge. The view from the Castle Keep of the layout at the east end of the station is one of the best railway panoramas in the country as HST and DMU enter and leave the station, and diesel locomotive hauled freight trains pass on the goods lines on the south side of the station. Gone are the days of steam when the service required numerous light engine and empty stock movements to be fitted in with the train working, and gone also are the days of the electric trains threading their way into the station from the Manors direction, or bringing north-south traffic to a stop as they clattered over the diamond crossings, bound for South Shields.

41

And what is left? To the north there is only the main line to Berwick, Edinburgh and beyond; to the south there is the main line to York, where routes to London, Penzance and Liverpool diverge, with summer trains to Blackpool, Paignton and Yarmouth etc. Along the coast Sunderland, Hartlepool and Stockton are served by the almost hourly service to Middlesbrough, with a single HST working reversing at Middlesbrough to go forward to Kings Cross, and one DMU continuing from Middlesbrough to Whitby.

To the west the Carlisle line is still open, although the section between Newcastle and Blaydon, along the north bank of the river, was closed from 4 October 1982 and trains now run via Dunston over a section of line last used for regular passenger services in 1926. As a result of this re-routing (which did not affect any intermediate stations) the remaining bay platforms at the west end of Newcastle Central were made redundant.

'This is York' has been a familiar sound to travellers since 1927, when loudspeakers were first used at this fine station. Previously a megaphone had been used and a contemporary account records of the new system 'a controlling genius in the signalbox can call out the destination of trains in a loud, supernatural voice that rolls under the station roof'. By 1927 the station was 50 years old as it was opened on 25 June 1877, replacing the cramped 1841 terminus inside the City Walls. The 1877 station faces the exterior of the Walls and in spring the ramparts are covered with daffodils which must, over the years, have gladdened the heart of many passengers.

The 1877 station is little changed structurally since the day it opened. Lighting, signalling, refreshment rooms, toilets, etc, have all been modernised but the platforms, apart from being lengthened, and the roof, except for renewals and repairs necessary after more than a century of British weather, are virtually still the same. Platforms have been added on the west side of the station, and lost on the east side, but it is still possible to stand on the platforms and admire the curve of the magnificent roof, with the highest arch (48ft) over the through lines and platforms, and the smaller arches (40ft high) on each side over the bay platforms. An additional arch (36ft high) on the east side covers other bay platforms, but is split in two parts by the station buildings. The spans are 81ft, 55ft and 43ft respectively.

The motive power has changed, and no longer do steam locomotives emit steam, smoke and smuts, annoying passengers with the dirt and noise, although at the present time York is one of the few stations to have a regular steam worked service, namely the Scarborough Spa Express; this train, now in its third year, runs on Tuesdays, Thursdays and Sundays during the peak of the summer season.

But when York station opened steam was in complete charge, hauling six-wheel coaches on the East Coast expresses between London and Scotland, and four-wheel and six-wheel coaches on the services radiating north, south, east and west of the City. Larger coaches required larger engines, and larger trains required longer platforms, so that many of the platforms, particularly at the south end, have been extended more than once. Since the final extensions took place in the first decade of this century the length of the main up platform has been 1692ft; however, not all of this is available to main line trains because the north end curves away to serve the Scarborough branch, but this enables Scarborough–Leeds trains to stand at the north end of the platform, allowing an East Coast route train to Kings Cross to draw up in front of it at the south end of the same platform. This allows an easy exchange of passengers without using the footbridge, and because of the scissors crossover at the centre of the platform and the four tracks to Chaloners Whin junction, two miles south of the station, the trains can be despatched independently. Since 1983, Chaloners Whin junction, the divergence of the routes south to Selby, Doncaster and London, and south-west to Normanton, is a junction no more, for with the opening of the new Selby diversion line East Coast route trains now leave the Normanton route a few miles on at Colton junction.

At one time the main up platform, now numbered 8A and 8B, was also signalled and used for down East Coast expresses which, before the introduction of dining cars on ECJS trains in 1893, had to make a meal halt at York. As the large refreshment room was adjacent to platform 8 (then No 4) it was prudent to work the trains into that platform rather than No 9 (then No 5) which would have resulted in a mad scramble through the subway; the footbridge was built in 1900.

The platforms were renumbered from 26 September 1938 with the addition of platforms 15 and 16 on the west side of the station. Originally the platforms were numbered 1–7 at the south end of the station and 8–13 at the north end, with No 14 (added 1900) outside the west wall, and it was considered more sensible to have 1–8 on one side of the footbridge and 9–14 on the other. Platforms 15 and 16 are reached by an extension to the footbridge. The platforms were renumbered:

Old	New	Remarks
1	1	South end bay. Track removed.
2	2	South end bay.
3	3	South end bay.
4	8	Through. Now 8A and 8B (formerly 8S & 8N).
5	9	Through. Now 9A and 9B (formerly 9S & 9N).
6	10	South end bay.
7	11	South end bay.
8	13	North end bay.
9	12	North end bay.
10	7	North end bay.
11	6	North end bay.
12	5	North end bay.
13	4	North end bay.
14	14	Through; added 1900.
15	15	Through; added 1938.
16	16	Through; added 1938.

In the remainder of this section the new platforms numbers will be used. Platforms 4, 5, 6 and 7 cannot be used for main line trains and accommodate Scarborough branch trains starting from York (until 1960s also used by Hull and Whitby trains), and platforms 12 and 13 cannot be used for Scarborough branch trains and are used for Harrogate trains (formerly by Pickering branch trains and by main line trains to and from Darlington and the north). At the south end of the station the bay platforms can be used by any trains to the south.

The original York terminus was opened in 1841 to cater for York & North Midland trains to and from Normanton and Great North of England trains to and from Darlington, and when the station was built it was not realised how railways would develop; consequently within a few years the station was found to be too small and platforms had to be added to accommodate trains on the Scarborough branch, opened in 1845. The opening of a route to London via Knottingley and Doncaster, and to Edinburgh over the fine bridges at Newcastle and Berwick, brought more traffic but there was no space in which to expand, bounded as it was by Tanner Row and Toft Green on one side and the City Walls on the other. Some slight amelioration was brought about by lengthening the platforms but as the station was a terminus there was no getting over the inconvenience caused to East Coast trains by the need to reverse. Even trains for the Scarborough branch could not reach their correct route without a reversal outside the station.

An Act for a new station was obtained in 1866 but it was 1871 before work started in earnest on planning a new station which would fit in with the existing lines, and even then it was another three years before the advertisements for tenders appeared. The insertion of the station was accomplished successfully by diverting the lines from the south directly into the new station, and by making a connection at the north end on to the adjacent Scarborough line as it headed for the bridge across the River Ouse. The most difficult length was the connection with the line from the north, which had to diverge from the 1841 course at what is now York Yard North and swing round to the east in a large loop to enter the new station at the north end. The old main line south of York Yard North (formerly Severus Junction) to York Yard South (formerly North Junction) became the goods lines, with sidings on both sides. The only section which had to be removed was from York Yard South to the 1841 station, which cut across the south end of the new station, but the old station could still be reached from the south and remained in use for carriage storage until 1967.

At first the 1877 station handled only local traffic and the East Coast services, but the opening of the Swinton & Knottingley Joint line in 1879 opened up a new route to the south-west and through trains and coaches to various points began to develop. In addition there was heavy traffic through York to the east coast, particularly Scarborough, sometimes worked through by 'foreign' engines. Parties bound for the seaside would hire a saloon and these, together with the regular through coaches, made York a hive of industry as the station pilots transferred the vehicles from one train to another.

York, being the operating if not the physical boundary between the North Eastern and the Great Northern, saw much engine changing on trains to and from the south, but the advent of the LNER and larger locomotives reduced this as it became possible for engines to work through between London and Newcastle, or even London and Edinburgh, although many trains were remanned at York. The rapid spread of dieselisation and the 'cure' prescribed by Dr Beeching in the 1960s, followed by the introduction of High Speed Trains in the 1970s, has virtually eliminated engine changing and in 1982 York Motive Power Depot was closed. It is now possible to enter the station with not a single train in sight!

The station has a smallish portico accommodating taxis, and many of the City's buses stop outside, there being no bus station. From the portico access is given to the booking hall, with the present booking office on the left and the entrance to the refreshment room on the right; the busy enquiry office adjoins the booking office (both to be replaced by a new travel centre) and passengers enter a circulating area, with W. H. Smith's drab bookstall ahead, left luggage office on the left, and ladies' room on the right. On the wall is one of the NER's maps of the system depicted on glazed ceramic tiles mentioned in Chapter 2.

To the right and left of the bookstall are ticket barriers, although only those on the south side of the bookstall are used now; until 1930 York was an 'open' station with most tickets collected on trains before they reached York, or at the exit from selected platforms using movable barriers. In North Eastern days ticket platforms were popular and were erected to serve lines entering the station from north, south and east.

Access between platforms was originally by subway, which is still there but used for luggage and parcels only, and passengers now use the footbridge erected in 1900 when No 14 platform was commissioned. The footbridge gives an excellent view of the layout of the station, and of the cast iron replicas of the North Eastern's coat-of-arms incorporated in the roof spandrels, which have been painted in their correct heraldic colours – although the crest was not recognised by the College of Heralds!

Adjoining the footbridge at the landing at the east end is what was until 1951 the Platform signalbox, the sole surviving reminder of the four manual boxes which once controlled the working of the station. In 1877 there was Locomotive Yard at the south end and Waterworks at the north end. Leeman Road box, also at the north end, was added with Platform 14 in 1900, and a new Locomotive Yard box (with 295 levers) was opened in June 1909. All the manual boxes were made redundant with the opening of the electric box in 1951. At the same time South Points and Chaloners Whin boxes controlling the tracks to the south, and Clifton box, controlling the tracks to the north, were also closed.

Damage was caused to the roof by German bombing in April 1942, particularly over platforms 1, 2, 3 and 4, where one of the main roof columns was destroyed; this can still be distinguished because the replacement does not match the 1877 columns. In the same raid some of the offices on the east side of the station were set alight by incendiary bombs, and many coaches of a sleeping car train standing at platform 9 were destroyed by fire. However, the station was back in use again later in the same day.

4

THE MAIN LINE FROM
SHAFTHOLME TO DARLINGTON

The North Eastern's portion of the East Coast main line falls readily into four distinct sections, namely Shaftholme Junction to York, York to Darlington, Darlington to Newcastle, and Newcastle to Berwick. Each length has its own style of architecture depending on when the line was built and by what company.

At the southern end the first train service was provided by the York & North Midland Railway (Y&NM) between York and Normanton, where connection was made with the North Midland Railway onwards to Derby, then the Midland Counties (Derby to Rugby), or the Birmingham & Derby, and finally the London & Birmingham into London (Euston Square). Various schemes for a line up the eastern side of the country eventually crystallised as the Great Northern Railway heading for Doncaster and York, but on the final stretch some shrewd moves by George Hudson persuaded the Great Northern that it would be unnecessary to build 25 miles of line if it were to use the Lancashire & Yorkshire line from Askern Junction to Knottingley, a new Y&NM connection from Knottingley to Burton Salmon, and the Y&NM main line onwards to York.

This route came into use in 1850 but as traffic developed it was found to be inconvenient having to rely on the good offices of the L&Y, which had little interest in north-south traffic and was more interested in east-west movement. Consequently in 1863 the North Eastern Railway (as successor to the Y&NM) applied for Parliamentary powers to build a direct line from Chaloners Whin, two miles south of York, to join the Hull & Selby line at Barlby, north of Selby, using the existing line to reach Selby station, and then a second new stretch from Selby to join the Great Northern at Shaftholme Junction, four miles north of Doncaster and adjacent to the point where the Great Northern made an end-on junction with the L&Y Knottingley line. The new line via Selby was opened on 2 January 1871.

Stations on the two new sections were Naburn, Escrick, and Riccall north of Selby, and Temple Hirst, Heck, Balne, and Moss south of Selby, with undistinguished buildings; a station was considered for Bishopthorpe, just south of York, but it was decided that there was 'No necessity at present'. Of these seven stations three were closed in June 1953, three in December 1958, but one – Temple Hirst – remained open until March 1961.

Now, as mentioned in the previous chapter, much of the line has been replaced by a new route swinging away to the west at Temple Hirst, to skirt the new Selby coalfield. The possibility of mining subsidence on a route heavily used by the East Coast High Speed Trains (HST) was not acceptable to British Rail and at the National Coal Board's expense a completely new line has been built for some 10½ miles – without a single station.

The new route diverges from the 1871 line just south of the bridge over the River Aire, ¼-mile south of the site of Temple Hirst station, and as the new line curves away from the existing line, over the new concrete Aire bridge, the surviving Temple Hirst station buildings can be seen to the east. The diversion strikes across level land with rivers, canals, and a high water table, passing under the Selby–Leeds line (carried on a new embankment and overbridge) near Hambleton, and on to join the Normanton–York line at Colton, so that the approach to York from London is once again over the Y&NM route of 1839, which lost its London trains in 1871 with the opening of the Selby route. The only other station site south of York which is encountered is Copmanthorpe, closed in January 1959 and since demolished. The 1871 line between the new junction at Temple Hirst and Selby remains in use for a Doncaster–Selby–York service, involving a reversal at Selby towards Hambleton junction, but the section between Barlby Junction and York (Chaloners Whin) has been closed and will be removed.

The line between York and Darlington was built by the Great North of England Railway (GNE) and opened to passenger traffic on 30 March 1841, sharing the station inside the City walls at York with the York & North Midland company. Most of the stations on this 44 miles were provided when the line was built, although the junction station at Pilmoor did not materialise until the Boroughbridge branch was opened in 1847, and that at Dalton (later Eryholme) until the Richmond branch was opened in 1846. Unusually for the NER neither of these stations had road access and could be reached only by footpaths, emphasising their main use as interchange stations.

The Plain of York is a fertile agricultural area and it was farm produce which provided the main traffic from the wayside stations; even the humble potato gave a worthwhile amount of revenue as in 1923 Thirsk despatched 5175 tons, Raskelf 2859 tons, Tollerton 2727 tons, Sessay 1696 tons, and Alne 1669 tons – 14,126 tons from five stations. Hay and clover put on rail in the area could amount to 1600 tons a year at some stations. The absence of quarries and mines meant that there was no bulk industrial traffic for the railway to carry and the emphasis was on the through main line traffic – meat and fish from Aberdeen, passengers from Edinburgh, coal from Newcastle, and engineering products from the industrial north-east.

However, the level land was eminently suitable for RAF airfields, which started appearing in the 1930s, with others following after the outbreak of World War II. These required supplies of petrol and bombs, and the personnel required rail transport for duty postings and leave, so that some of the stations were busier than they had been for some time.

However, Beningbrough, Alne, Raskelf, Pilmoor, Sessay, Otterington, Danby Wiske and Cowton were closed in 1958, but Tollerton (with one train a day) lasted until November 1965, and Croft Spa until March 1969: all have since had their platforms removed, and often the station buildings as well so that it is difficult to tell where the stations were, especially when travelling at 125mph!

Some of the cottages had at first floor level – usually between the bedroom windows – a large shield-shaped stone built into the front wall and inscribed GNER Co. 1843; a row of cottages south of Pilmoor had two such stones and still exists.

Another feature of the main line is the absence of level crossings: flat countryside is a breeder of level crossings as there are no contours which can be used to advantage for overbridges and underbridges. Over the years the North Eastern steadily abolished level crossings on the main line, leaving the LNER to remove the last one between York and Darlington, at Overton, south of Beningbrough.

Gas operated automatic semaphore signals controlled by track circuits were installed between Alne and Thirsk in 1905 and remained in use until 1933, when colour light signals were installed. These also worked automatically but manual control was available if required, especially at Thirsk and Sessay Wood (later renamed Pilmoor South and eventually Pilmoor) boxes.

Due to various widening schemes carried out between 1899 and 1959, particularly between York and Northallerton, many of the original station buildings have been demolished to make way for up and down slow lines, necessitating new platforms and station buildings. Northallerton station escaped because of convenient avoiding lines at a lower level, and between Northallerton and Eryholme (renamed from Dalton Junction in May 1901) the widening was in the form of lengthy running loops between stations so that no rebuilding was necessary.

The first widening took place under the Act of 1894, from north of Beningbrough to south of Alne, leading to the demolition of the original Tollerton station and its replacement by a new station set outside the new slow lines. No photograph of the old station has been located but what appears to be the original stationmaster's house, cut back to allow the laying of the down slow line, still stands south of the road overbridge, whereas the new station was built north of the bridge. The latter was authorised in 1899 at a cost of £1054 10s 11d (£1054.55), plus £783 13s 3d (£783.66) for a house for the stationmaster, and a cottage. A new electric signalbox was opened at Tollerton in January 1961, on the up side south of the station.

Further widenings in North Eastern days were restricted to loops between pairs of stations and it was not until the 1930s that more main line stations were affected as the LNER took advantage of a Government assistance scheme. Thus the four track section between Beningbrough and Alne was extended southwards to the River Ouse bridge just north of York, requiring the replacement of Beningbrough station, and northwards, on the down side only, to Pilmoor, requiring the replacement of the down side buildings at Alne and Raskelf. Further north the extension northwards of the Thirsk–Otterington loops almost to Northallerton meant the replacement of Otterington station.

Beningbrough station served the nearby village of Shipton-by-Beningbrough and, in fact, was known as Shipton until 1898. In NER days the platforms were staggered, with the up platform south of the road overbridge and the down platform to the north. The widening of 1933 brought up and down platforms north of the bridge, with new station buildings on both platforms, and a new station house on the down side for the stationmaster. The old signalbox, with brick base and wooden cabin, situated north of the overbridge, was extra high to allow the signalman a view over the bridge to see trains approaching

North Road Station, Darlington: (*above*) The interior of North Road in 1973. Much of the interior dates from 1842 although the layout was changed a number of times over the years, the final pattern having the Darlington to Barnard Castle line between the edge of the platform in the foreground and the cast iron railings. The buildings outside the main roof at the east end (left in the photograph) were for many years the Stockton & Darlington Railway's mineral offices. (*Author's collection*); (*below*) For the 150th anniversary in 1975 the station was converted into a Railway Museum housing locomotives – including *Locomotion No 1* built by George Stephenson in 1825 – and small exhibits. It was opened by HRH The Duke of Edinburgh on 27 September 1975, 150 years to the day since Stephenson trium- phantly trundled from Shildon to Stockton with a train of cheering passengers, many hitching a ride on the wagons of coal. (*Author's collection*)

On the Newcastle and Carlisle Railway: (*above*) Rosehill, one of the small but very attractive Newcastle & Carlisle stations, renamed Gilsland in 1869. Note the light, delicate awning to give protection from the weather to waiting passengers. (*Author's collection*); (*below*) Gilsland in British Rail days. Dormer windows have been added to the main building. In the period covered by these two views the station had a large hipped roof awning over the space in front of the station buildings, and the post in the foreground appears to have been one of the roof supports left in place because it accommodated one of the station oil lamps. The circular hole was for the pipe from the rain water guttering on the roof and the rain water drained through the inside of the cast iron column. (*W. Fawcett*)

from the south. With the 1933 widening a new box was provided roughly in the same position as the old but set back to allow the new up slow line to be laid; this box was also built to give a view over the bridge. At the same time the road bridge was converted from a single arch to three, with the large centre arch continuing to accommodate the up and down fast lines, and the additional arch on each side taking the up and down slow lines. The goods yard was behind the up platform. This location was a favourite site for H. G. Tidey, the noted railway photographer.

At Alne, work on the down side left untouched the Alne & Easingwold bay at the north end of the up platform and this remained in use until December 1957, although after the passenger service was withdrawn in November 1948 it dealt only with parcels traffic. The old station building on the down side was a square solid structure housing the offices and the stationmaster, with a wooden waiting shed on the up side; a standard cast iron footbridge joined the two platforms. Straddling the north end of the platforms was a three-arch road bridge, the centre arch taking the up and down fast lines; the arch on the up side allowed the Easingwold trains access to the bay platform, and that on the down side gave access to the goods yard situated behind the down platform. On widening to three tracks in 1933 the western end of the bridge was rebuilt, with the goods yard arch adapted for the new down slow line, and an extra arch added to reach the goods yard. At the same time all the buildings on the down side were replaced, with a new signalbox on the platform.

In 1959 the final phase of widening took place on the up side, from north of Pilmoor to south of Alne, completing four tracks from Northallerton to the Ouse Bridge north of Skelton Junction (York), and this meant the demolition of the up platform at Alne, together with the disused Easingwold bay. The Easingwold Railway, an independent line 2½ miles long was authorised in 1887 and opened in 1891; it ran from the NER station at Alne to a small single platform station on the northern outskirts of Easingwold, a country market town 13 miles north of York. To accommodate the Easingwold trains a short bay platform was inserted at the north end of the up platform at Alne, and for this the company paid a rent of £20 a year. However, this was gradually increased over the years and by 1912 had reached £60 a year, although from 1 January 1912 the NER allowed the Easingwold company £25 a year for shunting carried out at Alne by the Easingwold engine. This involved the Easingwold engine crossing the main line to the goods yard to collect wagons for Easingwold left by the NER pick-up goods.

In Great North of England days the goods warehouse at Alne was south of the station, at right-angles to the line and built at the foot of a low embankment; it is assumed that wagons entered the building at the east end at embankment/first floor level, leaving the ground floor of the warehouse for storage. However, the building was found to be too large for the traffic available and many years ago it was converted into five cottages, which are still occupied and well kept.

Back at the station the 1933 signalbox was demolished in May 1961 after it had been replaced by the new box at Tollerton earlier in the year.

At Raskelf in 1933 the down platform was converted to an island serving the down fast and slow lines, but although the up platform was unaffected it received new buildings to replace those that had formerly stood on the down platform. Until BR days the NER brick-built signalbox remained at the south end of the up platform but latterly it opened only when the pick-up goods required to drop or collect an odd wagon from the small goods yard. Closure of the station in 1958 allowed the buildings and platforms to be demolished in the following year. This also allowed the down slow line to be straightened, taking out the curves which had been necessary to pass on the west side of the island platform, and on the up side allowing the 1959 Pilmoor–Alne widening to go ahead.

Wartime necessity brought about the next spell of widening in 1942; this affected more main line stations and it was on the down side from south of Pilmoor to north of Thirsk, and on the up side from north of Thirsk to north of Pilmoor. This meant new platforms for the main line and the Boroughbridge branch, new station buildings, and a new stationmaster's house all on the down side at Pilmoor. In 1980 the house was offered for sale by a Thirsk estate agent, who described it as 'A superior double-fronted modern detached house, with large gardens, occupying a unique position, especially appealing to the country lover seeking a house in an isolated position'. He conveniently forgot to mention the HSTs flashing past at over 100mph a few yards away!

New platforms and buildings were necessary on both sides at Sessay, together with a detached house for the stationmaster; in 1978 this was offered for sale by BR at £17,500.

At Thirsk the up and down platforms were converted to islands, with the new slow lines on the outside. More recently the inner faces of these island platforms have been removed and trains stopping at Thirsk can only be accommodated at the outer faces. Sidings to the north of the station were brought back into use in World War II, with a regular pilot engine to shunt main line goods traffic, which could be despatched to the south either via York or via Harrogate and Leeds.

The Leeds & Thirsk Railway, opened in 1848, originally ran into its own station at Thirsk and this was much nearer the centre of the town than the GNE station; this meant the Leeds & Thirsk crossing the GNE line on a bridge south of the main line station, but before doing this the Thirsk bound trains first ran into the main line station and then, after station duties were completed, backed out to the junction and set off to the L&T terminus.

The Leeds & Thirsk opened its line from Melmerby to Stockton in 1852, by which time it had changed its name to Leeds Northern Railway – but it was found more convenient to work the trains from Melmerby to Thirsk, then along the York, Newcastle & Berwick main line to Northallerton, before turning off the main line for Stockton. After the Melmerby–Northallerton section was doubled in 1901 this practice decreased and some Leeds Northern line trains terminated at Thirsk and others at Northallerton (if not running through to Stockton, West Hartlepool and beyond). At times Thirsk was also the terminus for trains from Malton, via Gilling, which joined the main line at Pilmoor.

Another station affected by the 1933 widenings was Otterington, between Thirsk and Northallerton, where new up and down slow lines required new buildings on both sides of the main line. As at Alne the signalbox was on the platform, but on the up side. The station closed in September 1958 and was partly demolished in May 1961. At the stations affected by the 1933 widenings – Beningbrough, Alne, Raskelf and Otterington – the buildings were to a contemporary design favoured by the LNER in the 1930s, built of a high quality brick and with steeply sloping tiled roofs. A similar design was followed for the buildings affected by the 1942 widening, namely at Pilmoor and Sessay.

Throughout all these changes Northallerton station was virtually unchanged, retaining its 1841 buildings on the up platform although with some strange additions built to the same profile. However, recent demolition of awnings on the up platform has revealed the western elevation of the original building. Over the years bay platforms were

55

added, one at the north end to accommodate Hawes branch trains, and one at the south end for trains bound for Harrogate and Leeds. In 1911 the down platform was converted to an island so that trains from the Leeds direction could use the station without blocking the down main line. Previously, according to a contemporary account 'These trains have often to be run out of the station on to a siding until express trains get past, causing much delay'.

The goods yard at Northallerton was on the up side at the north end of the station and nearby was the engine turntable, although the engine shed itself was on the lower level adjacent to the original Leeds Northern line, which passed on the west side of the main line station and then burrowed under the main line to reach Stockton.

In 1852, eleven years after the opening of the Darlington–York line, the Leeds Northern line from Melmerby to Stockton was opened and provided with a station at the north end of the town. With the installation of a curve in 1856 joining the two lines, from north of the GNE station to west of the LN station, Leeds–Stockton trains commenced to run from Melmerby to Northallerton via Thirsk; this led to the closure of the Leeds Northern station, as interchange between main line and Leeds–Stockton trains could be provided at the main line station. However, as there was no direct connection into the station off the Melmerby–Northallerton line a platform was erected on the low level line, west of the main line station and adjacent to the engine shed site.

In 1901 the Melmerby–Northallerton line was doubled and at the same time a connection was put in to allow trains from the Melmerby direction to run into the main line station at Northallerton; the 1856 curve at the north end allowed them to continue to Stockton. This made the low level platform redundant, but platforms serving up and down lines were erected on the same site forty years later as a World War II emergency measure. However, their only use was after the war when engineering operations at week ends isolated the main line station.

Also in 1901 the down Longlands Loop was installed to allow trains from the York direction to join the Leeds Northern route on the lower level, before passing below the main line bound for Stockton and Middlesbrough, thus avoiding the conflicting movements which were necessary with trains running through the station and crossing the up main line. An up Longlands Loop was constructed in 1933, leaving the low level line and passing below the main line south of the station,

NEWCASTLE, FERRYHILL, STOCKTON, AND MIDDLESBROUGH, via LEAMSIDE.

Light Type—a.m. Dark Type—p.m.

		WEEKDAYS.	WEEKDAYS—continued.	SUNDAYS.

NEWCASTLE ... dep
Gateshead East
Felling
Pelaw
Usworth
Washington
Penshaw
Fencehouses ... arr
Leamside ... dep
Sherburn Colliery
Shincliffe ... arr
Ferryhill ... dep
Sedgefield
Stillington
Carlton
Stockton ... dep
Thornaby
Newport
MIDDLESBROUGH ... arr

A Runs on 12th July and each alternate Saturday.   **B** Wednesdays and Saturdays only.

		WEEKDAYS.	WEEKDAYS—continued.	SUNDAYS.

MIDDLESBROUGH ... dep
Newport
Thornaby
Stockton ... dep
Carlton
Stillington
Sedgefield
Ferryhill ... dep
Shincliffe
Sherburn Colliery
Leamside ... dep
Fencehouses
Penshaw
Washington
Usworth
Pelaw
Felling
Gateshead East
NEWCASTLE ... arr

A Saturdays only.

For complete service between Newcastle and Stockton, Thornaby, and Middlesbrough, see page 36.

DURHAM AND WATERHOUSES.

		WEEKDAYS.		WEEKDAYS.

DURHAM ... dep
Ushaw Moor
WATERHOUSES ... arr

WATERHOUSES ... dep
Ushaw Moor
DURHAM ... arr

A Saturdays only.   **B** Saturdays excepted.

The Newcastle–Leamside–Ferryhill–Middlesbrough service served stations on the 'old main line', and from Ferryhill used former Clarence, Leeds Northern and Stockton & Darlington lines to reach Middlesbrough. (*K. Hoole Collection*)

(*overleaf*)

In LNER days the staff at the larger stations were provided with booklets listing all the trains serving, or passing through, the station, with details of the coach and engine workings. This is a two-page extract from the Darlington (Bank Top) booklet for the summer of 1939. Note that the up and down Coronation streamlined trains were due to pass in the space of 5½ minutes. (*K. Hoole Collection*)

57

DARLINGTON STATION WORKING SUMMER 1939

WEEK-DAYS

Station From	Arrival Time.	Platform	Dept. Time.	Station To	Set. No. in Roster.	Set. Working.	Remarks.	Engine Working.
Tow Law ...	p.m. 6 13	1	p.m. ...	Darlington ...	183D	9-3 a.m. to Crook 12-45 p.m. to Bd. Castle (Sun.) to 10th Sept	Detach T (SO) ...	7-38 p.m. to Richmond
Aberdeen (SX) ...	...	Pass	6 11	King's Cross	...	...	Braked Fish and Meat	...
Richmond ...	6 12	4	6 15	Darlington ...	183E	6-55 p.m. to Tow Law	...	6-55 p.m. to Tow Law
Newcastle (Parcels)	6 1	1	...	York ...	695	...	Detach XM (MO) 3 XM (SO) 2 XM (SX)	...
Saltburn ...	6 17	2	...	Darlington ...	215	6-59 p.m. to Saltburn	...	7-26 p.m. to Saltburn Ex Shed (SO) 4-56 p.m. ex Middleton-in-Teesdale (SX)
Darlington ...	...	5	6 18	Middleton-in-Tees dale (SO) Barnard Castle (SX)	80 (SO) 88 (SX)	12-18 p.m. ex Newcastle (SO) 4-56 p.m. ex- Middleton-in-Teesdale (SX)	...	
Leeds ...	6 22	4	...	Darlington ...	12 (SX) 32 (SO	7-40 a.m. to Newcastle next day 5-45 p.m. to Redcar (Sun.)	Detach XM (SX) 2XM (SO)	To Shed
Darlington ...	...	3	6 26	Saltburn ...	212	5-47 p.m. ex Saltburn	...	5-13 p.m. ex Saltburn
Newcastle (Slow) ...	6 38	1	6 43	York ...	...	...	...	...
King's Cross (SO) ...	6 47	4	6 50	Newcastle ...	...	Runs 15th July to 2nd Sept. ...	...	...
Darlington ...	...	4	6 55	Tow Law ...	183E	6-12 p.m. ex Richmond	...	6-12 p.m. ex Richmond

Station		Line		To	No.			
Saltburn ...	6 48 / 6 49	3 (SO)	...	Darlington ...	211	7-26 p.m. to Saltburn ...	......	8-26 p.m. to Saltburn
Darlington ...	...	2 (to 9th Sept.)	6 59 / 7 2	Saltburn (SO)	215	6-17 p.m. ex Saltburn	......	5-47 p.m. ex Saltburn
Bishop Auckland ...	7 2 / 7 7	1 (SO)	...	Darlington ...	183F	8-55 p.m. to Bishop Auckland	......	7-55 p.m. to Bishop Auckland
King's Cross (SO) ...	Pass		7 1	Edinburgh ...	Pass	Stops Darlington on 16th and 23rd Sept.	......	......
Newcastle ...	7-0(SX) / 7-11(SO)	1	...	Darlington ...	26 (SX) / 506 (SO)	4-30 a.m. to Saltburn. 8-35 a.m. Edinbro' (Mon.) 5-50 p.m. to M.-in-Tees. Sun. to 10th Sept.	Detach 4 TKLV (SO) Aug. 3 TKLV (SO) July & Sept.	To Shed
Edinburgh (SX) ...	...	Pass	7 12½	King's Cross	Pass	"Coronation" ...	Does not run 4th and 7th Aug.	......
Scarbro. (SO) ...	7 9	4	7 14	Newcastle ...	158	......	XMQ and XM (SO) attached	......
King's Cross (SX) ...	...	Pass	7 18	Edinburgh ...	...	"Coronation" ...	Does not run 4th and 7th Aug.	......
Scarbro. (SX) ...	7 6	4	7 21	Newcastle ...	158	......	XMQ and XM (SO) attached	......
Appleby ...	7 21	1	...	Darlington ...	713	......	No. I Express Parcels detach XM	To Shed
Saltburn ...	7 22	2	...	Darlington ...	210	7-59 p.m. to Saltburn	......	7-59 p.m. to Saltburn
Darlington ...	...	3	7 26	Saltburn ...	211	6-48 p.m. ex Saltburn	Conveys H. & C. traffic for Saltburn and Guisbro', not empty stock	6-17 p.m. ex Saltburn
Lowestoft (SO) ...	7 24	4	...	Newcastle ...	...	Runs to 9th Sept.	......	......
Tebay ...	7 27	1	...	Darlington ...	181	7-38 p.m. to Richmond	I T detached (SX)	9-0 p.m. to Kby. Stephen

to allow trains from Teesside to York to reach the up slow line without occupying the main line through Northallerton station.

Northallerton provided connections for passengers between main line trains and the branch service to Leyburn, Hawes and Hawes Junction away to the west, reached by traversing the length of beautiful Wensleydale. This line was closed to passengers in 1954 but there is still stone traffic from Redmire. There was also a substantial flow of traffic between Leeds, Northallerton and West Hartlepool, whilst some trains from York took the same route to reach Newcastle. With the introduction of Pullman trains in the 1920s these ran via Leeds, Harrogate and Northallerton but continued along the main line to serve Darlington and Newcastle.

Using the coast route via Sunderland and joining the main line at Northallerton is the HST Cleveland Executive, which does not take the direct route from Stockton but runs via Middlesbrough, where reversal is necessary; it stops at Northallerton.

Over the last few years the condition of the station and the train service provided have been the subject of numerous complaints, especially when it is considered that it is the County town and the headquarters of the North Yorkshire (formerly North Riding) County Council.

North of Northallerton Danby Wiske station was not opened until 1 December 1884, having been authorised on 5 June 1884 at a cost of £381 6s 4d (£381.31), but the next station to the north, Cowton, dated from the opening of the line in 1841. The handsome station buildings on the down side were designed by Benjamin Green (who also designed Northallerton station) but since closure in 1958 they have been somewhat disfigured by the new occupier.

There were four tracks between Northallerton and Wiske Moor and water troughs were laid on the fast lines, while four tracks existed from north of Cowton to south of Eryholme, not affecting either station.

Dalton Junction station was built to serve the Richmond branch, opened in 1846, and G. T. Andrews, the York architect responsible for the stations on the branch also designed the junction station. The buildings were on the down side of the main line, in the V of the junction, with platforms to main line and branch; an up main line platform was situated south of the junction and trains from Richmond to Darlington were accommodated at a platform on the branch just before the junction was reached. Renaming to Eryholme took place on

Between Newcastle and Berwick: (*above*) Many of the stations on the main line north of Newcastle were large and impressive buildings. This is Warkworth from the road entrance after conversion to a private residence. Four ball finials, and three that have lost their ball, are visible. (*K. Hoole*); (*below*) Christon Bank station. (*P.B. Booth*)

Stations designed by G.T. Andrews: (above) The west end of Malton station, with the stationmaster's house and the train shed. The generally similar refreshment room block is in the left background (K. Hoole); (below) The south end of Filey station in 1962. The end screens have been removed, as has the covering over the girder spanning the tracks. The footbridge, of standard NER pattern, would not fit within the walls and has been erected through the wall on the west side, with another opening through the wall at the foot of the stairs to allow passengers to reach the platform. (K. Hoole)

Stations designed by G.T. Andrews: (*above*) Rillington station (west end) originally the junction station for the Pickering branch, which can be seen diverging to the left beyond the down platform. This layout required a signalbox at the far end of the station and a gatebox at the near end. (*K. Hoole*); (*below*) The skeleton of Rillington roof before it was completely demolished in 1955, with a Scarborough–York train passing through. This shows the method of supporting the roof used at the various Andrews stations with overall roofs. (*J.W. Armstrong*)

Stations designed by *G.T. Andrews*: (*above*) An Andrews wayside station, Ruswarp, near Whitby, opened in 1847 when the line was converted from horse to steam operation. Note the elaborately carved barge boards, and the relieving arches above the entrance to allow the latter to be more delicately constructed. (*K. Hoole*); (*below*) Cayton station, with the bay window at the south end of the building instead of facing on to the platform. An unusual bay window has been added at the front of the building. (*Author's collection*)

1 May 1901 and closure followed on 1 October 1911, when Croft Spa became the interchange station, although with main line trains not stopping at Croft Spa connections were given at Darlington.

After the closure of Eryholme a mid-day train from Richmond to Darlington stopped on Saturdays to pick up 'Company's employees' wives' and they returned later in the day after their weekly shopping trip. During World War II certain Richmond branch trains stopped at Eryholme to cater for RAF personnel stationed at a nearby airfield.

Croft is a small village on the Yorkshire bank of the River Tees, and from the train can be seen the old church where Charles Dodgson's father was Rector (and where the author was married); young Dodgson is best remembered as Lewis Carroll! The station on the main line was on the other side of the Tees, in County Durham, in a village properly known as Hurworth Place; the station was plain Croft until 1896 when it became Croft Spa. There were no goods facilities at the station, merely horse loading docks. The NER signalbox was another tall structure designed to give a view over the road bridge which spans the line at the south end of the station, but about 1913 it was replaced by a low wooden box south of the bridge.

This stretch of the main line was the first to see automatic colour light signals of the approach lit type, which were introduced between Eryholme and Black Banks on 12 February 1928. Croft Spa cabin was retained, but it was downgraded to a ground frame, which opened only when necessary to operate the crossover and loading dock points; on such occasions the relevant colour light signals were manually controlled.

These early colour light signals were of the three-aspect type, battery lit by 6-volt bulbs, but in 1939 this pioneer scheme was replaced by modern four-aspect 'searchlight' signals as part of the Eryholme and Darlington South resignalling programme.

The goods facilities for the area, latterly handling only coal, were provided at a lower level, nearer the Tees, at the end of a branch which originally diverged from the east-west Stockton & Darlington Railway near its North Road station. This branch was opened in 1829 and at one time a twice daily horse drawn coach service was provided for passengers between Darlington and Croft. In 1839 the branch was purchased by the Great North of England Railway in readiness for incorporating it into its Gateshead–York line as it passed through Darlington, and some of the branch is still in use as part of the East Coast main line. The southern section of the branch was left in place and continued to serve Croft Depot until 27 April 1964. The main line station was closed five years later, on 3 March 1969; it was a casualty brought about by the closure of the Richmond branch as since 15 September 1958 Croft Spa had been served only by Richmond branch trains since no main line trains deigned to stop.

Darlington Bank Top, with its clock tower, standing at the head of Victoria Road, was built in 1887, replacing an earlier station on the same site. The station is actually built on loops off the main line, allowing trains not stopping at Darlington to pass outside the east wall without the severe restriction in speed necessary to enter the platforms. The station is laid out in the form of an island, with bays let in at each end, those at the south end at one time accommodating Richmond and Saltburn branch trains, and those at the north end trains heading over former Stockton & Darlington lines to Crook, Kirkby Stephen, Penrith etc. The outer faces accommodate main line trains but in busier times the central crossovers allowed two trains to be handled at one platform so that convenient connections could be made.

Until 1975 the old Stockton & Darlington locomotives *Locomotion* and *Derwent* stood on a plinth at the buffer stop end of the southern bays, visible to passengers in trains calling at Darlington but not to passengers in expresses passing outside the station. Both engines are now displayed at North Road Station Museum, a building converted from the Stockton & Darlington station of 1842, although trains on the Darlington to Bishop Auckland service call at a platform under the same roof but outside the Museum itself.

Bank Top station can be approached from Victoria Road by a subway, or from Parkgate by an inclined roadway, with access to the platforms by passing ticket collectors. The overall roof is in three spans, with the centre span divided by the station buildings which run along the centre of the island. Each span is 60ft wide and the outer spans are 1000ft long. A local newspaper reported in 1935 that when the A4 Pacific engine working the Silver Jubilee streamlined train let off steam at the safety valves it dislodged panes of glass from the roof!

Unfortunately Darlington station has been the site of two serious collisions, both of which were attributed to human error; the first, in 1928, occurred at the south end of the station and the second, in 1929, at the north end. In addition two accidents have occurred when East Coast passenger trains were unable to stop in the station, both involving Class 55 Deltic locomotives. In the first incident, on 11

December 1968 with locomotive No 9017, the brake pipes had been incorrectly coupled between engine and train at Newcastle and as no brake test was carried out this error went unnoticed. Locomotive and train ran through the up platform at Bank Top until derailed at a sand drag at the south end of the platform, which protected the lines outside the station. On the second occasion, with 55.008, a piece of metal on the track damaged the brake pipes and the shut-off cocks so that the driver could not apply the brakes through the train. The train passed through the station at speed, collided with an empty diesel unit at the north end, and did not stop until it had run on to the Bishop Auckland branch, some 1600yd from where it should have stopped.

5

OLD AND NEW MAIN LINES BETWEEN DARLINGTON AND NEWCASTLE

North of Darlington the replacement of stations was not so prevalent and only three major widening schemes were carried out, Ferryhill–Tursdale Junction, Durham–Newton Hall Junction, and Birtley–Low Fell. However, it must be remembered that north of Ferryhill the present line is on a new course through Durham, adopted in 1871 in preference to the 'old main line' through Leamside and Washington. From Darlington to Rainton Crossing (between Leamside and Fencehouses) the original line was built by the Newcastle & Darlington Junction Railway, a company backed by George Hudson, and again he commissioned the York architect G. T. Andrews to design the stations at Aycliffe, Bradbury, Ferryhill, Shincliffe, Sherburn and Leamside. However, Hudson also provided stations on the sections of line over which he did not have complete control and thus an Andrews station was built as far north as Gateshead, as well as at Brockley Whins (later Boldon Colliery), and possibly at Fencehouses and Washington.

The new main line struck off at Tursdale Junction, north of Ferryhill, through Croxdale, to join the Bishop Auckland–Leamside line at Relly Mill, south of Durham; the Bishop Auckland branch was then used through Durham, to Newton Hall Junction, where a further section of new line branched off to run via Plawsworth, Chester-le-Street and the Team Valley to Gateshead. The section between Ferryhill and Relly Mill Junction was opened to passengers in January 1872, preceded by that from Newton Hall Junction to Gateshead in 1868. This was followed in June 1877 by the opening of a spacious island station at Ferryhill; the outer faces were used by through trains and there were bay platforms let in at each end. The new station was built to the east of the fast lines used by East Coast expresses, but the remains of the original station, on the west side of the fast lines, were not demolished until 1968. The 1877 station closed in March 1967 and the site was subsequently cleared completely, leaving another open space which it is difficult to visualise as a once thriving station.

In 1834 the Clarence Railway from Port Clarence used the Ferryhill Gap to reach Coxhoe, and later Byers Green, and in 1844 the Newcastle & Darlington Junction Railway, on its way from Darlington to Gateshead, ran alongside through the same natural gap in the hills. Because the railways used the gap the line was 1½ miles from the town of Ferryhill, but a separate community developed around the station and to this day it is known as Ferryhill Station – although the actual station closed in 1967. Ferryhill became an important rail centre with services to and from Coxhoe (withdrawn 1902), Bishop Auckland (cut back to Spennymoor in 1939 and service withdrawn 1952), Hartlepool (withdrawn 1952), and Stockton (also withdrawn 1952); stopping and semi-fast trains between York and Newcastle serving Ferryhill were withdrawn from 6 March 1967, bringing about the closure of the station, which was demolished in 1969.

The hills through which the Ferryhill Gap passes have been quarried and mined for many years and in 1913 88,772 tons of roadstone, gravel and sand were put on rail at sidings under Ferryhill's control. Although having two large coal mines in its area – Mainsforth and Dean & Chapter – the output carried by rail did not pass through the station accounts and thus is not dealt with in this work; the mineral traffic on the NER was so large that it warranted a separate Mineral Department, which handled its own accounts.

At Durham the original station cost £2,610 when it was merely a stopping place on the Bishop Auckland branch, but the structure provided for its new role as a main line station led to an initial expenditure of £11,329 14s 2d being authorised on 16 December 1870; the station has been added to and modified many times since then, and it is now a hotch-potch of old and new! Bay platforms at both ends catered for local traffic and at one time the NER – and the LNER for that matter – ran a comprehensive service of buses into the station yard from many of the surrounding villages which were not served by the railway. To house the buses the NER erected a corrugated iron garage at the south end of the yard, on the up side, and this was not demolished until BR days; 60 years ago the buses slowly climbed the steep hill to the station and the service was eventually abandoned, only to be resumed in 1980.

North of Durham the stations on the Team Valley line were at Plawsworth (closed April 1952), Chester-le-Street, Birtley and Lamesley and on 1 February 1867 a tender of £8,108 1s 10d was accepted for their construction. A further station, Bensham, between Low Fell and Gateshead, was opened on 1 November 1892 and cost £6,830 although built largely of wood! Chester-le-Street is the only station to remain open on this stretch, although for a time the premises were occupied by the local Labour Party. At Ouston Junction, south of Birtley, the main line is joined on the down side by the branch dropping down from Consett, opened throughout in 1896; in the following year the NER received powers to lay an additional pair of tracks from Ouston Junction to Low Fell, necessitating extra platforms at Birtley, Lamesley and Low Fell. Lamesley lost its passenger service in June 1945, Low Fell in April 1952, and Birtley in December 1955 following the withdrawal of the Consett services earlier in the year. Bensham closed in September 1954. Much of the area between Birtley and Low Fell is now covered by the large Tyne Marshalling Yard which was formally opened by Lord Hailsham on 28 June 1963.

Of the remaining stations Aycliffe, the first station north of Darlington, changed little over the years; its main source of traffic was not passengers, but limestone from the quarries south of the station, which despatched 33,524 tons in 1923. The station closed to passengers and goods in 1953. The next station, Bradbury, catered for an estimated 610 inhabitants – and more than half of those lived on the western side of Sedgefield and would have to pass Sedgefield station (on the Stockton–Ferryhill line) to reach Bradbury station. However, joining a train at Bradbury was far more convenient if travelling south to Darlington and beyond, as to reach the same destinations from Sedgefield station meant travelling north to Ferryhill, there to change into a southbound train calling at Bradbury! Because of its lack of traffic Bradbury was closed to passengers and goods in 1950.

On the 'old main line' Shincliffe station was adjacent to the highway from Stockton to Durham and a mile south of the village; it was similar in design to Brockley Whins and both were built of stone. However, the blocks used at Shincliffe were noticeably smaller than those used at Brockley Whins, and whereas Shincliffe had a typical Andrews bay window on the platform Brockley Whins, being in the junction of two lines, had two. The bottom of the bay window at Shincliffe was level with the platform, indicating that the original platform had been much lower.

The next station, Sherburn Colliery, was a nondescript building and may have been by Andrews; for the first 30 years of its existence it was known as Sherburn but in 1874, to avoid confusion with the other Sherburns on the NER, it had Colliery added to its name. Both Shincliffe and Sherburn Colliery were early candidates for closure and both lost their passenger service on 28 July 1941.

Two miles north of Sherburn there was once a station at Belmont Junction, the junction being between the 'old main line' and the branch to Durham (Gilesgate). Both Gilesgate and Belmont Junction were closed to passenger traffic in 1857 with the opening of the new Durham station on the branch to Bishop Auckland, but Gilesgate continued in use as the goods station for Durham City until 1966, and still remains but now in private hands. Traces of the station at Belmont Junction remained until the 1960s, and in the vee of the junction there was an interesting water tank, with pumphouse below, and a handsome stone chimney, all dating from 1845. Because of their age and design they were to have been dismantled and re-erected at Beamish Open Air Museum but they were unceremoniously reduced to a heap of stones by British Rail in January 1971. Gilesgate station itself was a handsome little terminus, with passenger train shed, goods shed, office block and stationmaster's house, all designed by G. T. Andrews.

The original station at Leamside was a single storey building but it was replaced in 1857 by a station more suitable for the interchange facilities required with the opening of the Bishop Auckland branch, which diverged south of the station. The second station was built as a large island, with the up line on the east side and the down line on the west. A single track bay platform was inserted at both ends. The buildings were grouped together in the centre of the island, the most noticeable feature being two large rectangular wooden erections on the roof. I have only recently discovered that they were two disguised water tanks, that at the south end being made by E. Thompson of York in 1856 and holding 4,000 gallons, with a similar but larger tank holding 5,000 gallons, but of unknown origin, at the north end. Leamside closed to passenger and goods traffic in October 1953 but it was used for years after that by Newcastle–York trains diverted because of week-end engineering works on the main line and unable to call at Durham. From Durham a shuttle service ran over the four miles to Leamside to connect with the diverted trains. In its busier days Leamside's main goods traffic was bricks, the average annual quantity despatched amounting to 10,000 tons.

Fencehouses station was on what was originally the five mile long

Durham Junction Railway from Rainton to Washington, taken over by the Newcastle & Darlington Junction in 1844 to form part of Hudson's empire and a link in the chain of railways from London to the Tyne. The buildings contained features of Andrews' work but it did not follow any of his fairly standard designs. On the east side of the station two tracks were used by National Coal Board trains and the BR signalbox at the south end of the station operated the level crossing gates for each pair of tracks.

Penshaw (Pensher until 1881) was an island station, rebuilt in 1913 after the earlier buildings had been destroyed by fire. Here again the main outward traffic was bricks, with 19,406 tons in 1913, although this had dropped to 7,172 tons in 1923. In 1913 2,474 tons of creosote, tar and pitch were despatched, no doubt produced by the coke works in the vicinity, and this had increased to 6,372 tons for 1923.

Between Penshaw and Washington the River Wear is crossed by the Durham Junction's most striking memorial, the Victoria Bridge, 125ft high and 811ft long. North of the bridge connection was made with the Stanhope & Tyne line through Washington, a station of indeterminate age and of no apparent distinction. Yet again bricks accounted for most of the goods traffic – 25,547 tons in 1913, 13,340 tons in 1923, but down to 9,585 tons in 1924; 1,861 tons of 'composition' were despatched in 1913 and 4,271 in 1923. This is a pitch-like substance described in NER records as 'for cementing clay channels etc (ducts) used in electrical work' and it was no doubt produced at the large chemical works at Washington.

Originally the expresses from the south, introduced in 1844, used the Stanhope & Tyne between Washington and Brockley Whins, where at first an awkward reversal was necessary to join the Brandling Junction line. A rapidly constructed wooden viaduct soon eased the situation and the curve over the viaduct joined the Brandling Junction immediately west of Brockley Whins station which, as already mentioned, was similar to Shincliffe but with two bay windows, one overlooking the Brandling Junction line between Sunderland and Gateshead, and the other the curve. Thus it seems probable that there was a platform of sorts on the curve, but as it became redundant in 1850 with the opening of a cut-off from Washington direct to Pelaw, all traces have long since disappeared, although the wooden viaduct remained standing until 1940.

On the last lap into Gateshead the East Coast trains passed through the 1842 Brandling Junction station at Felling, a handsome little building which still stands and now sees Tyneside Metro trains passing its doors, although it is no longer in railway use. The Brandling Junction, opened in 1839, originally had its terminus in Oakwellgate, but this was small and insignificant and certainly not up to George Hudson's flamboyant style so he commissioned Andrews to design a fine station at Greenesfield, perhaps the north's earliest and largest white elephant!

The station at Greenesfield was built very quickly in 1844 to cater for the long distance passengers arriving from the south via Darlington, Leamside and Washington; it had a train shed 352ft × 88ft and a very imposing frontage on the north side facing across the river to Newcastle. It was obvious when it was built that within a few years the Tyne and Tweed would be bridged to enable trains to run through between London and Edinburgh, and with the completion of the permanent bridge across the Tyne in 1849, and the opening of Newcastle Central station in 1850, Greenesfield station became redundant after only six years!

The layout was unusual for an Andrews station, and instead of having arrival and departure platforms on opposite sides of the train shed they were both on the same (north) side; half the length of the platform was available for arriving trains and the other half, for departures, was narrower to accommodate a track between the platform face and the arrival track. Inside the train shed there were also three sidings and all the tracks were connected by turnplates at both ends of the station and in the centre.

In 1851 the redundant train shed became a locomotive repair shop and formed the nucleus of Gateshead Locomotive Works, eventually being known as No 1 erecting shop. It continued in use for locomotive repairs until the 1960s. Also used as part of the Works was the eastern half of the station offices but both former offices and Works were demolished in 1968. The 1844 building included a station hotel at the eastern end and although this still stands it has not been used for its intended purpose for more than 130 years, but it is still used for railway purposes.

Gateshead East station, to use its more recent name, was built on the curve giving access to the High Level Bridge across the Tyne and it took the place of Greenesfield as Gateshead's main station; it was replaced by a new and much larger station in 1885. Seventeen years earlier Gateshead West station had been opened alongside on the curve from the new Team Valley line on to the High Level Bridge.

Although the northern end of Gateshead East's down platform and Gateshead West's up platform joined at the south end of the High Level Bridge the opposite ends of the two platforms faced east and west respectively. In the 1960s Gateshead West was served only by a few trains from Darlington entering Newcastle Central at the East End but these ceased on 1 November 1965. Gateshead East continued to be served by South Shields and Sunderland trains until closure of the station was brought about by the withdrawal of these services so that work could begin on the Metro system, first to Heworth and later to South Shields.

6

THE LEEDS NORTHERN – AND ON
TO NEWCASTLE

West of the East Coast main line the Leeds & Thirsk completed its line in 1849, but it closed north of Harrogate in 1967, together with the 1852 extension from Melmerby to Northallerton. Stations worthy of mention include Arthington (closed 1965) where the original station was adjacent to the Pool–Harewood road. The opening of the branch to Ilkley in 1865 required platforms at the junction some distance to the south but it was not until 1875 that a permanent station at the junction was authorised at a cost of £1,425, although the actual cost when completed was £1,588; rebuilding of the station was authorised in 1895 at an estimated cost of £729 9s, but this time the actual cost was lower and came out at £631 9s 5d.

The Leeds & Thirsk did not pass through Harrogate but kept to the Crimple valley and passed on the east side of the town with a station at Starbeck to serve Harrogate. The York & North Midland branch from Church Fenton got much nearer to the centre of Harrogate by bridging the Crimple valley, but a tunnel was required to reach the Brunswick terminus on the south side of the town. The building of a new central station in 1862 allowed Brunswick to close and all that remains to be seen is a commemorative stone erected in 1949. The 1862 Harrogate station changed little over the years apart from extensions and improvements, which were carried out in 1873 (£1319 3s 7d) and 1897/8 (£12,433 18s 4d).

Harrogate was a well-kept station and in the 1920s and 1930s it was notable for its flower displays, especially when Queen Mary used the station on her visits to her daughter at nearby Harewood House. In the mid-1960s an extensive modernisation and development scheme was carried out by BR and Copthall Holdings, resulting in the nine storey Copthall Tower House and three storey Copthall Bridge House office blocks, the former at the front of the station facing Station Parade, and the latter built across the tracks at the south end of the station; both blocks have shops at ground level.

Harrogate, because of its spa status, warranted a Pullman service from July 1923; at first the Harrogate Pullman ran between London, Harrogate and Newcastle but from July 1925 it was extended northwards to Edinburgh; in 1928 it was renamed Queen of Scots. The West Riding Pullman, introduced in 1925, also served Harrogate and Newcastle from May 1928, but from September 1935 it ran only between London and Harrogate and the service was renamed Yorkshire Pullman. Both services were resumed after World War II but eventually succumbed under BR's standardisation policy.

Goods facilities were originally provided at Brunswick and Starbeck stations, and even after Brunswick closed to passengers it continued in use for goods traffic until the facilities at Starbeck could be enlarged. However, a large goods station was built in Bower Road in Harrogate in 1896, served by its own tracks from Dragon Junction (where the lines to York and Ripon diverged north of the station).

Services remaining consist of dmu trains from Leeds and York, some of which run through from York to Leeds via Harrogate, and two HST 125 trains from Kings Cross each day.

Ripon, 11½ miles north of Harrogate, was a two-platform station at the north end of the city and at one time the North Eastern operated a motor bus service between the station and Ripon Market Place. From 1902 Ripon was served by through trains to Kings Cross (via Harrogate) worked by Great Northern engines and coaches, but the most frequent service was provided by Leeds–Northallerton trains terminating at Saltburn, Stockton or West Hartlepool. Ripon was also the terminus of some of the local trains to Masham, which diverged from the Leeds Northern line at Melmerby, three miles to the north.

Melmerby was originally a wayside station between Ripon and Thirsk, but the opening of the line between Melmerby and Northallerton in 1852 made it into a junction station, later joined by the Masham branch (1875). Until 1913 there was a signalbox at the south end of the station controlling the Thirsk line junction and the level crossing gates, and another at the north end controlling the Masham branch junction. Abolition of the North box was obtained by resiting the Masham branch junction further south so that it could also be controlled by Melmerby South box, which then became plain Melmerby. Until the Masham branch closed to passengers on 1 January 1931 an engine was stationed at this rural terminus for working both the passenger and goods service on the branch, but subsequently the freight service was worked by the Starbeck engine

WHITBY AND STOCKTON.

Light Type—a.m.   Dark Type—p.m.

WEEKDAYS.

		A	B						C	B	B
WHITBY	dep	7 8	8 10	10 5	30	3 30	5 31	—	7 48		9 45
Ruswarp	,,	7 13	.	10 10	35	..	5 36	—	7 53		
Sleights	,,	7 18	8 18	10 15	40	..	5 41	—	7 58		
Grosmont	,,	7 28	8 28	10 25	51	3 44	5 51	—	8 8		
Egton	,,	7 33	8 32	10 30	57	3 49	5 56	—	8 13		
Glaisdale	,,	7 37	8 36	10 35	2	3 54	6	—	8 18	10 7	
Lealholm	,,	7 42	f	10 41	9	4	6 7	—	8 24		
Danby	,,	7 51	8 47	10 50	18	4	9	6 16	—	8 33	
Castleton	,,	7 56	8 58	10 55	23	4 13	6 20	—	8 38	1021
Commondale	,,	8 1	..	11 0	28	4 18	6 25	—		
Kildale	,,	8 10	9 8	11 9	37	4 28	6 34	—	8 49	
Battersby	arr	8 14	9 11	11 13	41	4 32	6 37	—	8 54	2 1034
	dep	8 19	9 16	11 17	46	4 34	6 40	—	9 8	3 1038
Ingleby	,,	8 22		11 20	49	4 37	6 43	—		
Stokesley	,,	8 30	8 30	11 27	58	4 45	4 52	6 50	7 22	9 10
Sexhow	,,	8 37	8 37	11 34	3	4 52	4 56	6 57	7 29	
Potto	,,	8 42	8 42	11 38	9	4	6	7 33		
Trenholme Bar	,,	8 49	8 49	11 44	16	5	7	7 39		
Picton	,,	8 55	8 55	11 49	21	5	7	7 45		9 30
Yarm	,,	9 2	9 2	11 56	28	5 14	7	7 52		9 38
Eaglescliffe	arr	9 6	9 6	12 3	32	5 18	7	7 56		9 41
	dep	9 8	9 8	12 5	45	5 24	7	7 59		9 44
STOCKTON	arr	9 14	9 14	12 9	5	5 30	7	8 5		9 47

WEEKDAYS.

		D			B		A		E	
STOCKTON	dep	7 42	10 27	—	46	4 29	5 32	8 12	
Eaglescliffe	arr	7 48	10 33	—	52	4 35	5 38	8 18	
	dep	7 53	10 38	—	57	4	5	8	
Yarm	,,	7 57	10 42	—	2	4 30	4 43	5 50	8
Picton	,,	8 5	10 50	—		4	4 50	5 53	8
Trenholme Bar	,,	8 11	10 56	—		4	5	6	8
Potto	,,	8 16	11 1	—		4	5	6	8 49
Sexhow	,,	8 20	11 5	—		4	5 15	6	
Stokesley	,,	8 27	11 12	—		4 34	5	6 22	8
Ingleby	,,	8 34	11 18	—		4	5	6	8
Battersby	arr	8 37	11 13	1 29	2 43	4 53	4 57	6 28	8
	dep	8 38	11 27	1 34	45	4 57	5 23	6 34	9 12
Kildale	,,	8 43	11 32	f		4	5	6	9
Commondale	,,	8 52	11 41			5 12	5	6 44	9
Castleton	,,	7 58	8 57	11 46	1 28	3	5 17	5	6 49	9 31
Danby	,,	8 3	9 3	11 51		3 14	5	6 54	9
Lealholm	,,	8 10	9 10	11 58		3	5 27	6	9
Glaisdale	,,	8 15	9 15	12 4	3 2	3 23		5 34	6	9
Egton	,,	8 19	9 19	12 7			6 7	9
Grosmont	,,	8 24	9 24	12 12	2 10	3 41	6 20	7 10	9 52
Sleights	,,	g	9 34	12 22		3	6	7	
Ruswarp	,,		9 39	12 27		3	6	7	
WHITBY	arr	8 43	9 45	12 33	2 23	3 52	5 50	6 31	7 28	10 13

A Wednesdays only. **B** Will not run after 13th September. **C** Will commence on 15th September. **D** Saturdays only. **E** Will not run between Stokesley and Whitby after 13th September. **f** Stop when required. **g** Stops when required to set down.

RIPON AND MASHAM.

WEEKDAYS.

RIPON	dep	9 18	12 5	4 15	8 20
Melmerby	,,	9 25	12 12	4 22	8 27
Tanfield	,,	9 35	12 22	4 32	8 37
MASHAM	arr	9 41	12 28	4 38	8 43

WEEKDAYS.

MASHAM	dep	7 25	10 35	3 6	6 20
Tanfield	,,	7 31	10 41	3 12	6 26
Melmerby	,,	7 41	10 51	3 22	6 36
RIPON	arr	7 48	10 58	3 29	6 43

Trains shewn in italics do not run daily throughout

NORTHALLERTON AND HAWES.

Light Type—a.m.   Dark Type—p.m.

WEEKDAYS.

			A								
NORTHALLERTON	dep	7 35	10 0	10 50		35	3 55	6 30	9 40	—
Ainderby	,,	7 43	10 8	10 57		42	4	6 37	9 47	
Scruton	,,	7 48	10 12	11 1		46	4	6 41	9 51	
Leeming Bar	,,	7 52	10 16	11 5		50	4	6 45	9 55	
Bedale	arr	7 56	10 21	11 9		54	4 16	6 49	9 59	
	dep	7 58		11 11		56	4	6 51	0	
Crakehall	,,	8 4		11 17	2	2	4	6 57	0	7
Jervaulx	,,	8 15		11 21	2	4	4 55	2	12	
Finghall Lane	,,	8 20		11 26	2 19	4 40	7	10 17	
Constable Burton	,,	8 24		11 30	2 23	4 44	7	10 21	
Spennithorne	,,	8 28		11 34	2 27	4 48	7	10 25	
Leyburn	arr	8 32		11 38	2 32	4 52	7 20	10 30	
	dep	8 38		11 44	2 37	4 59	7 30	
Wensley	,,	8 44		11 49	2 43	5 5	7 36	
Redmire	,,	8 49		11 54	2 48	5 10	7 41	
Aysgarth	,,	8 56		12 1	2 56	5 17	7 49	
Askrigg	arr	9 6		12 11	3 5	5 56	8	
	dep	9 15		12 20	3 14	5 38	8	
Hawes	arr	10 10		12 22	—	5 37	8 10	
HAWES JUNCTION and GARSDALE	arr	10 25		12 36	—	5 52	8 25	—
Hawes Junc. & Garsdale	dep	10 32		1 12		6 22	9 38	
Skipton	arr	11 40		2 39		7 14	10 27	
Hawes Junc. & Garsdale	arr	11 33		12 42		5 58		
Carlisle	dep	12 0		2 28		7 40		

WEEKDAYS.

			B		A					
Carlisle	dep					8 40	11 0	—	5 8
Hawes Junc. & Garsdale	arr					10 32	12 52	—	6 20
Skipton	dep					9c11	11 5	—	4 40
Hawes Junc. & Garsdale	arr					10c33	12 32	—	5 58
HAWES JUNCTION and GARSDALE	dep			—	7 10	—	10 50	—	5 8	6 25
Hawes	,,		7 6	7 22		11 2	5	3 38	6 25
Askrigg	,,		7 9	7 30		11 10	25	4	6 45
Aysgarth	,,		7 19	7 39		11 19	34	56	6 54
Redmire	,,			7 46		11 25	41	4	7
Wensley	,,			7 51		11 30	46	6	
Leyburn	arr	6 0	7 31	7 56		11 35	51	4 13	7
	dep	6 6	7 37	7 58		11 40	56	4 18	7 24
Spennithorne	,,	6 5		8 2		11 45	4	4 22	7
Constable Burton	,,	6 9		8 6		11 49	4	4 26	7
Finghall Lane	,,	6 12		8 9		11 52	8	4 29	7
Jervaulx	,,	6 21		8 18		12 1	4	4 38	7
Crakehall	,,	6 26	7 45	8 23		12 6	22	4	7 51
Bedale	arr	6 30	7 49	8 25	11 3	12 8	25	4 47	7
	dep	6 34	7 55	8 30	11 8	12 14	29	4 50	7 51
Leeming Bar	,,	6 38		8 34	11 12	12 22	37	4 58	8
Scruton	,,	6 38		8 34	11 16	12 22	37	4 58	8
Ainderby	,,	6 42		8 38	11 16	12 22	37	4 58	8
NORTHALLERTON	arr	6 50	8 2	8 45	11 20	12 30	45	5 8	8 12

A Tuesdays only. **B** Mondays only. **c** On Mondays and Thursdays leaves Skipton at 7.5, and arrives at Hawes Junction and Garsdale at 8.38.

NORTHALLERTON AND RIPON.

WEEKDAYS.

		A	AB	C	AB	D
NORTHALLERTON	dep	7 35	10 15	10 54	2 56	7 40
Newby Wiske	,,	7 41	10 21	11 0	3 2	7 46
Sinderby	,,	7 52	10 32	11 11	3 13	7 57
Melmerby	,,	7 58	10 37	11 16	3 19	8 3
RIPON	arr	8 6	10 43	11c42	3 25	8c24

WEEKDAYS.

		D	A	AB			
RIPON	dep	8 40	12 27	3 50	7c52	—
Melmerby	,,	9 4	12 34	3 57	8 0	—
Sinderby	,,	9 10	12 40	4 3	8 6	—
Newby Wiske	,,	9 21	12 51	4 14	8 17	—
NORTHALLERTON	arr	9 28	12 58	4 21	8 24	—

A Stops at Pickhill (between Newby Wiske and Sinderby) on Thursdays. **B** Thursdays only. **C** Thursdays excepted. **D** Stops at Pickhill (between Newby Wiske and Sinderby) on Wednesdays. **e** Connection at Melmerby.

the period for which this time table is issued.

The Ripon–Masham, Northallerton–Hawes and Northallerton–Ripon services have all disappeared, but the Whitby–Stockton service still operates between Whitby and Battersby, where trains reverse to reach Middlesbrough via Great Ayton. (*K. Hoole Collection*)

At wayside stations waiting sheds, often of wood, were usually provided on the platform opposite to that on which the station buildings were erected. They were of many types and this is the structure at Weeton. (*W. Fawcett*)

which shunted at Ripon all day and then, at the end of its stint, worked loaded and empty wagons to Starbeck. Masham station, with its spacious goods yard, still stands at the side of the road into the town from the east.

The service over the original Leeds & Thirsk route between Melmerby and Thirsk ceased from 14 September 1959, bringing about the closure of the two intermediate stations at Baldersby and Topcliffe.

With the doubling of the Melmerby–Northallerton section in 1901 the route through Sinderby, Pickhill and Newby Wiske increased in importance and it eventually carried the Newcastle–Liverpool dining car trains and the LNER and BR Pullman trains. Beyond Northallerton the newly named Leeds Northern Railway looked for routes to the north and finally reached Stockton in 1852, crossing on the way the original Stockton & Darlington Railway's 1825 line at a site which is now known as Eaglescliffe, although between 1853 and 1878 it was known as Preston Junction.

The two lines crossed on the level and the station was established east of the intersection, with a single platform allowing cross-platform interchange. However, the trains of each company kept to their own side of the platform even though serving the platform in both directions, bringing down the criticism of the Board of Trade Inspector and a particularly vociferous resident at nearby Preston Hall, Marshall Fowler. Extensive alterations to the station were authorised in 1893 at a cost of £13,553 12s 1d, resulting in two long island platforms, trains on the Darlington–Saltburn service normally using the outer tracks, and those on the Stockton–Northallerton service the inner pair of tracks.

At Stockton the Leeds Northern shared the station with the West Hartlepool Harbour & Railway until both became part of the North Eastern, leading eventually to the provision of a new station in 1893. In readiness for the opening of the new station (on a site slightly to the east of the earlier station) the name was changed in 1892 from North Stockton to Stockton, and at the same time South Stockton station, on the former Stockton & Darlington line between Eaglescliffe and Middlesbrough, was renamed Thornaby. The 1893 Stockton station consisted of two through platforms with two bays at the north end, one on the east side and one on the west, the through platforms covered by a single span roof of typical Bell design 80ft wide and 557ft long; an additional span 69ft 7in wide was required at the north end to cover the east bay and three carriage sidings. A portico 96ft × 40ft graced the entrance from Bishopton Lane. A sign of the times is the removal of the station roof and the appearance of the area has not been helped by the destruction by fire of the nearby Queen's Hotel, situated on the station approach road but not owned by the railway company or BR.

At Billingham the lines to Port Clarence (originally Clarence Railway) and West Hartlepool (originally Stockton & Hartlepool Railway) diverged immediately east of the station and level crossing but in November 1966 a new island platform station was opened on the Hartlepool line, on a site considered more convenient than the old position on the west side of the town. In November 1970 the old station was one of 15 railway properties on Teesside advertised for sale by BR.

West Hartlepool station became plain Hartlepool in 1967 with the combination of the two communities, the older Hartlepool (also known as East Hartlepool in railway terminology) and the more recent West Hartlepool. The existing station dates from 1880, with additional platforms opened in December 1904. From September 1964, to save expense in renewals, all through passenger traffic in both directions has used the former down platform. Protection from the weather for passengers is provided by umbrella roofs with girder bracing spanning the tracks.

Serving a population of 65,110 in West Hartlepool and the

surrounding area, the station issued 552,408 tickets in 1911, while the goods department loaded 534,054 tons of iron ore and 532,494 tons of timber in 1913. The timber was mainly pit props for the Durham collieries, brought in by the shipload from Scandinavia and stored in extensive yards, notably on the south side of the town towards Seaton Carew. Unfortunately on occasions these concentrations of timber caught fire and burned for days, destroying not only the wood but the timber bogies and sleepers, twisting the rails into unusable shapes.

Going north from Hartlepool the station at Hart had four platforms, two serving the original Hartlepool Dock Company's lines up and down Hesleden Bank, opened in 1835, and two serving the coast line to Seaham, opened 70 years later. The station was closed between 1941 and 1946 as a wartime economy measure, and finally closed to passengers in August 1953, although it remained open for parcels until 1959.

At first the new line between Hart and Seaham, opened in 1905, warranted only an 'autocar' service serving one station, that at Horden. From 1 July 1913 Easington station opened, but Blackhall Rocks (opened in 1912 but only on Wednesdays and Saturdays in the summer) did not become a fully fledged station until October 1919. The original plan was for it to be called Blackhalls. These three stations were closed to passengers in the 1960s.

Where the new line joined the Londonderry Railway, purchased by the North Eastern in 1900, Seaham Colliery station was erected and the former Londonderry terminus remained as Seaham; however, in 1925 Seaham Colliery became Seaham, and the LR station became Seaham Harbour. The latter was by far the most interesting station of the two, served by trains from Sunderland until September 1939; it had a single platform and an extensive range of buildings, including a very convenient hostelry adjoining the back of the platform! Seaham station is still open.

For some years the expresses running from Newcastle via Sunderland and Stockton to York and beyond continued to use the older route south of Sunderland, up Seaton Bank and via Wellfield to

---

(*opposite*)

The layout of the station working booklets differed slightly from station to station. This is a page from the Sunderland version, again for the summer of 1939, with more explicit details of the engine workings. A locomotive inspector would be stationed on the platform at busy periods to supervise the engine and crew workings. (*K. Hoole Collection*)

SUNDERLAND STATION WORKING SUMMER 1939

UP—(Nos. 1 and 2) PLATFORM WORKING—SATURDAYS ONLY.

FROM	Arrival pm	Platform	Departure pm	To	Set Number in Roster	Set Working	Engine Working	Engine Working Number
Wearm'th Ety.	4 10	2	4 22	Pittington	77	2-20 pm ex Hesleden	Same as set	Sunderland 14
Newcastle	4 17	1	4 20	East Sidings	68	5-15 pm to W. Hartlepool	To Shed	Sunderland 10
South Shields	4 26	1	4 30	Durham	83	—	Same as set	Tyne Dock 1
East Boldon †	4 29	2	4 35	Manchester	520	—	Same as set	—
Newcastle	4 36	2	4 38	Leeds A & Liverpool	521	—	Same as set	Leeds 1
South Shields	4 44	2	4 52	Seaham Harb.	64	2-4 pm ex Blackhall Rocks	Same as set	Durham 2
East Boldon	4 55	1	5 7	Wellfield	81		Same as set	W. H'pool 7
South Shields	5 6	2	5 13	Durham	78		Same as set	W. Auck'ld 1
East Sidings	5 10	1	5 15	W. H'pool A	68	2-20 pm ex Hesleden	Same as set	W. H'pool 8
Newcastle	5 19	2	5 22	Pittington	88	4-17 pm ex Newcastle	Same as set	Sunderland 8
South Shields	5 26	1	5 33	Seaham Harb.	86		Same as set	Sunderland 4
Wearmouth	5 30	2	5 38	Durham	61	2-7 pm ex Durham	Same as set	Durham 17
Newcastle	5 37	1	5 39	Middlesbro' A	208		Same as set	Gateshead 17
South Shields	5 47	2	5 55	Villette Road	75	7-40 am to S. Shields Mon.	Same as set	Tyne Dock 3
Newcastle	6 1	1	6 5	W. H'pool A	63		Same as set	Sunderland 9
South Shields	6 6	2	6 22	Pittington	69		Same as set	Tyne Dock 4
Newcastle	6 17	1	6 34	Durham	70		Same as set	Heaton 12
South Shields	6 26	2	6 32	W. H'pool B	85		Same as set	W. H'pool 4
Newcastle	6 37	2	6 39	Middlesbro' A	209		Same as set	Gateshead 5
Wearm'th Ety.	6 45	2	6 50	Seaham Harb.	77	5-47 pm ex Pittington	Same as set	Sunderland 14
South Shields	7 4	1	7 22	Pittington	80		In, 8-22 pm to So. Shields / Out, Ex Shed	Durham 12
Newcastle	7 17	2	7 27	Seaham Harb.	56		Same as set	Sunderland 15
South Shields	7 26	1	7 30	Durham	22		Same as set	Tyne Dock 2
Newcastle	7 36	2	7 38	Middlesbro' A	206		Same as set	Middlesbro' 6

† Not after 3rd September.   (A) Via Coast Line.   (B) Via Wellfield.

Stockton, but they gradually moved to the easier coast line until this became the recognised through route, which is still used today.

North of Seaham, at Hall Dene, was a small private station for use by the Londonderry family when they resided at Seaham Hall before moving to Wynyard. This station had a single storey house on the up side, and a signalbox on the down side controlled the level crossing. The right to use it as a private station was extinguished from 1 February 1925.

Where the lines to Sunderland converged at Ryhope there were two separate stations, the 1894 station on the 1834 Durham & Sunderland line up Seaton Bank, and Ryhope East, a small structure opened in 1900 on the Londonderry line. The former closed in 1953 but Ryhope East lasted another seven years.

The two routes are not connected until Ryhope Grange, where they diverge to reach Hendon and South Dock (early termini of the railways south of Sunderland) and the 1879 Sunderland station. The latter was built in connection with the first railway bridge across the Wear to Monkwearmouth, and brought all the various services around the town under one roof. The station was built in a cutting adjacent to the new commercial centre of the town, which had moved away from the dock area and Sunderland Moor. Because of its cramped position it was only possible to include two island platforms, the whole covered by a single span roof carried on semi-circular arched ribs between the retaining walls on each side.

The main buildings at Sunderland were at the north end, surmounted by a clock tower, but there was a secondary entrance at the south end. The open forecourt at the north end depicted in early prints was later built on to form an extended concourse, with shops at the outer corners. The station was damaged by German bombing in World War II and some of the roof girders had to be removed, but others were left in place until the station was partially rebuilt in 1953. In 1965 the station was completely remodelled in connection with town centre improvements and it was formally reopened on 4 November; the main passenger facilities were relocated at the south end instead of the north, and although the two island platforms were retained one was given over to parcels traffic, leaving the two faces of the other island to accommodate the up and down passenger trains.

After crossing the Wear the first station is the much illustrated building at Monkwearmouth, the southern terminus of the Brandling Junction Railway opened in 1848, with its imposing frontage. This

Nikolaus Pevsner described as 'one of the most handsome railway stations in existence'. Long thought to be to the designs of John Dobson of Newcastle it has now been found to be the work of Thomas Moore of Sunderland. Until 1928 the platforms were roofed to 'an old design involving columns between the platform lines and instead of perpetuating its objectionable features it has been decided to replace it by a smaller verandah roof on each platform'. The exterior may have been well photographed but I have never been able to locate a photograph of the station with its overall roof.

Seaburn station was opened by the Mayor of Sunderland on 3 May 1937 to serve housing development in the area; it is about a mile from the sea, situated just south of the point where the line turns north-west to head for East Boldon; for this reason it was expected that it would provide access 'to the attractions of Roker and Seaburn'. The platforms as built were 504ft long and access to the platforms was by means of a Passimeter booking office which the LNER favoured at that time.

Before reaching Boldon Colliery station the Sunderland to Newcastle line crosses the site of the former Stanhope & Tyne over which the 9F-hauled iron ore trains used to run on their journey to Consett, but latterly the only traffic has been coal from Boldon Colliery to Westoe (South Shields) hauled by an NCB locomotive, but the colliery has recently closed.

Boldon Colliery station was known as Brockley Whins until 1926 and in 1844, under that name, it was notable as the location where complicated shunting movements had to be carried out to get the London–Gateshead trains off the Stanhope & Tyne line and on to the Brandling Junction line.

Pelaw was overlooked on its north side by CWS factories, but it is now no more as the line to South Shields is closed and in the process of being converted to Metro use. At the time of writing the Metro ends at Heworth, where there are interchange facilities with British Rail, and where new platforms have been provided. On this stretch there were four tracks, with platforms on the southern pair at Felling, now utilised as a Metro station. This means that the first BR station out of Newcastle is now Heworth as Gateshead East has been closed and demolished. There is a new above-ground Metro station at Gateshead Stadium but Gateshead (Metro) is underground.

The Metro line between Pelaw and South Shields takes a more easterly course between Tyne Dock and South Shields to serve the

Chichester area of the town; the 1879 station at South Shields is to be abandoned and the Metro will terminate at a new station to the south of the old. The intermediate stations at Hebburn and Jarrow will be modernised for Metro use, with new stations at Bede, Tyne Dock and Chichester.

By the courtesy of the PTE and its then Marketing & Information Officer, Richard A. Wood, I was able to spend a full day exploring the Metro system, travelling over all the lines except Heworth to South Shields, which was due to be energised a few days later. I was particularly interested in the former North Eastern stations now used by the Metro, and I was struck by the cleanliness of the stations, all unattended. At Heworth there was a constant stream of passengers off the buses and on to the trains to Newcastle and although the journey does now involve a change of vehicle I feel that the rapid service into the centre of Newcastle outweighs a bus into the centre of the city, with the possibility of a long traffic hold up on the Tyne Bridge! In any case why run a bus into the centre of Newcastle when there is a train? Let us have an integrated transport system rather than merely pay lip service to the idea.

7

YORK TO SCARBOROUGH, AND THE WORK OF G. T. ANDREWS

A line from York to Scarborough was first discussed in 1839 and in 1841 the York & North Midland Railway announced that it was to introduce a Bill for such a branch, but George Hudson's pre-occupation with a line from Darlington to Gateshead (as part of an East Coast main line) meant that the idea had to be temporarily shelved. However, it was resurrected in 1843 and an Act was obtained in the following year; because of the level nature of the 42 miles over which it had to pass the line was ready in 1845. At that time Scarborough attracted a few seasonal visitors, who had to endure travel by coach over the poor roads of the period and the Y&NM line, by offering improved speed and comfort to travellers to the coast, fostered Scarborough's eventual rise to be the 'Queen of Watering Places', although I must admit that her crown is now somewhat tarnished!

Hudson commissioned his favourite architect, George Townsend Andrews, to design the stations, station houses, crossing keepers' cottages, and goods sheds, his most notable work being the terminus at Scarborough, set in what is now the centre of the town. The wayside stations were of various types, depending on their position and importance; many of them included typical Andrews features, such as flattish hipped roofs and wide overhanging eaves. Some were built in brick and others in stone, notably those in the Malton area where the stone was obtained from nearby Hildenley Quarry. This cream coloured stone creates an impressive picture, with the joints in the stonework almost invisible as the blocks are held together with their own weight and the interlocking of grooves and projections on adjoining blocks. Built of this stone are the stations at Kirkham Abbey, Castle Howard, Huttons Ambo, and Malton, with the station houses at the first three now privately occupied.

When the Scarborough branch was under discussion a station was proposed at Bootham, where the line passes under the main road from

York to Thirsk and the north, but this did not materialise as a permanent station. However, in 1848 a station was opened hereabouts to serve events such as cattle shows and flower shows held on Bootham Stray, and a ticket dated August 1871 is in the National Collection.

Between Haxby and Strensall, adjacent to Strensall No 2 level crossing gatebox, a small halt platform was opened in 1926 and served by the York to Strensall and Flaxton local service, which was worked by a petrol railbus and push-and-pull steam autocars; stopping trains between York and Scarborough called at Strensall but not at Strensall Halt. However, the Halt closed in 1930 when all the stations between York and Scarborough, except Malton and Seamer, were closed, although the final traces of the Halt have only recently disappeared. Although the Scarborough branch could accommodate stopping trains and expresses during most of the year it became a difficult operation in the busy summer months when the slow trains had to be fitted in with the increased summer service boosted by numerous excursions and specials. Consequently the branch was the first in the north east to see mass closure of the intermediate stations when, in September 1930, twelve were closed to passengers. However, most of them remained open for goods and parcels traffic for a further 30 years or more, and some of them handled occasional excursions, notably to the Blackpool illuminations.

Brickworks adjacent to the station accounted for the heaviest amount of traffic at Strensall in 1913 and 1,037 tons were despatched. The other traffic was mainly agricultural, such as hay, clover, barley and potatoes; the latter accounted for 296 tons in 1913 but 1,179 tons in 1924. Flaxton handled similar traffic.

At Barton Hill the Andrews station house was built adjacent to the road leading to Barton-le-Willows and the box controlling the level crossing also controlled the goods yard. Another signalbox 300yd nearer York, at the west end of the station platforms, controlled the level crossing over the Malton–York road but this was closed in 1936 when the road was realigned and converted to dual carriageway.

Kirkham Abbey station is at the point where the line enters the valley of the River Derwent, with the line keeping the river company to ensure a level course rather than tunnel through the Howardian Hills as first proposed. However, use of the river bank required numerous curves and these have necessitated a speed restriction up to the present day. Across the river from the station are the remains of Kirkham Priory and Andrews obviously took care to ensure that the

platform elevation

street elevation

rear elevations

Haxby Station

Haxby, also by Andrews, was one version of his standard design, with the building at right angles to the track so that the most imposing frontage was to the road. The typical bay window allowed the stationmaster to look both ways along the platform. (*W. Fawcett*)

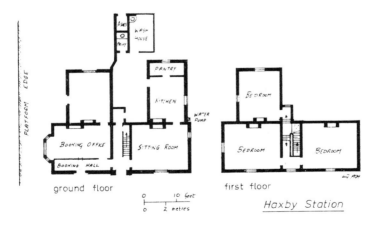

ground floor

first floor

Haxby Station

Ground floor and first floor plan of Haxby. (*W. Fawcett*)

87

station buildings did not clash with the picturesque ruins on the far bank.

Latterly the platforms were staggered, one on each side of the level crossing which carries a minor road dropping down from the A64 to cross first the railway and then the river, the latter on an ancient three-arch stone bridge. It seems probable that originally both platforms were on the east side of the level crossing, but when it became necessary to extend and raise the platforms there was insufficient space adjoining the station buildings and the up platform was moved to the west side of the crossing. Confirmation of this comes from the fact that the station house still has the typical pointed bay window favoured by Andrews, which gave the stationmaster a view along the platform.

The goods yard was on the up side of the line at the Malton end of the station, with 12 coal cells and a fixed yard crane. The brick signal box at the level crossing probably dates from the 1870s, when most NER boxes were introduced with the adoption of the block system. A NER fogging disc is still in place east of the cabin, beyond the end of the down platform; if this is not visible from the cabin because of fog it is time to call out the fogsignalmen.

There is no adjacent village and Kirkham Abbey station served a few nearby cottages and the villages of Whitwell-on-the-Hill (1 mile), Westow (1½ miles), Leavening (4 miles), Burythorpe (4 miles) and Acklam (5 miles), catering for a total population in 1911 of only 806. This resulted in 6,132 tickets being sold in the year, averaging 118 passengers per week outward and presumably about the same number inward.

The station house and yard were sold by auction in 1973 and realised £18,000; they were sold again in 1980 for £85,000, and have since been resold for use as a garden centre and coffee lounge.

The next station, Castle Howard, is only ¾ mile away nearer Malton, and it was built to serve the Vanbrugh mansion of the same name some 2½ miles away to the north-west. Situated deep in the valley of the Derwent the station, now a private house, is in an idyllic situation, with the passing trains hardly noticeable as they rumble past at a sedate 45mph. Now, of course, there are not so many trains, whereas at one time there was a constant procession of trains to Scarborough in the morning and back in the evening, laden with excursionists and holiday-makers from inland towns and cities intent on enjoying a day at the seaside.

Two-level stations: (*above*) Norham, between Tweedmouth and Kelso, was closed to passengers in 1964 and is now used as a private residence, and houses a small railway museum, by a former BR employee who worked at the station. (*J.C. Dean*). The lower picture shows the rear of the building. (*J.C. Dean*)

Stepped gables: (*above*) The Lanchester Valley station at Consett had an operational life of only five years as in 1867 it was replaced by Benfieldside, a short distance to the north, with the opening of the line from Blaydon. (*K. Hoole*); (*below*) Goathland was completed in 1865 when the Beck Hole incline diversion was opened. This view was taken in 1964 on the occasion of a BBC TV special headed by Class K4 2–6–0 No 3442 *The Great Marquess*. This station is now operated by the North York Moors Railway. (*K. Hoole*)

The station had a small goods yard on the down side west of the station, and the stone signalbox on the opposite side of the line controlled a down relief siding into which stopping trains were reversed to allow expresses to pass. In the 1950s the wooden waiting shed on the up platform was let as a holiday home. This picturesque station saw many notable visitors to Castle Howard, with polished coaches and shining horses waiting in the yard to pick up guests bound for the mansion. The most notable of all was Queen Victoria, who spent two nights there as the guest of the Earl of Carlisle as she was on her way to open Newcastle Central station and the Royal Border Bridge at Berwick on 29 August 1850. When the inaugural train ran five years earlier the Earl of Carlisle provided 'a supply of strong ale from the cellars of Castle Howard for all those who chose to partake'.

Huttons Ambo, plain Hutton until 1885, was a little used station and served a population of only 533 residing at High Hutton (1 mile), Low Hutton (adjacent to the station), Menethorpe (¾ mile) and Westow (2 miles). Westow was also served by Kirkham Abbey station, from which it was 1½ miles distant, but the NER estimated that approximately 25% of the Westow inhabitants (73) would use Huttons Ambo station and the remaining 75% (220) would use Kirkham Abbey station.

The small village of Menethorpe was on the opposite side of the Derwent from the station but the line crossed the river immediately east of the station and the villagers used the railway bridge to get to and from the station. The flagrant and persistent trespassing eventually led to the railway company erecting a footbridge across the river in 1885 and £50 of the cost of £300 was borne by the local landowner. When the station was closed in 1930 the bridge was taken over from the LNER by the North Riding and East Riding county councils and is still in use. Partly built of old rails the bridge is visible from the train. During the summer of 1982 the bridge was the focal point for the search for the gunman Barry Prudom as the river bank provided excellent cover for anyone wishing to evade capture.

The station named Malton is actually in Norton and until the 1974 boundary changes the two towns were in different counties, Malton in the North Riding of Yorkshire and Norton in the East Riding, but both are now in North Yorkshire. The station has always been the most important between York and Scarborough, serving a wide richly agricultural area as well as being at one time the junction for passenger and goods traffic radiating to Driffield, Thirsk and Whitby. For many years it was the interchange point for the Pickering and Whitby line although the actual junction was at Rillington, four miles to the east.

Malton was a milling and brewing town and large quantities of flour and ale were put on rail, together with barley; livestock was handled in large numbers and 3,232 wagons were despatched in 1913. A number of racing stables in the area meant a larger than average amount of horsebox traffic to race meetings all over the country, but I can hardly think that this accounts for the 4,971 tons of manure despatched in 1913! In the 1930s the LNER provided a fleet of motor horseboxes for the traffic to the various racecourses, but BR pulled out of the business and sold off the vehicles.

The station house and offices, all designed by Andrews, are accompanied by a train shed with an overall roof; originally it covered both up and down tracks and platforms but this meant that the platforms were very narrow and when the time came to widen them it was necessary to put the up platform outside the south wall of the station, with access by means of large archways cut through the wall, and passenger protection from the weather by an awning. This left a single track through the roofed section and this served the down platform; to reach the up platform a wheeled drawbridge was run across the down track, but this could only be done when no train was standing at the platform and when the signals at the west end were at danger.

The stationmaster's house stands at the west end of the down platform, later joined by a somewhat similar building to the east of the station entrance and this now houses a privately run refreshment room. Glazed awnings were added at the east end to protect passengers joining trains in the Whitby bay, with cross platform interchange from York–Scarborough trains. Only one track in the bay was served by a platform as the other track was used as a carriage siding. Both tracks have been removed and the area is now used for storing miscellaneous motor vehicles and farm machinery; a proposal to build a supermarket on the site has been turned down.

A signalbox opposite the up platform controlled movements through the station and adjacent to it was the locomotive turntable and a steam coaling crane, serving the two-road engine shed at the west end of the station; all these have now been swept away. At one time there were also signalboxes at Malton West and Malton East but the former has now gone and Malton East has become plain Malton,

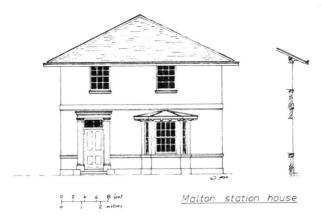

Malton stationmaster's house at the west end of the station. It has the wide overhanging eaves favoured by Andrews. (*W. Fawcett*)

controlling all the points and signals and the level crossing now with lifting barriers. A by-pass has considerably reduced road traffic over the crossing and the extensive traffic jams, which sometimes stretched for miles, have now moved elsewhere.

In 1966 the up platform was abandoned and up and down trains booked to stop at Malton began to use the former down platform in the train shed. However, the up line remained in place and allows non-stop up trains to pass outside the train shed.

Giving access to the station from the Malton side of the river is a girder bridge across the Derwent; this, and the earlier wooden bridge, carried a rail track to a mill on the north side and at one time, when the Derwent was navigable, stone was tipped from railway wagons on the bridge into boats on the river. The once busy goods yard lost its warehouse in 1957, destroyed by fire, but at the entrance there still stands an Andrews (or Andrews pattern) house in brick, probably occupied at one time by the goods agent. The whole area is liable to flooding when water which has fallen on the hills around Scarborough reaches Malton, and on occasions the water has been so deep that train services have had to be suspended. This meant that the York–Scarborough service had to be diverted via Bridlington and Market Weighton, a route which is no longer possible.

The next station to the east, Rillington, was built for use as the interchange station for Pickering (with forward progress to Whitby by horse-drawn rail coach) and thus the station was provided with an overall roof (removed 1955). However, it soon became more convenient for passengers to change at Malton, and Rillington became a wayside station of no special importance. The junction for the Pickering line was immediately east of the station and the signalbox was built nearby (on the up side); this required a gatebox at the west end of the station where the line was crossed by a minor road, but in 1959 a new box was built adjacent to the level crossing to operate the gates, and also the junction at the opposite end of the station. However, the junction became redundant following the withdrawal of the Whitby passenger service in 1965 and of the Pickering goods service in 1966.

The stations between Rillington and Seamer – Knapton, Heslerton, Weaverthorpe and Ganton – are in brick, although Ganton has now been demolished. They are in various Andrews styles, usually with the buildings end-on to the track so that the main frontage is presented to the road. Weaverthorpe is unusual in having a hipped roof and here the goods yard remained open until 1981 to handle steel traffic for a local construction firm. Heslerton was originally a minor station warranting only a single storey building, but an upper floor was added c1872. Knapton also handled goods traffic until recently but only to and from the private siding serving the Associated British Maltsters silo. The station house at Knapton is currently being fitted with modern style windows.

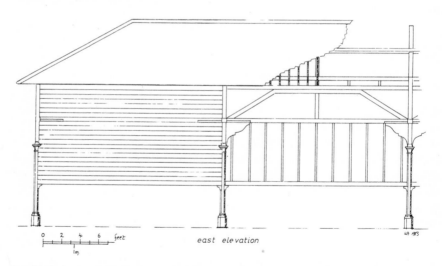

0 2 4 6 feet
1m

east elevation

Goods sheds, too, differed in design and size. G. T. Andrews favoured a pattern built up on cast iron columns, with the side opposite the loading platform boarded to within about 5ft from the ground. This shed at Seamer was four spans long. (*W. Fawcett*).

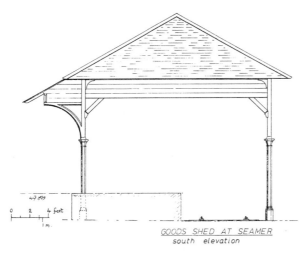

GOODS SHED AT SEAMER
south elevation

End view of the Seamer goods shed. It has now been demolished. (*W. Fawcett*)

It appears that Seamer station originally had up and down platforms separated by two tracks but that at some date, as yet not located, it was converted to an island platform station for ease of interchange between York–Scarborough and Scarborough–Hull trains to serve Filey and Bridlington. The original signalbox was some distance away from the level crossing and the gates were operated by a gateman under the control of the signalman. When it was required to place the gates directly in the hands of the signalman, using a gatewheel, the new box was built adjacent to the level crossing (c1911) but the old box was left in place and still stands.

Attractive single storey gatehouses were provided along the branch, particularly east of Malton, where numerous minor roads and tracks lead to the farms on the flat lands south of the Derwent. The through roads are limited to the level crossings at Knapton and Heslerton, both leading to the bridge over the river at Yedingham – the main York–Scarborough road before the coming of the railway – and the level crossing at Weaverthorpe carries the Sherburn–Brompton road. Heslerton and Weaverthorpe signalboxes give the impression that they were built incorrectly, at 90deg to the track, as the frames are across one end of the box rather than along its length.

The goods sheds at the smaller stations consisted of a timber framed slate roof supported on cast iron columns, with the boarded sides not reaching down to ground level.

8

THE EAST RIDING

George Hudson was rapidly expanding his empire in the 1840s, particularly east of York. The York–Scarborough line of 1845 was followed by Hull–Bridlington (a Hull & Selby Railway project taken over by Hudson) and Seamer–Filey in 1846, Filey–Bridlington and York–Market Weighton in 1847, and Market Weighton–Selby in 1848. In addition the horse-drawn Whitby and Pickering was converted for locomotive operation in 1847. On all these lines the stations were designed by G. T. Andrews, their most notable features being the overall roofs at the stations serving the larger communities at Beverley, Bridlington, Driffield, Filey, Market Weighton, Pickering and Pocklington, and the stone entrance porticos at Bridlington, Market Weighton and Pocklington and at the smaller unroofed stations at Bempton, Flamborough, Lockington and Nafferton. The standard design of stone doorcase used at Barton Hill, Kirkham Abbey, Rillington and Weaverthorpe on the Scarborough branch also appeared at Hutton Cranswick and Londesborough (on a single storey extension to the main building) and at Cayton (on the main building itself). Invariably Andrews provided a bay window in the station offices or house, looking out on to the platform so that the stationmaster could look both ways along the platform; these were to a standard design but at Market Weighton and Pocklington they were under the overall roof and were smaller bow windows.

The bay window at Cayton is another exception because it is at one end of the building, which is parallel to the track and not at the more usual 90deg. If the building was turned round through 90deg it would fulfil Andrews' principles of door to road and bay window to platform, but as it stands it looks as if Cayton was built incorrectly – by accident or design? An inappropriate bay window was added to the front of the building at some time. The station building also stands further away from the track than usual.

Of the roofed stations in East Yorkshire only the roof at Pocklington remains in its entirety, and there the ends of the roofed

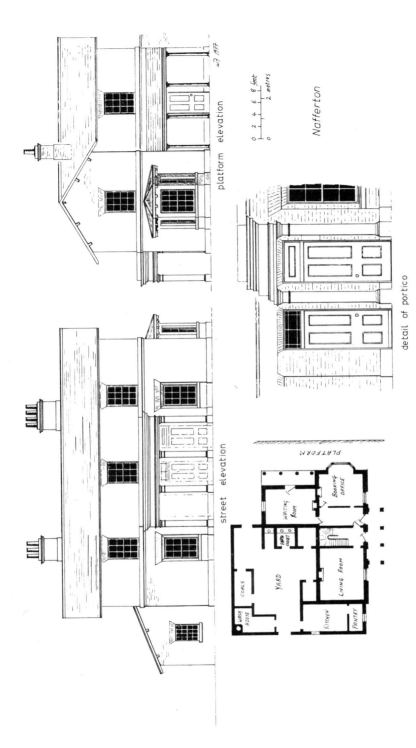

platform elevation

w? 1977

Nafferton

0 2 4 6 8 feet
0 2 metres

street elevation

detail of portico

PLATFORM

WASH HOUSE
COALS
YARD
WRITING ROOM
ROOM CLOSET
BOOKING OFFICE
KITCHEN
PANTRY
LIVING ROOM

At some of his stations Andrews provided a small portico with stone pillars. This is Nafferton, a modified version of Haxby. (*W. Fawcett*)

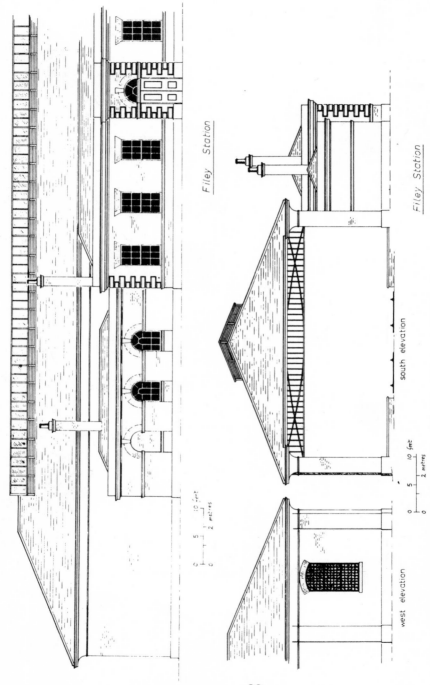

Filey Station

Filey Station

west elevation

south elevation

Filey station buildings remain in use but most of the train shed roof has now been removed. The lower drawing shows a south end view of Filey. The unusual pattern of girders was later covered by wooden panelling and end screens were erected on both platforms. (*W. Fawcett*). See plan opposite

98

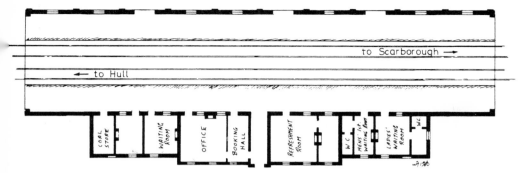

Plan of Filey when there was a refreshment room. The use of the various rooms has been changed on a number of occasions. (*W. Fawcett*)

portion of the station have been filled in to make a gymnasium for Pocklington School. Filey roof is partially dismantled; the roof at Beverley was replaced in 1908 and those at Bridlington, Driffield and Market Weighton have been removed. In fact Market Weighton station has disappeared completely and the site is now occupied by a housing estate. At Flamborough the stone portico was removed after the station closed.

On the Hull–Bridlington section single storey gatehouses were provided but north of Bridlington two-storey cottages were preferred.

The wayside stations on the Hull–Scarborough line handled the usual agricultural traffic, with Burton Agnes outstanding, despatching 4,815 tons of grain in 1913 and handling 414 wagons of livestock. Flamborough loaded 386 tons of fish in the goods yard and the wagons were allowed to run by gravity on to the back of the Scarborough–Hull slow passenger trains standing in the up platform.

Beverley handled cement (5,356 tons), oil cake (4,315 tons) and grain (2,631 tons) in 1924, together with 775 wagons of livestock, although the latter figure was 344 down on the 1913 total. As a tanning centre 'Tanning materials' accounted for 1,196 tons in 1923, and another entry for that year accounts for 135 tons of 'wagons on own wheels'. Driffield was a centre for milling and in 1913 9,034 tons of oil cake were loaded. Bridlington handled agricultural traffic from the surrounding area and the station was notable for the large number of 'day trippers' that used the station but, unfortunately, no details are available. The resort was served by trains which terminated at Bridlington and also by excursions which ran through to Scarborough. At busy times between 20 and 30 excursions brought in thousands of passengers, old and young, all bound for the sea front, usually

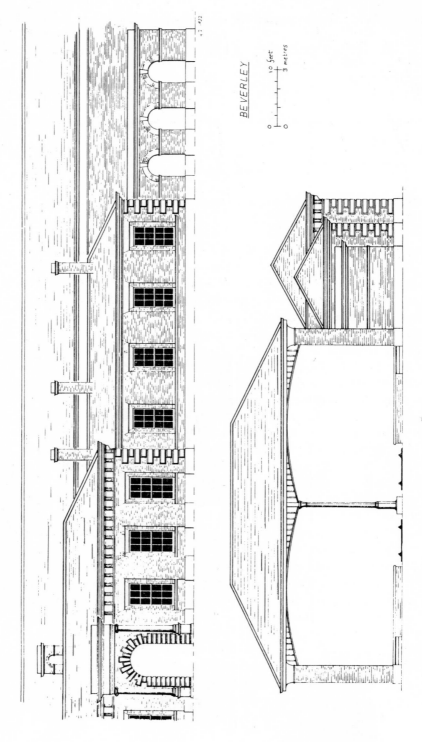

BEVERLEY

0   10 feet
0   3 metres

The handsome frontage of Beverley station, again by G. T. Andrews, opened in 1846. In the end elevation the original roof is shown, with columns between the tracks. This was replaced in 1908. (*W. Fawcett*)

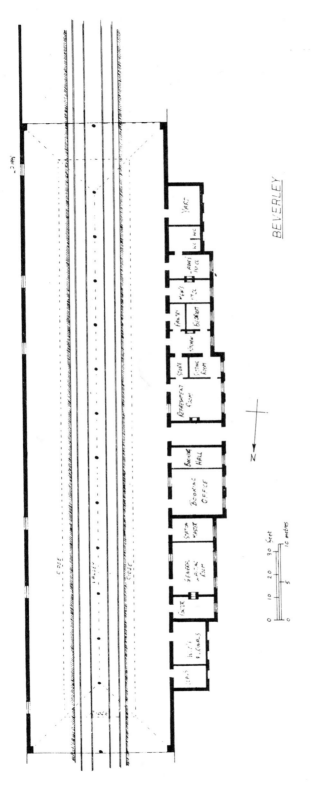

Plan of Beverley station, with original roof. (*W. Fawcett*)

returning to the station in the evening weary but happy!

Although Hudson planned to build a line from York to Beverley only the York–Market Weighton section was opened (in 1847) and it was 1861 before the Market Weighton–Beverley section was completed. Thus the stations east of Market Weighton do not follow the same pattern as those in the York direction, the latter being by Andrews. Over the years there was a spate of renaming: Earswick was originally Huntington, Warthill was Stockton-on-Forest, Holtby was Gate Helmsley, Nunburnholme was Burnby, and Londesborough was Shipton; only Stamford Bridge, Fangfoss, Pocklington and Market Weighton retained their original names.

In 1913 Pocklington loaded 3,300 tons of vegetables in bulk and 2,302 tons of potatoes, but in 1924 there was a mere 163 tons of vegetables but 5,033 tons of potatoes. Market Weighton handled 1,639 tons of barley, 847 tons of grain, and 564 tons of wheat in 1913, the products of the large fields on the Yorkshire Wolds north of the town.

Two small resorts on the coast were connected to Hull by independent railways, Withernsea by the Hull & Holderness Railway in 1854, and Hornsea by the Hull & Hornsea Railway ten years later, but both soon became part of the NER. I have no record of the architect who designed the Hull & Holderness stations but the Hull & Hornsea stations were designed by Rawlins Gould of York, an employee of G. T. Andrews before the latter's death in 1855. Thus it is not surprising that there is a similarity between the portico at Whitby by Andrews (1847) and that at Hornsea by Gould (1864).

Travelling west out of Hull on the 1840 line to Selby the stations between Hessle and Staddlethorpe (now Gilberdyke) were rebuilt or replaced when widening to four tracks took place in 1904. This meant that Hessle, Ferriby, Broomfleet and Staddlethorpe acquired platforms on the outer (slow) lines only, but Brough had platforms on all four tracks.

As the major part of the widening took part on the south side of the line this allowed some of the earlier buildings to remain on the down side at Hessle, Ferriby and Brough. However, in more recent times the virtual disappearance of freight traffic to and from Hull has meant that four tracks are no longer required for the whole distance and now only Broomfleet to Gilberdyke is four track, with three tracks between Ferriby and Melton Halt. This has meant alterations to the platforms of certain stations and, for instance, at Hessle each platform has been

HULL AND WITHERNSEA.

Light Type—a.m.   Dark Type—p.m.

WEEKDAYS

					A			B			C		
HULL	dep	5 47	6 33			9 40					3 11		4 30
Botanic Gardens	,,	5 51	6 37	9 32		9 44			3 15		4 37
Stepney	,,	5 54	6 40	9 35		9 47			3 18		4 37
Sculcoates	,,	5 57		9 38		9 50			3 21		4 40
Southcoates	,,	6 2	6 45	9 42		9 54		1 20	3 25		4 44
Marfleet	,,	6 7	6 50			9 59			3 30		4 49
Hedon	,,	6 13	6 58	9 52		10 6		1 31	3 37		4 56
Rye Hill	,,	6 19	7 3			10 12			3 43		
Keyingham	,,	6 23	7 8			10 17			3 48		
Ottringham	,,	6 28	7 13	10 3		10 21			3 52		
Winestead	,,	6 34	7 19			10 27			3 58		
Patrington	,,	6 38	7 24			10 33	2 53		4 3		
WITHERNSEA	arr	6 45	7 31	10 15		10 40		1 54	4 10		

WEEKDAYS—continued.   SUNDAYS.

				D						
HULL	dep	5 35	6 20	7 23	9	5 10 55	7 45	2 15	7 15	—
Botanic Gardens	,,		6 24	7 28	9 10 59	7 49	2 19	7 19	—
Stepney	,,		6 27				7 52	2 22	7 22	—
Sculcoates	,,				9 15	7 55	2 25	7 25	—
Southcoates	,,	5 43	6 32	7 33	9 17	8 2 2 29	7 29	—
Marfleet	,,		6 37		9 11		8 4 2 34	7 34	—
Hedon	,,	5 52	6 43	7 42	9 25	8 11 2 41	7 41	—
Rye Hill	,,		6 49				8 17 2 47	7 47	—
Keyingham	,,	6 0		7 53		8 22 2 52	7 52	—
Ottringham	,,	6 4	6 55	7 57		8 26 2 56	7 56	—
Winestead	,,	6 10				8 32	—
Patrington	,,	6 15				8 37	3 2	—
WITHERNSEA	arr	6 22	7 11	8 9	9 5 11 52	8 44	3 14	8 14	—

WEEKDAYS

WITHERNSEA	dep	6 55	8 0	8 50	10 53	3 17	5 50	6 39	7 40
Patrington	,,	7 3	8 8	8 58	11 1	3 25	5 58	6 47	7 48
Winestead	,,	7 6	8 11		11 4	3 28		6 50	7 51
Ottringham	,,	7 12	8 17	9 5	11 10	3 34	6 5	6 56	7 58
Keyingham	,,	7 16	8 21		11 14	3 38		7 0	
Rye Hill	,,	7 21	8 26		11 19	3 43		7 5	
Hedon	,,	7 27	8 32	9 15	11 25	3 49	6 15	7 11	8 8
Marfleet	,,	7 33			11 31	3 56		7 18	
Southcoates	,,	7 40	8 44	9 24	11 37	4 4	6 24	7 23	8 17
Sculcoates	,,	7 44			11 41	4 8		7 28	
Stepney	,,	7 47			11 44	4 11		7 31	
Botanic Gardens	,,	7 50	8 49		11 47	4 14	6 29	7 33	8 22
HULL	arr	7 57	8 56	9 32	11 54	4 18	6 40	7 40	8 32

WEEKDAYS—continued.   SUNDAYS.

					E				
WITHERNSEA	dep	8 15	8 30	10 20		8 55	5 20	8 28	8 45
Patrington	,,			10 28		9 3	5 28	8 36	8 53
Winestead	,,					9 6			
Ottringham	,,		8 42	10 36		9 12	5 37		
Keyingham	,,			10 40		9 16	5 41		
Rye Hill	,,		8 49	10 45		9 21	5 46		
Hedon	,,		8 55	10 51		9 27	5 52	8 53	9 17
Marfleet	,,			10 58		9 34	5 59		
Southcoates	,,	8 43	9 1	11 3		9 39	6 4	9 3	9 24
Sculcoates	,,			11 8		9 43	6 8		
Stepney	,,	8 48	9 12	11 11		9 46	6 11	9 10	
Botanic Gardens	,,	8 51	9 18	11 47		9 49	6 14	9 13	
HULL	arr	8 56	9 22	11 18		9 54	6 21	9 21	9 46

A Will run from 12th July to 30th August. **B** Mondays, Thursdays, and Saturdays only. **C** Tuesdays only. **D** Tuesdays and Saturdays only. **E** Will not run after 14th September. **f** Stops when required.

On Monday, 4th August (Bank Holiday), the ordinary train service between Hull and Withernsea will be suspended. For particulars of the service on that day see special bills.

HULL AND HORNSEA.

Light Type—a.m.   Dark Type—p.m.

WEEKDAYS.

				A				B		C			D E
HULL	dep	5 55	7 20	—		9 45		1 35	1 55			3 30
Botanic Gardens	,,	5 56	7 24	9 40		9 49		1 39	1 59			3 34
Stepney	,,	6 2	7 27	9 43		9 52		1 42	2 2			3 37
Sculcoates	,,	6 5		9 45		9 55						3 40
Wilmington	,,	6 8	7 31	9 47		9 58		1 46	2 6			3 43
Sutton-on-Hull	,,	6 13	7 36			10 3		1 51				3 48
Swine	,,	6 19				10 9						3 54
Skirlaugh	,,	6 23				10 13						3 58
Burton Constable	,,	6 27	7 47	10		10 17		2 20			
Whitedale	,,	6 30				10 20					
Sigglesthorne	,,	6 34				10 24					
Hornsea Bridge	,,	6 43	7 57	10 14		10 34	2 58	2 8	2 31			4 18
HORNSEA	arr	6 45	7 59	10 16		10 36		2 10	2 33	2 56		4 20

WEEKDAYS—continued.   SUNDAYS.

									F			
HULL	dep	4 18	5 50	6 12	7 8	9	7 50	2 20	7 40
Botanic Gardens	,,	4 22		6 16		9	4 10 51	7 54	2 24	7 44
Stepney	,,	4 26		6 20			7 10 54	7 57	2 27	7 47
Sculcoates	,,	4 29		6 22			10	8 0	2 30	
Wilmington	,,	4 31		6 25	7 14	9	3 10 58	8 3	2 33	7 51
Sutton-on-Hull	,,	4 36	5 59	6 30	7 19	9	18 11 3	8 8	
Swine	,,	4 42		6 36			9 24 11 9	8 14	2 44	
Skirlaugh	,,	4 46		6 40	7 26	9	28 11 13	8 18	
Burton Constable	,,	4 50		6 44	7 30	9	32 11 17	8 22	
Whitedale	,,	4 53		6 47		9	35 11 21	8 25	
Sigglesthorne	,,	4 57		6 51			9	8 29	3 1	8 21
Hornsea Bridge	,,	5 6	6 16	7 0	7 40	9	9 11 30	8 39	
HORNSEA	arr	5 8	6 18	7 2	7 42	9	51 11 30	8 41	3 11	8 30

WEEKDAYS.

				G							
HORNSEA	dep	6 55	7 57	8 30	9	0 10 50		8 24	8 30
Hornsea Bridge	,,	6 58	8 0	8 33	9	3 10 53		8 27	
Sigglesthorne	,,	7 5	8 7		9	9 10 59			6 35
Whitedale	,,	7 9	8 11	8 40		11 3			
Burton Constable	,,	7 13	8 15		9	15 11 6			6 45
Skirlaugh	,,	7 18	8 19		9	19 11 10			
Swine	,,	7 23	8 23			11 14			
Sutton-on-Hull	,,	7 30	8 29	8 51	9	25 11 20		8 45	6 54
Wilmington	,,	7 35	8 34	8 56	9	31 11 25		8 50	6 59
Sculcoates	,,	7 37	8 36	8 58		11 27		8 52	
Stepney	,,	7 40	8 39			11 30		8 55	
Botanic Gardens	,,	7 43	8 42	9 2		11 33		8 58	7 2
HULL	arr	7 50	8 49	9 9	9	40 11 40		9 6	7 14

WEEKDAYS—continued.   SUNDAYS.

				C				H		
HORNSEA	dep	7 15	8 0	8 15	10 19		9 0	5 20	8 30	8 40
Hornsea Bridge	,,	7 18	8 3	8 18			9 3		
Sigglesthorne	,,	7 24		8 24	10 19		9 9	5 28	8 48
Whitedale	,,	7 28		8 28	10 10		9 13	5 32	
Burton Constable	,,	7 31		8 31	10 14		9 16	5 35	8 40
Skirlaugh	,,	7 35		8 35	10 18		9 20	5 39	
Swine	,,	7 39		8 39	10 45		9 24	5 43	
Sutton-on-Hull	,,	7 45	8 23	8 50	10 45		9 30	5 49	8 50	
Wilmington	,,	7 50	8 23	8 56	10 10		9 36	5 54	8 56	
Sculcoates	,,						9 37	5 56	8 57	
Stepney	,,	7 54	8 27	9 3	10 46		9 40	5 59	9 2	
Botanic Gardens	,,	7 57	8 30	9 3	10 49		9 43	6 2	9 3	
HULL	arr	8 4	8 38	9 15	10 55		9 50	6 9	9 11	9 39

A Will run from 12th July to 30th August. **B** Thursdays and Saturdays only. **C** Mondays, Thursdays, and Saturdays only. **D** Tuesdays only. **E** Stops at Goxhill (between Sigglesthorne and Hornsea Bridge), to set down from Hull. **F** Tuesdays and Saturdays only. **G** Stops at Goxhill (between Hornsea Bridge and Sigglesthorne), on Tuesdays to take up for Hull. **H** Will not run after 14th September.

On Monday, 4th August (Bank Holiday), the ordinary train service between Hull and Hornsea will be suspended. For particulars of the service on that day see special bills.

Trains shown in italics do not run daily throughout the period for which this time table is issued.

The Hull–Withernsea and Hull–Hornsea tables in the NER 1902 pocket timetable. Both services were withdrawn in October 1964. (*K. Hoole Collection*) extended outwards by about 8ft to serve what were the fast lines, while at Ferriby the down platform alone has been extended to serve what was the down fast; the up slow is retained through the station and thus the up platform has not been affected.

At Brough the two slow line platforms have become bays for trains from the Hull direction. Broomfleet has had a chequered existence. It appears as a market day stopping place in Bradshaw until 1853 but then disappears, until in July 1861 platforms were authorised and it reappeared in the timetable, still open only on market day (Tuesday) in Hull. From 1907 two or three trains in each direction stopped 'when required', the only trains with a mandatory stop being the market day trains. Finally in 1920 it became a normal full time station. In the last century Crabley Creek, at a minor level crossing 1¾ miles nearer Hull, also had market day stops but in this case it did not materialise as a fully fledged station.

West of Gilberdyke the 1869 line to Goole diverges, and the Selby line continues as double track through Eastrington and Howden, renamed South Eastrington and North Howden respectively in 1922 to avoid confusion with the Hull & Barnsley stations with similar names, although both ex-NER stations lost their prefix in 1961. Because of the range of old station buildings west of the level crossing at Howden the down platform, when raised in height, had to be removed to the east side of the crossing, making the platforms staggered.

In peacetime Howden's main traffic was manure, despatching around the 3,000 ton mark in 1913, rising to 3,500 tons in 1923. In World War I a gigantic airship shed 800ft long × 400ft wide and 175ft high was erected on level land 1½ miles north of the station; the construction materials and workmen brought a great influx of traffic, and a single line branch was laid to the site. The airship R100 was built in the shed but after that had been launched the building became redundant because of the unfortunate experiences with this type of transport and in 1933 a start was made on dismantling the shed for scrap, bringing about the movement back to Howden of some 10,000 tons of traffic consigned from the Sheffield firm of dismantlers. It seems probable that following World War I some surplus locomotives were stored at the airship shed, or on the Royal Naval Airship Siding, as in 1923 1,307 tons of 'Locomotives and tenders on own wheels' were accounted for at North Howden station.

Hemingbrough, closed to passengers in 1967, was named Cliffe until 1874, the village of that name being much nearer to the station than Hemingbrough village. From Staddlethorpe westwards the villagers attended Selby market rather than Hull, and were served by a Mondays Only 10.25am from Staddlethorpe which ran out from Selby as an empty train. From July 1923 the 6.52am Selby to Staddlethorpe was worked by the ex-NER Leyland bus with rail wheels; this then worked the 7.35am Staddlethorpe to Goole, and back to Selby direct at 8.02am. This interesting vehicle was destroyed by fire at Selby shed in November 1926. On Sundays in the late 1920s a Selby-based Sentinel steam railcar worked a service between Doncaster and Staddlethorpe to connect with Leeds–Hull trains. Hull based Sentinel cars also worked services to Goole and Thorne North, the limit of the North Eastern Area, and there was also a school term service between Goole and Thorne North operated by the Goole based Sentinel car belonging to the LNER/LMS Axholme Joint Railway.

The first railway to reach Selby was that from Leeds in 1834, and although planned to go through to Hull it was left to the separate Hull & Selby company to build the East Riding section of the line. The Leeds & Selby terminated at a station which is still standing, but when the River Ouse was bridged to continue the line to Hull a second station was built to the west of the original. The rural branch to Market Weighton opened in 1848, and in 1871 the opening of the Chaloners Whin Junction to Shaftholme Junction route put Selby on the main line, although this is a status which it has now lost with the opening of the Selby coalfield diversion.

With the building of a new bridge across the river in 1891 the station had to be rebuilt and it was provided with loops serving the platforms so that trains calling at the station did not delay East Coast expresses. Additional services to use the station commenced on 1 July 1904 (to Cawood) and 1 May 1912 (to Goole) but the former service was withdrawn from 1 January 1930 (although the goods traffic continued for a further 30 years) and the latter on 15 June 1964; the Market Weighton service (extended to Driffield and Bridlington in 1890) was withdrawn on 14 June 1965.

Selby was an important market town, with a rich agricultural hinterland, but it had industries of its own, particularly milling and shipbuilding; the former accounted for 99,121 tons of oil cake traffic in 1924, together with 30,764 tons of flour and bran, and 32,564 tons of oils. The shipbuilding materials, being inwards traffic, does not appear in the station returns, although the 1,516 tons of scrap iron and steel could account for some of the waste material from the shipyard, where vessels were launched sideways into the river.

Passengers travelling to some North Eastern stations were dismayed to find their train passing through without stopping. This occurred at Selby, where trains from Bridlington ran through on the main line before reversing into the up side bay, giving connections into a York–Kings Cross train in the up platform.

The Alnwick & Coldstream pattern stations: (above) Two interesting stations were provided on the link between Burnhouse Junction (near Spennymoor) and Bishop Auckland opened in 1885. Extensive use was made of wood and glass for the passenger accommodation. This is Coundon in 1950, eleven years after closure to passenger traffic. (*J.W. Armstrong*); (below) This design of station was used extensively on the line between Alnwick and Coldstream, opened in 1887. The buildings were to a similar basic design modified to suit the site and the importance of the station. This is Wooperton about 1905; it was closed to passengers in 1930. (*Lens of Sutton*)

Single platform stations on double lines: (*above*) Crook (second station). The NER service was from Darlington to Blackhill (originally Benfieldside) but between 1956 and 1965 Crook was the terminus after the Crook–Tow Law section had been closed, and before it was further cut back to a Darlington–Bishop Auckland service. Class A8 4–6–2T No 69872 has just arrived at Crook from Darlington and is about to run round its train ready for the return journey. (*T.J. Edgington*); (*below*) Seghill, on the former Blyth & Tyne line to Bedlington. Note that the signal indication authorises movement over the crossover on to the down line as the train is bound for Blyth or Newbiggin. (*J.W. Armstrong*)

9

NEWCASTLE TO BERWICK

Without a doubt the most imposing wayside stations on the NER were those on the main line between Newcastle and Berwick, which started life as the Newcastle & Berwick Railway but which almost immediately became part of the York, Newcastle & Berwick. The company's early days were fraught with arguments between the advantages of steam (favoured by George Hudson) or atmospheric traction (supported by Lord Howick) but Parliament decided that steam power should be used and the Hudson line was opened on 1 July 1847.

The line actually started at a junction with the Newcastle & North Shields Railway north of Heaton and at first the northern terminus was at Tweedmouth (where the station premises included a small hotel) until the temporary bridge across the Tweed to Berwick was ready for use from 10 October 1848. The permanent bridge followed on 29 August 1850, when it was opened by Queen Victoria.

The more important stations were fine buildings, designed in a neo-Tudor style by Benjamin Green of the Newcastle architectural practice of J. & B. Green, and the smaller stations, crossing keepers' houses and platform waiting sheds were to the same style but on a smaller scale. The buildings were invariably decorated with large stone ball finials, some stations having as many as 14!

Some stations, such as Beal, Lucker and Tweedmouth, have been demolished, but others, notably Warkworth, are now in private occupation and have been sympathetically restored. In fact Warkworth, with its imposing flight of stone steps up from the road, now looks more like a 'gentleman's country residence' than a former station! Even the small goods sheds and weigh cabins were carefully designed to fit in with the station houses, but it is a pity that two goods sheds, at Acklington and Christon Bank, have been described as 'Gothic engine sheds' in a recent comprehensive work on railway architecture.

The station houses were large structures with spacious accommodation, but they must have been cold in winter without the benefit of

Chathill, one of the fine Newcastle & Berwick stations. (*W. Fawcett*)

Chathill. Station approach elevation. (*W. Fawcett*)

central heating. There appears to have been little attempt at standardisation except in details and no two stations were exactly alike, although there was a fairly close similarity in some of them. Perhaps the closest were Beal, Longhirst and Stannington, with square bay windows at ground and first floor level. Then came Belford and Warkworth, both with a small entrance portico but Belford, being on level ground, lacked the flight of steps which was necessary at Warkworth.

Acklington and Christon Bank bore some resemblance to one another, but whereas Christon Bank had a small gable at each end Acklington had a similar gable at one end only; both had an awning between the two wings of the main house/office block, but Acklington had an additional shelter for passengers provided by an awning along the front of a single storey building at the north end of the main buildings. Of the small stations and cottages Smeafield was similar to

110

The waiting shed on the up platform at Acklington; one of the distinctive smaller buildings on the north main line. (*W. Fawcett*)

Goswick, Newham was similar to Chevington, and Forest Hall (with two storeys) was generally similar to Plessey (with one), but all three pairs quoted differed in one way or another. Because the line through Longhoughton station was built on an embankment the entrance to the station buildings was at ground floor level from the yard but at first floor level from the platform.

The first station north of Newcastle Central is Manors, now only a pale shadow of its former self and served only by the local service to Morpeth and Alnmouth, although at the time of writing a single Newcastle–Edinburgh train stops at 17.19. A station in the Manors area first appeared with the opening of the Newcastle & North Shields Railway in 1839, but within a decade it was also necessary to provide accommodation for the Newcastle & Berwick trains which had to wait to reach the new Central station opened in 1850.

The Blyth & Tyne Railway reached Newcastle in 1864 and established its terminus at New Bridge Street, only a short distance away from the NER Manors station, but there was no connection between the two routes until 1909, although the B&T had been taken over by the NER in 1874.

The Tyneside electrification of 1904 was a most important 20th century development and the first electric trains commenced running between New Bridge Street and Benton on 29 March 1904; this service was gradually extended until on 1 July 1904 the electric trains reached Newcastle Central via Backworth, Tynemouth, North Shields, Heaton and Manors.

A scheme to link Manors and New Bridge Street was then put in hand and was completed on 1 January 1909, when Manors North station opened replacing New Bridge Street, and at the same time the original platforms serving the main line and the Tynemouth line became Manors East. However, there was only a limited service over the new connection and this ran between Central and Benton hourly in the middle of the day, with the main service still from Manors North, via Backworth, Tynemouth and Manors East to Central station (and in the opposite direction). It was not until 1 March 1917 that a circular service commenced in both directions, so that a train from Newcastle to Tynemouth, Whitley Bay and back to Central station called at Manors East on its outward journey and at Manors North 58 minutes later on its inward journey, covering the section between Manors and Central in both directions.

In 1901 the city and its surrounding areas were invaded by the electric tram, which made a great difference to NER traffic. In 1901/2 trams commenced running between Newcastle, North Shields and Whitley Bay but operated by three separate concerns. The NER could not compete for short distance traffic and passengers decreased:

STATION	PASSENGERS BOOKED	
	1901	*1911*
Byker	100,401	28,741
Heaton	1,151,158	519,350
Manors East & North	984,781	565,231
St Anthonys	32,428	11,283
St Peters	112,636	37,111
Walker	172,563	37,247
Walkergate	116,481	56,278
West Jesmond	353,021	112,440

On the middle distance traffic it more or less held its own:

Cullercoats	259,499	271,939
North Shields	1,123,490	1,107,300
Percy Main	227,991	228,273
Tynemouth	375,523	356,302

but it was on the longer distance traffic, where the NER was able to provide a fast, clean and reliable service, that building developments took place for the season ticket holders:

Monkseaton	80,219	241,313
Whitley Bay	320,733	509,974

Eventually a 20 minute service operated round the circle in both directions calling at all stations, with an additional hourly service outwards via the Riverside branch providing a fast service back to Newcastle, running non-stop between West Monkseaton and Manors East or North depending on the route. In the reverse direction trains ran non-stop between Manors and West Monkseaton, returning via the Riverside branch.

10

NEWCASTLE TO CARLISLE

The need for efficient, reliable and faster communication across the country from Newcastle to Carlisle was realised in the 19th century and thoughts centred on a canal, until it was pointed out that a canal would cost three times as much as a railway. This led to the formation of the Newcastle & Carlisle Railway in 1825 and the company obtained its first Act on 22 May 1829. Work commenced at both ends of the line in 1830, but it was another eight years before the line was opened throughout, and then from Gateshead and not from Newcastle. It was October 1839 before a branch from Blaydon gave access to Newcastle, crossing the Tyne at Scotswood, and it was not until 1 January 1851 that the Newcastle & Carlisle trains commenced using the west end of Newcastle Central station, four months after the opening of the east end.

The Newcastle & Carlisle, which originally favoured right hand running, built some picturesque neo-Tudor houses, mostly small and, as there were no platforms to consider, not always close to or parallel to the line. Consequently when platforms were eventually erected the station house was not always in a convenient position relevant to the line and had to be left to stand isolated or, where platforms could be built adjacent to the house, the platform level was level with the window sills and steps had to be provided down into the house or offices.

For most of its length the N&C was in Northumberland, although between Scotswood Bridge and just east of Wylam it was in County Durham; a short distance west of Rose Hill (later Gilsland) it passed over a tributary of the River Irthing and into Cumberland. Incidentally in J. W. Carmichael's notable 'Views on the Newcastle and Carlisle Railway' (originally published in parts between 1836 and 1838) he illustrated the most westerly station in Northumberland, Rose Hill, which changed little over the years, except for the erection of a dormer window on each side of the central gable. However, over much of its life the station frontage was obscured by a canopy, a small and charming feature in N&C days, but an extra large and clumsy version in NE and LNER days.

Riding Mill also had an N&C building and partially staggered platforms, but its most unusual feature was the barrow crossing cut through the down platform in line with the west end of the up platform – for milk traffic? When not in use the gap in the down platform was covered with timber (sleepers?) so that the platform surface was level and unbroken. Sturdy gateposts and a substantial wooden gate formed part of the stanchion and tube fence along the rear of the platform. Main traffic from the station was locally felled timber, which amounted to 2,569 tons in 1923.

Corbridge, where the station is south of the Tyne and the town is on the north bank, was another station with an overtrack signalbox but, in common with a few other boxes of this type, it was destroyed by fire in 1957. This station was unusual in that a road bridge ran across the centre of the station, spanning platforms and tracks. According to J. M. Fleming this was because the N&C omitted to obtain powers to cross the turnpike road (now A68) on the level and in 1847 built a bridge to carry the road, necessitating the demolition of the original

Fourstones

Many Newcastle & Carlisle Railway buildings remain but this is one of the NER replacement buildings, at Fourstones, dating from 1879/80. (*W. Fawcett*)

station house on the south side of the line and its replacement by a house on the north side. Arches through the embankment leading up to the bridge on the south side of the line accommodated tracks into the goods yards.

In its early days Hexham had a roofed train shed but this disappeared a century or so ago, when it was replaced by typical NER platform awnings. In more recent times the station footbridge has lost its covering, and the large NER enamelled station nameboard lettered HEXHAM FOR ALLENDALE has gone. There was a bay platform at the west end for use by Allendale branch trains, and another at the east end used by local trains to Newcastle; the latter platform could also be used by trains from Allendale, which ran through the station and reversed into the bay to give connections with a following Carlisle–Newcastle train brought to a stand at the up through platform. Signals were operated from an overtrack box east of the station, which controlled the outlets from the goods yard and the engine shed, both on the south side of the line, with Hexham West at the Carlisle end of the station, but this box was closed in 1966.

Many Newcastle & Carlisle buildings have undergone alterations during their 145 years' existence, such as an increase in living accommodation, or alterations to the windows, and some stations have disappeared completely as they have become redundant; Blaydon station, referred to in 1911 as 'one of the oldest and best known landmarks in the town' was replaced in 1912. The old station was a small single storey building, with narrow platforms, but the new station in red pressed bricks, had 'large door and window openings treated in a simple manner'. Each platform was covered with a light iron-framed glazed roof carried on ornamental cast iron pillars, with glazed windscreens at the ends. However, 65 years later this station, 'neat in design and grouping', according to a 1912 account, was in a disgraceful condition, with roofing removed and some rooms still showing signs of damage by a fire which occurred three years earlier. In addition some spray-paint addicts had been at work and British Rail even admitted that it was 'the eyesore of all eyesores'.

Wylam, with its connections with early coal mining, iron making, William Hedley, George Stephenson, and the development of the steam locomotive, still retains its N&C station house on the down platform, with its corbelled gable, although the house has been extended on each side of the gable by the addition of extra rooms on the first floor. The platforms are now staggered, with the down

115

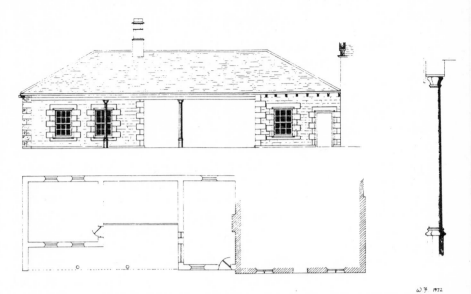

The booking office and waiting room at Wylam was a Newcastle & Carlisle building and adjoined the station house. (*W. Fawcett*)

platform east of the level crossing and the up platform to the west. It retains its overtrack signalbox.

Prudhoe has a high hipped roof signalbox and the station buildings are of a style used about 1880; it was renamed Prudhoe for Ovingham in 1937 but reverted to Prudhoe in 1971. The main goods traffic in 1913 was earthenware drain pipes.

At Stocksfield a small attractive house in stone, with porch, was built on the down side but set at an angle to the running lines and adjacent to the line into the goods yard. The platforms were partly staggered and both provided shelter for passengers in open fronted waiting sheds common on the N&C line, with very deep front valances. To accommodate the down platform and the cast iron footbridge the north-east corner of the goods shed was cut off.

The station house at Hexham, illustrated by Carmichael, still stands on the west side of the entrance, although considerably altered over the years, and latterly supporting the end of the entrance canopy.

In addition to the Newcastle–Carlisle service, and the local services, there was the North British Hawick and Riccarton Junction to Newcastle service, which joined the Carlisle line at Border Counties Junction, a mile west of Hexham. Before the 1923 Grouping these trains were worked by North British engines, and in LNER days ex-North British engines were stationed at Blaydon shed for this

116

Overbridge stations: (*above*) Some stations utilised wooden offices on an overbridge, as at Heaton, built in 1887 when four tracks were provided from Manors to the divergence of the Berwick and North Shields lines at Heaton Junction. (*Author's collection*); (*below*) A brick office block on the overbridge, also opened in 1887, was at Dinsdale, on the new line built to allow Stockton & Darlington line east to west trains to use the new Bank Top station at Darlington. The goods facilities were retained at the station it replaced, Fighting Cocks, on the original route of 1825. (*Author's collection*)

Roofs: (*above*) The interior of Leeds City station in 1959. This was the North Eastern and London & North Western portion built in 1869, with the original mansard roof in the foreground and a dissimilar extension roof in the background. The station was completely rebuilt in the 1960s, replaced by a conglomeration which does no credit to one of our larger cities. (*British Rail*); (*below*) In spite of the ravages of time and German bombing, York station roof has changed little in its lifetime. It was opened in 1877, replacing an earlier station within the city walls, and its sweeping curve makes an impressive picture, especially when the sun is streaming through the openings. (*British Rail*)

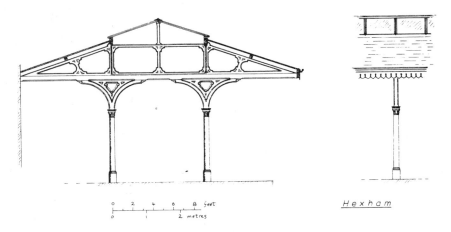

The style of roof on the platforms at Hexham, dating from 1871. (W. Fawcett)

working. There were also Saturday trains between Hexham and Bellingham or Kielder but the NB line closed on 15 October 1956. The NER Allendale branch, which also joined the Carlisle line at Border Counties Junction, closed to passengers much earlier (22 September 1930) but remained open for goods traffic until 20 November 1950.

At Fourstones, closed in 1967, the station buildings were replaced in 1880 at a cost of £880, and a further £69 was spent on converting the old buildings into a house for the stationmaster. A wooden waiting shed with stone base and deep valance, remained until closure. This was a busy station in North Eastern days, handling lime, minerals, stone and paper, as well as the livestock and other traffic associated with a rural station.

For a time Haydon Bridge was the terminus of the line from Newcastle and originally had a roofed train shed. However, in 1877 £2,291 was allocated for new station buildings and goods warehouse, and those erected on the platform were of the double gable type, with canopy between, similar to those built at Fourstones, but with a different arrangement of windows. The original station house, with a three-arch arcade in front, was left adjacent to the tracks into the goods yard, at the east end of the station. Until the opening of the Allendale branch in 1869 Haydon Bridge handled the lead obtained from the hills to the south, Allendale being only five miles away across the bridge over the Tyne depicted in Carmichael's drawing. Latterly the main traffic at Haydon Bridge was roadstone.

Bardon Mill was another station latterly with staggered platforms, the two adjacent ends being joined by a sleeper crossing; yet another deep wooden front valance waiting shed was provided, but in this example the front of the shed was enclosed with wood pierced by three windows and a door.

It is unusual to find as important a station as Haltwhistle with staggered platforms, but the constraints of the river and the bridge carrying the Alston branch led to the Newcastle bound platform being sited east of the station buildings, with the Carlisle platform sited to the west, the adjoining ends being served by a footbridge. The down platform was latterly an island and until 1976 the outer face (that nearest the river) was used by the Alston branch trains, which departed from the east end and then immediately headed south over the river. The N&C station buildings remain on the north side. A locomotive turntable was provided at the west end of the station, with a water column for use by engines turning there, and there were also water columns at the ends of the two through platforms, all supplied from a tank dating from 1861 situated on a handsome stone base on the up platform.

Until 1 May 1869 Gilsland was known as Rosehill, although N&C timesheets refer to it as Rose Hill. Being built on an embankment it was served by a subway between the platforms. Gilsland was the centre of much Roman activity and some excavation work was actually carried out on railway property; extensive remains were found at this Roman 'milecastle' site, including coins dated between 32BC and AD 324. Twentieth century excavations revealed that much damage had been caused to the site during the construction of the railway 75 years earlier.

West of the level crossing at Low Row the Naworth Coal Co Ltd had its own coal depot on the north side of the running lines, while on the south side a short siding was installed in 1921 for Carrick's Cumberland Dairy & Pure Milk Supply Co Ltd. The station closed in 1959.

Naworth (494ft above sea level) was at the summit of a 12 mile climb from Carlisle (67ft asl) and eastbound freight trains were often assisted in the rear as far as Low Row. Naworth started life as a private station for the use of the Earl of Carlisle at nearby Naworth Castle; it first appeared in the public timetable in 1871, but closed in 1952. Unfortunately the station's greatest claim to fame is a tragic one! On 30 August 1926 a new Hailey open charabanc was crossing the line when it was struck by the 1.18pm Newcastle to Carlisle express. Seven occupants of the charabanc were killed instantly and one passenger died later; three, including the motor driver, were seriously injured, and three received minor injuries and shock. The gatekeeper, who had only just taken up duty at Naworth, mistakenly opened the gates as the train was approaching and although the driver of the charabanc accelerated to try and get out of the way the vehicle was caught by the engine and wrecked.

Milton station and the Brampton area played a large part in the early days of the Newcastle & Carlisle Railway and readers are referred to *Lord Carlisle's Railways* by B. Webb and D. A. Gordon (RCTS 1978) for a detailed account. Suffice to say here that Milton station was opened in 1838, but was renamed Brampton in 1870, and Brampton Junction in 1885. It apparently reverted to plain Brampton in 1891 but became Brampton Junction again in 1913. British Rail renamed it Brampton (Cumberland) in 1971, only for it to become Brampton (Cumbria) in 1975 as a result of the local authority boundary changes. It is still open to passengers, but closed to goods traffic in 1965. Many of the old buildings remained until quite recently. The station is approached from two minor roads, one on each side of the line, with no vehicular connection between them, although there is a foot crossing at the east end of the station.

Rail transport to Brampton commenced in 1799 with a primitive wagonway conveying coal and lime; this was converted to 4ft 8in gauge in 1829 and by 1836 horse-drawn coaches were conveying passengers between Milton station and Brampton at a fare of 3d. Steam traction did not appear on the passenger service until 1881, although it failed to survive a Board of Trade inspection. For many years the service was operated by the local colliery company but after some years of discussion the NER was persuaded to take over the line from 29 October 1912, and after much rehabilitation work the line was reopened to passengers on 31 July 1913, using NER locomotives and coaches. World War I created difficulties and the service was withdrawn on 1 March 1917, only to reopen exactly three years later. However, the traffic to and from the single platform station at Brampton Town was insufficient to justify the line remaining open and it closed yet again, on 29 October 1923, never to reopen. Goods traffic survived until the end of the year. The Brampton Town service was operated by a BTP 0-4-4T engine and a single coach push-and-pull unit based at Carlisle and it was accommodated at the rear of the up platform at Brampton Junction.

BRAMPTON
TOWN STATION

Will be opened for Passenger Traffic

From 1st August.

AUTOCARS WILL RUN TO AND FROM BRAMPTON JUNCTION STATION ON WEEKDAYS

connecting with the NEWCASTLE-CARLISLE SERVICE.

	a.m.	a.m.	a.m.	a.m.	a.m	a.m.	a.m.	p.m.	p.m.	p.m.	p.m.	p.m.	p.m	p.m.	p.m.	p.m.
NEWCASTLE ....dep.	—	—	—	6 40	8 20	—	19 20	—	1 20	—	—	2 55	—	—	5 20	6 20	7 20
CARLISLE ...... „	6†40	7 15	—	7 35	9 25	10 0	—	1 42	2 18	—	3 50	4 25	5 0	5 55	6 40	—	8 55
							noon										
BRAMPTON JUNC. „	7 18	7 40	8 0	8 30	10 4	10 25	12 9	2 17	2 48	3 16	4 26	4 50	5 45	6 32	7 18	8 22	9 31
BRAMPTON TOWN arr.	7 23	7 45	8 5	8 35	10 9	10 30	12 5	2 22	2 53	3 21	4 31	4 55	5 50	6 37	7 23	8 27	9 36

	a.m.	a.m.	a.m.	a.m.	a.m.	a.m.	p.m.	p.m.	p.m.	p.m.	p.m.	p.m	p.m.	p.m.	p.m.
BRAMPTON TOWN dep.	7 28	7 50	8 10	9 48	10 12	11 45	2 5	2 27	3 3	4 15	4 37	5 35	6 18	6 52	8 8	9 8	9 40
BRAMPTON JUNC. arr.	7 33	7 55	8 15	9 53	10 17	11 50	2 10	2 32	3 8	4 20	4 42	5 40	6 23	6 57	8 13	9 13	9 45
							p.m.										
CARLISE .... „	8 20	—	8 49	10 31	—	12 18	—	3 4	3 42	5 11	—	6 17	—	7 43	8 47	9 47	10 14
NEWCASTLE .... „	9 18	9 55	—	11 55	2 50	—	4 5	—	6 9	—	9 —	—	—	8 26	—	11 0	—

* This additional train will stop at the intermediate stations between Carlisle and Brampton at the following times :—
Scotby, 6-47, Wetheral, 6-53, Heads Nook, 6-58, How Mill, 7-3, arriving Brampton at 7-12 a.m.

For further particulars apply to the District Passenger Agent, North Eastern Railway, Newcastle.

YORK, *July, 1913.*

11579 Petty & Sons (Leeds) Limited, Whitehall Printeries, Leeds.—2,000.

Wetheral was unusual in that, apart from a loading dock at the west end of the station, the main goods facilities were at Corby Gates on the opposite side of the River Eden gorge. However, the station could be approached from Corby Gates by a footpath along the north side of the fine viaduct spanning the river. At one time there was a ½d toll, although this was waived on Sundays for pedestrians attending church, or any other place of public worship in Wetheral, but only within one hour before or after the time of Divine Service. It was also waived on Monday, Friday, and Saturday evenings for the purpose of attending Divine Worship or choir practice, but not at any other time even if it was to attend a place of worship.

Because of the curvature of the line through the station at Wetheral the signalbox was placed in the centre of the station, high above the down platform, so that the signalman could obtain a good view in both directions. The station closed to passengers on 2 January 1967 but reopened on 5 October 1981.

(*opposite*)⎯⎯⎯⎯⎯⎯⎯⎯⎯⎯⎯⎯⎯⎯⎯⎯⎯⎯⎯⎯⎯⎯⎯⎯⎯
The opening of Brampton Town station by the NER took place on 1 August 1913 and was advertised by this handbill. It was served by autocars running from Brampton Junction on the Newcastle–Carlisle line, restoring a service which had been withdrawn many years earlier when it was operated by the local colliery company. (*K. Hoole Collection*)

11

A LOOK AT FOUR COUNTRY BRANCHES

1 Malton to Driffield

To me the most truly rural branch on the North Eastern was that between Malton and Driffield, passing through the rolling Yorkshire Wolds, with the small stations in remote locations and usually out of sight of the villages they served. At Settrington, North Grimston, Sledmere & Fimber and Garton the station buildings were set on the original low platforms, a mere 12in high, and although platform extensions were at a higher level the low platforms gave a striking impression of antiquity.

The line was built by the independent Malton & Driffield Railway connecting with the York & North Midland's York–Scarborough line at the Malton end, and with the same company's (leased) Hull–Bridlington line at the Driffield end, using the Y&NM station in each case. Most of the station buildings remain, even if altered, but Burdale and Sledmere & Fimber have been demolished, while Wetwang (a name which often provokes mirth) has been extended by its new owners.

The first station out of Malton, Settrington, was at one time noted for its well-kept gardens, but with only three or four passenger trains in each direction daily (all worked by engines from Malton shed) the stationmaster and porter-signalman would not be overworked and would have plenty of time to attend to the gardens. The shunting neck at Settrington ended in a stop-block adjacent to a railway cottage and in February 1949 J25 0-6-0 No 5656 demolished the stop-block and ended up in the cottage!

At double track stations it was often necessary to stagger the platforms when a platform of greater height and length was required. At North Grimston this was done on a single line, with the low platform and station house on one side of the level crossing and the increased height platform and waiting room on the other. The level crossing actually crossed the running line and two sidings, making it extraordinarily wide for a station of this size. The waiting room block, authorised in 1893, has now become a small private residence, with a picture window to the lounge looking out on to the former platform.

Wharram was a busier station handling between 4,000 and 5,000 passengers a year, with a long full-height platform. Before World War I its main traffic was agricultural, but the development of a large quarry on the Driffield side of the station meant that in the 1920s Wharram was despatching 101,994 tons of limestone a year; this stone was loaded at the quarry but passed through the station's accounts. The quarry ceased production after World War II.

Between Wharram and Burdale the line passed through the crest of the Wolds by means of Burdale Tunnel (1745yd) and another large quarry was opened out in the 1920s adjacent to Burdale station. Between the tunnel and Burdale station once stood a derelict cottage built of bricks lettered M D R (Malton & Driffield Railway) and when this fact was first published there was a minor goldrush to acquire one! The cottage was completely demolished some years ago and the rubble removed.

Sledmere & Fimber was the busiest station on the branch for passengers (6,546 booked in 1911) and goods (1,937 tons of barley, 1,105 tons of timber, 600 tons of wheat and 271 wagons of livestock in 1913). The barley was handled by a corn merchant who rented a large warehouse on the Driffield side of the station from the NER. This station was three miles from Sledmere House, the home of the Sykes family, and in 1948 King George VI and Queen Elizabeth arrived at Sledmere station in the royal train drawn by Class A2 Pacific No 60534 *Irish Elegance*. After closure the station was allowed to become derelict and the area has now been cleared in connection with road improvements. For some years the wooden waiting shed off the platform was used as a cricket pavilion in a nearby field, but it has now gone.

Wetwang was almost as busy as Sledmere & Fimber, handling more than 6,000 passengers in 1911 from the village only ¼-mile away. Main goods traffic was grain from the extensive fields which cover the Wolds and which are such a magnificent sight when the crops are ripe and ready for cutting.

Garton, the quietest station on the line could only attract 2,065 passengers in 1911! Nevertheless the line continued on its sleepy way but it became an early post-war closure and the passenger service was withdrawn from 5 June 1950, although goods traffic continued for another eight years.

Trains usually consisted of a small tank engine and one or two coaches, but as there was no restriction on the locomotives that could be used it was possible to route scenic excursions from Hull to Whitby over the branch, involving reversing at Driffield and Malton. The first of these ran in 1934 headed by a B16 4-6-0 locomotive and, except for the war period, these trains continued to run, latterly worked by B1 4-6-0 engines. Another pre-war innovation was the running of excursions to allow passengers to inspect the station gardens and on one occasion in 1937 C7 Atlantic 737 was observed standing at Wharram. As the usual engines were F8 2-4-2Ts and G5 0-4-4Ts from Malton shed the sight of a large green engine attracted some attention. The branch train was often referred to as 'the Malton dodger'.

The station houses and offices were generally very plain, built of brick and set parallel to the track, except at Garton where the buildings were at right-angles to the line. Sledmere & Fimber and Wetwang had both been extended at the Driffield end at some time, and since closure a single storey office building at Wetwang has had an extra storey added. The house at North Grimston is by far the most imposing and appears to have been built some time after the others on the branch.

Signalling was originally by staff & ticket but signalboxes were not provided except at Sledmere; instead the staff stations had a small wooden shelter on the platform and this accommodated the small lever frame. This shelter was to a design favoured by the NER for use on its minor branches and they were retained at Wetwang and Garton until complete closure of the line in 1958.

2 Northallerton to Hawes

Another fascinating rural branch was the line running west from Northallerton, along the valley of the Ure. This passed through lush countryside famous for its milk and cheeses, with the terrain gradually getting more harsh as the Pennines were approached. Through Ainderby, Scruton and Leeming Bar, where the level crossing over the old A1 road held up the traffic before the days of the by-pass; Bedale, with its trim gardens, used as an overnight stop for Royal Trains; Crakehall, Jervaulx, Finghall Lane and Constable Burton, the latter not to be confused with Burton Constable on the Hornsea branch. Perhaps it was such confusion that led to Burton Constable

Roofs: (*above*) The arcades formed by the columns, girders and roof, add an attraction to some North Eastern stations, as at Hexham (*British Rail*); (*below*) The old and new (comparatively) at Bridlington, looking along platforms 5 and 6, added in 1912, with platform 4 on the right. The buildings at the rear of platform 4 were once the extent of the original (1846) station, which had a typical G. T. Andrews portico. The approach road is now covered by platform 4, which has recently become the main down platform with the removal of the tracks through the original part of the station. (*L. Ward*)

Changes at North Shields: (*above*) North Shields (west end) in BR days, with an electric train of 1937 stock bound for Newcastle Central. (*N.E. Stead*); (*below*) North Shields (west end) after being taken over by the Tyne & Wear Metro. The additional platform in the foreground accommodates the daytime only service to and from St James which, with the trains on the coastal circle, gives a five minute service on the line through Wallsend and Percy Main. (*Tyne & Wear PTE*)

being renamed Ellerby in 1922? Then there was Leyburn, the market town centre of the lower dale, with its partly staggered platforms and small engine shed.

West of Leyburn came Wensley and Redmire, the latter 22 miles from Northallerton and now the terminus of the line, handling limestone for Teesside. Aysgarth for the beautiful waterfalls, sometimes only a trickle after long hot and sunny summer days, followed by Askrigg and then Hawes, where the goods shed has been converted to a fascinating museum illustrating the life of the dale as it used to be.

Stations along the line were of no great architectural merit; Ainderby yard frontage was two storey, with the frontage apparently single storey at platform level as the line was on an embankment. Leeming Bar showed some features more familiar in the East Riding, with a stone portico to the single storey house, and a later two storey house adjoining.

The whole branch was single line except for the section between Leeming Bar and Bedale, and through certain stations; if, however, there was double track through a station but no platform on one line then only a passenger train and a freight train, or two freight trains, could pass, but if there was a platform on both tracks then any combination of trains, including two passenger trains, were allowed to pass.

It always seems strange to me that Leeming Bar, at one end of the double track section, had two platforms whereas Bedale at the other end and serving a market town, only had one. Other stations with two platforms were Jervaulx, Constable Burton, Leyburn, Wensley, Aysgarth and, of course, Hawes. The buildings of the five stations between Bedale and Leyburn all have (or had) stepped gables on some part of the structure, although differing from the standard design of similar gables which appeared on certain NER stations ten years or so later. Those used on the Wensleydale line must have been a favourite design of the architect who designed the stations for the independent Bedale & Leyburn Railway Co which existed between 1853 and 1859.

Hawes station was jointly owned by the North Eastern and the Midland, with the NER running in from the east and the MR from the west, although for operating convenience many North Eastern trains worked through to Hawes Junction/Garsdale and, in fact, the NER rented engine shed accommodation from the Midland at Hawes Junction and there was, surprisingly, no engine shed at Hawes. The station at Hawes was of Midland design.

131

The stations on the branch handled the usual agricultural traffic – grain, potatoes and an odd wagon of livestock, but Leeming Bar in 1913 despatched 3,363 tons of ale from the brewery adjacent to the station, a building later used by the makers of VOM (Vale of Mowbray) pork pies and meat products. Bedale increased its livestock traffic from 53 wagons in 1913 to 674 wagons in 1923 and 774 in 1924, but Leyburn despatched 1,017 wagons of livestock in 1913. Leyburn loaded roadstone and Hawes loaded limestone but not in large quantities.

Cheese and milk traffic was sent by passenger train, some of the milk going direct for distribution in London, Newcastle, the Hartlepools, Scarborough and Hull, and other supplies going to the Wensleydale Pure Milk Society's dairy at Northallerton, established in 1905, and situated just north of the station. In the 1920s the milk loaded at stations on the branch amounted to 1,130,965 gallons in one year, almost wholly in churns, each of which had to be returned to the sending station for the farmer to collect and refill. Later glass-lined milk tank wagons were used and these ran until BR days. The milk traffic was so important that the branch was specially opened on Sundays to handle the 4.0pm No 1 braked parcels train from Northallerton, and the return at 6.0pm from Hawes to Northallerton and York.

The Pure Milk Society's dairy also despatched the cream off the milk and this could amount to 1,000 gallons a month. The cans of cream were conveyed between the dairy and Northallerton station by a specially built four-wheel hand propelled trolley which operated the track circuits. Cheesemaking was largely a farmhouse industry in Wensleydale and it is only in comparatively recent years that Wensleydale cheese has been produced in large quantities by specialised dairies.

The Midland Railway had running powers from Hawes eastwards as far as Leyburn but these were not exercised, although excursions did run from Bradford, via Skipton and Hawes Junction. North Eastern excursions ran from Hawes to such east coast resorts as Scarborough, but this meant leaving Hawes at 6.20am, picking up passengers at all the stations along the branch, and taking 4½ hours in a compartment with no toilet facilities, before the coast was reached!

Hardraw Scar, near Hawes (which the NER persisted in calling Hardraw Scaur), was famous before 1914 for its brass band contests and in 1903 nine excursions were run to Hawes from places as far apart as Newcastle and Manchester. Band concerts have recently been resumed in this open-air setting but there are no excursions taxing Hawes station to capacity as the present audience arrives by car, bicycle, or on foot.

3 Alnwick–Coldstream

There were few stations to beat those on the branch between Alnwick and Coldstream, built under the Alnwick & Cornhill Act of May 1882 and opened in 1887. However, once again it was 'last opened, first closed' as passenger services were withdrawn in September 1930, although the goods service continued into BR days. The stations were designed by the NER architect William Bell, and stations to the same basic design also appeared at Byers Green and Coundon (opened December 1885) on the new line between Burnhouse Junction (near Spennymoor) and Bishop Auckland, and at Witton-le-Wear, where the station on a new site replaced the 1847 station built for the Wear Valley Railway.

The line between Alnwick and Coldstream (the latter, on the Tweedmouth–Kelso line was known as Cornhill until 1873) was the result of a proposed line with the backing of the North British Railway which was intended to serve the same area. To protect its virtual monopoly the NER submitted a Bill of its own and it was this that was authorised in May 1882 in preference to the proposed Central Northumberland Railway.

The line, 35 miles 2 furlongs 2 chains and 5 yards long according to the Act, served ten intermediate stations of which the most important was Wooler, a market town where the population of 1,382, together with a further 558 citizens in the catchment area of the station, provided 13,199 passengers in 1911. However, Wooler's most numerous passengers were sheep; 1,672 wagons of livestock were handled in 1923, and with 40 sheep to a wagon that was a lot of sheep! I wonder if those counting them went to sleep on the job?

The first Alnwick station was opened in 1850 at the end of a three-mile branch from the main line at Alnmouth, but with the completion of the line to Coldstream a fine new station was opened at Alnwick, although with only two platforms. Its design, with a three-span roof, is reminiscent of some of the NER's larger stations, and it was undoubtedly built to show off what the NER could do for the royal and other distinguished visitors to the Duke of Northumberland's nearby Alnwick Castle.

The line served very scattered communities, with only Wooler and Ilderton having a population of more than 1,000 in 1911. The least used station at Edlingham, with only 1,819 passengers in 1911, was quoted by the NER as serving a population of 576 but this was made up of:

Village	Distance from Edlingham station	Population
Edlingham	1	73
Lemmington	1½	68
Long Framlington	7(!)	435

The inhabitants of Long Framlington could also use the North British station at Rothbury, which was only 5½ miles from the village. Is it any wonder that Edlingham was downgraded to a 'Halt' in the 1926 timetable? Even wagons of livestock were few and far between and amounted to only six in 1911.

Goods traffic at all the stations was light, the only commodity amounting to more than 1,000 tons in 1911 being at Wooler, where 3,328 tons of building stone were put on rail.

The stations survived largely unaltered until BR days, as a parcels and goods service ran over the southern half of the line until 1953, and over the northern half until 1965. Now most of these interesting houses have been converted into private residences, some showing little sign of their railway origin.

4 Wear Valley Junction to Wearhead

Contrasting with the leisurely tempo of the Coldstream line was the hustle and bustle of the line from Wear Valley Junction to Wearhead, built at three different periods. Wear Valley Junction station was unusual, built on the line from Bishop Auckland to Crook (opened 1843) to act as the interchange station with the branch along the Wear Valley, initially as far as Frosterley. Until the branch was opened in 1847 there was no station at the junction; the station was first known as Witton Junction and it was one of those stations where it was impossible to pinpoint the exact date of renaming because it appeared as Wear Valley Junction in the Saltburn to Benfieldside (Consett) table in one part of the timetable, and as Witton Junction in the table giving the branch service. However, from 1 May 1882 both tables corresponded and listed it as Wear Valley Junction.

The station layout was also unusual; the down platform was south of the actual junction and could be used by trains to Crook or

Wearhead, but the up platform was north of the junction and could only be used directly by trains from Crook to Bishop Auckland; trains off the branch had to reverse into the platform. At one time the branch coaches were detached from Darlington to Blackhill trains at Wear Valley Junction and, in the opposite direction, attached to Blackhill–Bishop Auckland trains, but later trains ran between Wearhead and Darlington worked by the engine stationed at Wearhead. At one time engines from a two-road shed at Stanhope and a part roundhouse at Wear Valley Junction also worked the branch services.

The first station on the branch was at Witton-le-Wear, where the original station still stands but in use as a private residence, for in November 1888 the NER authorised expenditure of £567 to erect a new station on a new site some distance to the east of the old; this latter station has completely disappeared since the passenger service on the branch was withdrawn in 1953.

Harperley was a later addition on the branch, opened in 1892 to split the 6⅜ mile section between Witton-le-Wear and Wolsingham, whereas the buildings at Wolsingham and the original terminus at Frosterley date from the opening of the line in 1847.

The prime objective of the Wear Valley Railway was to tap the huge mineral resources, and to cater for an even more productive area the line was extended a further two miles to Stanhope in 1862. Here a small terminal station with an overall roof was erected but when, after much pressure from the top end of the valley, the line was extended to Wearhead in 1895 the 1862 station became redundant as it was impossible to project the line from this point. Consequently a new station had to be built just west of the junction where the new line diverged from the old.

The stations west of Stanhope were just as undistinguished as the stations east of Stanhope were distinguished, and even at the new terminus at Wearhead there was on the single bare platform only a single storey building housing the offices, waiting rooms etc. However, the mineral traffic was the mainstay of the line, not the passengers, and limestone, ores and other minerals poured on to the branch in an effort to satisfy the increasing number of blast furnaces in North East England. Some traffic was loaded in station yards, or the traffic from a nearby siding was accounted for in the station's books, but much of the traffic was loaded in the various quarries and sent straight to its destination. Examples of both are quoted to illustrate the traffic passing along the branch:

Traffic handled at stations (tons) 1913:

	Clay and Gannister	Roadstone	Lime and Limestone	Ores	Bricks
Witton-le-Wear	26,431	—	—	—	18,127
Wolsingham	21,431	—	—	—	—
Frosterley	11,075	4,294	15,110	1,447	—
Stanhope	—	—	100,600	12,521	—
Eastgate	—	35,400	—	—	—
Westgate	2,671	1,390	—	4,295	—
St Johns Chapel	6,974	—	—	—	—
Wearhead	5,256	34,915	—	6,253	—

Traffic handled at quarries (tons) 1913:

			Lime and Limestone		
Rookhope	—	—	18,013	—	—
Rogerley	—	—	179,231	—	—
Parson Byers	—	—	236,485	—	—
Bishopley	—	—	12,519	—	—
Fineburn	—	—	49,454	—	—
Harehope	—	—	77,376	—	—
Newlandside	—	—	178,259	—	—
North Bishopley	—	—	1,053	—	—

Some of the quarries are still worked in a small way, but most of them are now very large holes in the ground, where men once toiled with picks and shovels to extract minerals from the earth, working under primitive conditions for a small wage.

However, there are still some signs of activity in the dale, and the line is still open to the cement works sidings at Eastgate. Readers may remember a series of programmes on television featuring Thora Hird as the matriarch of a quarry-owning family prone to squabbling among themselves. The action was supposed to take place in and around the cement works and the opening and closing shots provided some excellent views of the works and the surrounding Wear Valley countryside.

12

NON-PUBLIC STATIONS, AND RENAMING

The North Eastern Railway provided several additional stations and platforms for use during the summer months, or for special events; some were included within the station premises and did not warrant a separate entry in the timetable, such as at Bridlington, where platforms 7 and 8 were known as the Excursion Platforms and were used only on summer Saturdays and Sundays and on Bank Holidays, whereas Scarborough had a fully fledged seasonal Excursion Station totally separate from the main (Central) station. The only way for passengers from one to the other was by public roads. This Scarborough station, sometimes known as Londesborough Road, had only two platforms, one through and one bay, but it was designed to take advantage of the peculiar layout immediately outside Central station, where trains from Whitby had to reverse to enter the main station. The excursion station was last used in 1963 but some of the premises still exist. Hull (Paragon) also had some excursion platforms (Nos 13 and 14) although Nos 11 and 12 were also outside the main station and were used at times for excursion traffic.

Further north Redcar had its Special Platform outside the covered station and there are references to an Excursion Platform at Middlesbrough in the last century.

Horse racing warranted a special two-platform station at Wetherby (last used in 1959), and at Killingworth additional platforms were provided and these, too, lasted into BR days. The two substantial platforms at Holgate, south of York station, were used for passengers attending the races on the Knavesmire and these were last used for this purpose in 1939. At one time there was a Hedon Racecourse (near Hull), about which nothing definite is known, but better documented is Hedon Halt, opened in August 1948 to serve Hull Motor Cycle Speedway. Special trains ran from Hull (Paragon) and some Withernsea trains called when events were being held, usually in an

137

evening, but the halt remained open for only two seasons and it closed about October 1949.

On the other side of Hull there was Newington Excursion Station, situated adjacent to Anlaby Road and open for a few days each year to cater for the crowds visiting the large annual pleasure fair held on the City's fairground in Walton Street. The station was sited on what was originally the Bridlington branch out of Hull (Manor House Street), a line which was largely superseded in 1848 with the opening of Paragon station. However, the line provided direct access from the yards on the west side of Hull to the Bridlington and Scarborough direction and remained open until 1965, although Newington station appears to have closed because of World War I, never to reopen. Not far away, but situated on what was once a Hull & Barnsley Railway goods only line, is Boothferry Park, opened in January 1951 to serve Hull City AFC's ground.

In July 1936 the LNER opened Hawthorn Towers Halt, between Seaham and Easington, to serve a holiday camp specially designed for children. It too appears to have been a wartime casualty and the station buildings were demolished in 1944. A much larger holiday camp was built near Filey by Butlins, but although completed during World War II, it did not open to the public until 1947. It was served by its own station, opened on 10 May 1947, and was last used in 1977. It had a spacious layout with four platforms and stood at the end of two curves off the Hull–Scarborough line so that trains could arrive from north and south.

War delayed the opening of Filey Holiday Camp station but brought about the opening of at least seven stations serving Royal Ordnance Factories. Barnbow, near Cross Gates, on the east side of Leeds, appears to have opened in 1915 and closed in 1924, and in World War II Demons Bridge and Simpasture were opened to serve the large ROF at Aycliffe, north of Darlington. At Thorp Arch, near Wetherby, the World War II ROF was served by a circular railway running in the factory grounds and this warranted four stations so that the workpeople could alight near their place of work; they were named Ranges, River, Roman Road and Walton.

Scotswood Works Halt was opened in 1915 to serve the adjacent W. G. Armstrong-Whitworth works on the north bank of the Tyne; special trains for workmen ran from Newcastle Central and some ordinary trains called although the service was not listed in the public timetable. After the war, as work decreased, the train service was gradually reduced until the Halt closed at midnight on 27 September 1924. This station reappeared in 1941 and it warranted an entry in the working timetable until 1947, although not shown in the public timebook. It was demolished in 1948.

Another installation in operation in both wars was the Catterick Camp Military Railway. In World War I the passenger service was worked by the military using their own engines and rolling stock but in World War II it was operated by the LNER. At first the goods traffic was also worked by the War Department but as the camp was run down and the engines sold off the LNER took over the working of the goods traffic in September 1923. Trains conveying troops returning from week-end leave continued to run in the early hours of each Monday morning until November 1964, latterly worked by diesel multiple-units from Darlington.

Other stations serving particular works were Graythorpe Halt, on the Seaton Snook branch, near West Hartlepool, for Gray's shipyard; this was only open for a few years c1920–3, but occasional excursions were run until 1936 for the benefit of the residents of this remote area. Melton Halt, for Earle's cement works, situated on the Hull–Selby line, between Ferriby and Brough, was opened c1920, and Plenmeller Halt, between Haltwhistle and Featherstone Park, on the Alston branch, was open from 1919 to 1932 for miners at Plenmeller colliery.

Rowntree's Halt, on the Foss Islands branch at York, was opened in 1927 for daily use by staff, and for occasional visiting parties, and Warrenby remained in use from 1916 until replaced by a new halt named British Steel Redcar in 1978 when the running lines were diverted to give more space for the new steelworks on the site of an earlier ironworks.

Ridge Bridge was unusual in that it started life in 1912 as a public station, but two years later it was withdrawn from the public timetable and used only by miners from a nearby colliery. It was situated between Garforth and Micklefield on the Leeds–Selby line and it was officially closed from 1 January 1940, although the Working Timetable showed trains calling until 1944.

At least two stations were built primarily for workpeople but were open to the public; these were Belasis Lane Halt (1929–1961) between Billingham and Haverton Hill, and Bowers Halt, between Castleford and Kippax (1934–1951). The 'Halt' suffix was dropped from both stations in 1937.

The NER had a number of private stations, usually serving nearby estates and originating in the early days of railways when landowners could block a line by refusing permission for the line to cross their land, or demanding an exorbitant price. In some cases the railway was taken round the land of the offending owner, but in others the price of the land was the provision of a station, with the right to stop trains when required.

Broomielaw, between Darlington and Barnard Castle, was one such station, provided for the Bowes-Lyon family at nearby Streatlam Castle, to which there was a direct carriage drive. The Castle was sold in the 1920s by the Earl of Strathmore to Norman Field of Lartington Hall, who thus acquired the right to stop *any* passenger train at Broomielaw Halt for himself, his tenants and his employees to allow them to join or alight. An instruction to this effect issued by the LNER in 1936 reveals that by that time any train signalled as OP (Ordinary Passenger) could be stopped on request by the public, either to set down or take up, although the station did not appear in the public timetable until June 1942. It closed to passengers when the Darlington to Middleton-in-Teesdale service ceased from 30 November 1964.

Fallodon, between Christon Bank and Chathill on the main line north of Newcastle, was the seat of Sir Edward Grey, later Lord Grey of Fallodon, one-time chairman of the NER and a distinguished statesman. The origins of the station can be traced back to the building of the line between Newcastle and Berwick when, in January 1846, Sir George Grey agreed to sell to the Newcastle & Berwick Company a portion of land required for the new line; in return the railway company agreed to build a station, at which trains could be stopped when required by Sir George and his family, guests, and servants. Lord Grey died on 7 September 1933 and on 30 May 1934 an Agreement was signed between the LNER and Captain Graves, the new owner, allowing the right to be extinguished and the station closed. It was demolished some 30 years later.

In 1900 the NER took over the network of lines developed by the Londonderry family in the Seaham and Sunderland area. It was agreed by George Gibb, the general manager, that the Londonderry family could retain their right to use Seaham Hall station and stop 'other than express trains'. However, Lord Londonderry's agent imposed two conditions, namely that Seaham Colliery station should be renamed Seaham, and the ex-Londonderry Seaham station should be renamed Seaham Harbour.

The North Eastern renamed many of its stations, and some of them more than once as the system developed. These renamings ranged from a complete change of name to a small change in the spelling, such as Pinchingthorpe to Pinchinthorpe, and there was indecision as to whether a name should be rendered as one word or two, South Bank or Southbank, Kirby Moorside or Kirbymoorside, Stainton Dale or Staintondale to name a few. There were often discrepancies between the names as printed in the public timetable, the working timetable, and the nameboard on the station itself. For example one authority quotes Fence Houses as becoming Fencehouses in 1862, and yet the station nameboard was still lettered Fence Houses in the early years of this century. Another example concerns Heaton, consistently listed in the timetables as such whereas the station nameboard plainly stated 'Heaton for Byker'.

Exact dates of change of name also present a problem. These were often announced by an internal circular, with the public timetable not far behind, but the working timetable was a poor third. It is obvious that the time taken to print the timetables caused discrepancies, such as at High Westwood, where a new station was opened on 1 July 1909. A public notice announcing the opening, issued in June 1909 quoted the correct name, High Westwood, whereas the timetable for July 1909 listed it as Westwood. Presumably the notice required only a few days to print whereas the timetable had gone to press some weeks earlier, too early to amend the change of intended name.

Nor is Bradshaw too reliable. In one example the name of the station differs in the 'up' and 'down' tables, appearing as Wressel in one direction and as Wressle in the other. Bradshaw also adopted its own abbreviations, such as Heddon-on-Wall for Heddon-on-the-Wall consistently used in contemporary NER timetables.

The amalgamation with the Hull & Barnsley Railway in 1922 brought renamings to avoid confusion between NER and HBR stations at Howden and Eastrington. The two lines crossed near Howden and thus the HBR stations became North Eastrington and South Howden, and the NER stations became South Eastrington and North Howden.

The formation of the LNER on 1 January 1923 led to further renamings to avoid confusion with similarly named stations on other parts of the new company's system; Carlton became Redmarshall, Cockfield became Cockfield Fell, and Holme became Holme Moor, with many others.

Where there was more than one station in a town or city descriptive suffixes were sometimes used, such as Hull Paragon (or Paragon Street), Leeds New (retained until 1938, when the station was anything but new as it was opened in 1869!), and Newcastle Central, Newcastle Manors North and Newcastle Manors East. At Darlington in 1922 the Bank Top suffix was no longer in use for the main line station, but the former Stockton & Darlington station was known as North Road, with no indication of the town in which it was situated, which seems odd to me! But Darlington was prone to oddities because in an earlier timetable (1886) just before the opening of the Dinsdale line, the index to the public timetable does not differentiate between the two stations and covers both under the sole entry Darlington.

At one time the NER system boasted four stations named Sherburn, but in 1874 three were renamed: Sherburn (York, Newcastle & Berwick) became Sherburn Colliery; Sherburn (Durham & Sunderland) became Sherburn House; Sherburn (York & Scarborough) became Wykeham. The fourth, Sherburn (York & North Midland), was allowed to remain until 1903 when it became Sherburn-in-Elmet.

GAZETTEER
SECTION ONE

NER STATIONS

All NER stations are listed alphabetically *as existing at 31 December 1922* (except former Hull & Barnsley Railway stations taken over on 1 April 1922). The information given is:

Station name
LO   Date of opening of line
SO   Date of opening of station (only included if known to be later than date of opening of line)
PS   Population served by the station in 1911
TI   Tickets issued at the station in 1911
G   Principal goods traffic (in tons) loaded at the station in 1913. NF = no facilities for goods traffic. LF = Limited facilities for goods traffic.
L   Wagons of livestock loaded at the station in 1913
R   Station renaming(s)
CP   Date of closure to passenger traffic
CG   Date of closure to goods traffic
REM Remarks

NOTE: Any commodity loading less than 100 tons in the year is omitted, and thus a station with a Closed Goods date can have a blank in the Goods Traffic entry if no single commodity totalled more than 100 tons.

The larger stations handled passengers, parcels and mail, and the goods traffic was dealt with at purpose built goods stations and warehouses such as Leeman Road and Foss Islands at York, Forth and New Bridge Street at Newcastle, and the antiquated Marsh Lane at Leeds. At Hull goods traffic was handled at Hull Goods, Drypool, King George Dock, Marfleet, Salt End Jetty, Stepney, Wilmington and Stoneferry. Although this work deals principally with the passenger stations it may be as well to give some example of traffic handled at some of the larger goods stations:

143

HULL (total traffic from stations listed above for 1913) in tons

Timber	311,384	Wheat	43,127
Flour & bran	155,492	Potatoes	42,447
Oil cake	106,587	Manure/gas lime	37,966
Cement	92,179	Ashes & cinders	20,965
Fish	86,910	Iron/steel	19,875
Maize	63,008	Gravel/sand	19,602
Oils	35,618*	Paper making material	18,478
Oats	44,646	Manure	17,306
Barley	43,778	Vegetables	13,526
		Scrap iron & steel	11,108

Livestock 4,395 wagons
*Oil tonnage had risen to 132,590 tons by 1923.

Newcastle's largest total for 1913 was Flour & Bran at 52,594 tons, illustrating Hull's superiority in the grain and milling trade, but Newcastle loaded 16,832 wagons of livestock! Heading the Leeds figures was Manure & Gas Lime at 58,008 tons, followed by Iron & Steel at 25,825 tons; at York Flour/bran reached 101,863 tons, with the next highest Scrap Iron & Steel amounting to 13,215 way behind. As may be expected Middlesbrough's largest loadings were:

Pig iron	249,900	Scrap iron & steel	79,505
Bars, Joists & girders	220,009	Iron & steel	68,860
Iron ore	184,325	Rails, iron & steel	46,558
Blooms	91,644	Timber	43,553

West Hartlepool imported a large quantity of iron ore, 534,054 tons, with timber, largely pit props, a close second with 532,494 tons; iron and steel plates accounted for 136,778 tons, followed by pig iron at 91,254. The importance of quarrying in the area is illustrated by the 57,747 tons of chalk loaded in 1913. Sunderland also handled iron ore, 142,935 tons in 1913, and in the same year Tyne Dock loaded 399,211 tons together with 174,507 tons of timber.

At some towns the goods traffic, although originally handled at the passenger station, was moved to a separate goods station when additional accommodation was required at the passenger station; a typical example was Scarborough, where a new goods station was erected at Gallows Close at the turn of the century and the former goods shed provided with platforms and included in the passenger station. At other locations where a new passenger station was provided the goods facilities remained at the original station and the redundant buildings were taken over for goods traffic; such examples were at Stanhope and Wetherby. At Sandsend the station site was unsuitable for the goods shed and this was provided at East Row, some distance nearer Whitby. Even 80 years ago a station could be closed to passenger traffic and yet retain its goods facilities, such as Winestead (1904) and Stutton (1905).

A number of stations had no goods facilities, usually because there was another station nearby at which goods facilities were provided, or there were separate passenger and goods stations in the same city or town both operating under the same name. A good example here is Durham, where the passenger station did not handle goods traffic; this was dealt with at the 1840 Newcastle & Darlington Junction station at Gilesgate, on the other side of the city, which became redundant as a passenger station in 1857. Thus the legend NF in the Gazetteer applies to the passenger station only, even though it may be followed by a goods closure date. A few minor stations had no general goods facilities but could handle bulk traffic such as coal, limestone, roadstone etc and these are indicated by the legend LF.

It must be remembered that the stations listed are those in existence at 1 January 1923 and that some stations acquired goods facilities under LNER ownership, having previously dealt only with passengers.

KEY TO NER LINES AND BRANCHES

No	Line/branch	Between
1	Annfield Plain	Birtley and Blackhill
2	Ayton branch	Nunthorpe and Battersby
3	Alnwick and Cornhill	Alnwick and Coldstream
4	Alnwick branch	Alnmouth and Alnwick
5	Alston branch	Haltwhistle and Alston
6	Amble branch	Chevington and Amble
7	Axholme Joint line	Goole and Haxey
8	Axholme Joint line Fockerby branch	Reedness and Fockerby
9	Bishop Auckland and Barnard Castle	As title
10	Bishop Auckland and Consett	Bishop Auckland and Blackhill
11	Bishop Auckland and Ferryhill	As title
11A	Bishop Auckland and Weardale	Bishop Auckland and Shildon
12	Blyth & Tyne Main Line	Manors North and Blyth
13	Blyth & Tyne Morpeth branch	Newsham and Morpeth
14	Blyth & Tyne Newbiggin branch	Bedlington and Newbiggin

No	Line/branch	Between
15	Blyth & Tyne Tynemouth branch	Monkseaton and Tynemouth
16	Boroughbridge branch	Pilmoor–Knaresborough
16A	Brampton Town branch	Brampton Junction and Brampton Town
17	Cawood branch	Selby and Cawood
18	Church Fenton and Harrogate	As title
19	Consett branch	Scotswood and Blackhill
20	Darlington and Barnard Castle	North Road and Barnard Castle
21	Darlington and Saltburn	As title
21A	Darras Hall branch	Ponteland and Darras Hall
22	Dearness Valley	Durham and Waterhouses
23	Blank	Blank
24	Durham and Bishop Auckland	As title
25	Durham Coast	Hart and Seaham
26	Eden Valley	Kirkby Stephen and Penrith (LNWR)
27	Eston branch	Cargo Fleet and Eston
28	Ferryhill and Hartlepool	As title
29	Ferryhill and Stockton	As title
30	Guisborough branch	Middlesbrough and Guisborough
31	Guisborough and Brotton	As title
32	Hartlepool and West Hartlepool	As title
33	Hawes branch	Northallerton and Hawes
34	Helmsley branch	Gilling and Pickering
35	Hexham and Allendale	As title
36	Hornsea branch	Sculcoates and Hornsea
37	Hull and Doncaster	Staddlethorpe and Thorne
38	Hull and Scarborough	Hull and Seamer
39	Hull and Selby	As title
39A	Hull Riverside Quay branch	Hessle Road and Riverside Quay
40	Kelso branch	Tweedmouth and Kelso (NBR)
41	Knottingley branch	Burton Salmon and Knottingley (LYR)
42	Lanchester Valley	Durham and Blackhill
43	Leeds and Castleford	Garforth and Castleford
44	Leeds and Selby	Selby and Leeds New Station (Joint)
45	Leeds Northern	Holbeck (MR) and Stockton
46	Leeds and Wetherby	Cross Gates and Thorp Arch
47	Malton and Driffield	As title
48	Market Weighton and Beverley	As title
48A	Market Weighton and Driffield	As title
49	Masham branch	Melmerby and Masham
50	Melmerby and Thirsk	As title

Changes at Tynemouth: (*above*) When the line was extended from North Shields to Tynemouth in 1847 a handsome terminus was erected, which later incorporated the Royal Hotel. However, the station was closed to passengers in 1882 when it was replaced by the present Tynemouth station, but the old station continued in use for goods traffic until 1959. (*K. Hoole*); (*below*) The southern end of the 1882 Tynemouth station in LNER days. The Tyne & Wear Metro trains use only the two through platforms on the left. (*Author's collection*)

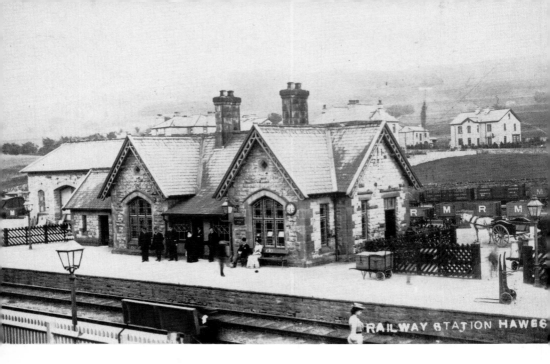

Some joint stations: (above) Hawes. Note the preponderance of Midland Railway wagons in the goods yard, together with a wagon of coal from Lofthouse Colliery, and one belonging to a Joseph Moore of Hawes, presumably a local coal merchant; it is his wagon No 2, and has dumb buffers formed from extensions of the solebars. (Author's collection); (below) Stanley, on the Methley Joint line, over which the passenger traffic between Leeds and Castleford was worked by the Great Northern Railway (K. Hoole)

No	Line/branch	Between
51	Murton and Durham (Elvet)	As title
52	Newcastle and Berwick	As title
53	Newcastle and Carlisle Railway	As title
54	Newcastle, Leamside and Ferryhill	As title
55	Nidd Valley branch	Harrogate and Pateley Bridge
56	North Yorkshire and Cleveland	Picton and Grosmont
57	Otley branch	Arthington and Otley
58	Otley and Ilkley Joint line	As title
59	Pelaw and South Shields	As title
60	Pelaw and Sunderland	As title
61	Penshaw branch	Penshaw and Sunderland
62	Pickering and Seamer	As title
63	Ponteland Railway	Gosforth and Ponteland
64	Port Clarence branch	Billingham and Port Clarence
65	Redheugh Deviation to Dunston branch	Dunston
66	Richmond branch	Eryholme and Richmond
67	Riverside branch	Manors and Percy Main
68	Saltburn and Whitby	Marske and Whitby
69	Scarborough and Whitby	Scarborough and Whitby (West Cliff)
70	Scotswood, Newburn and Wylam	Elswick and Prudhoe
70A	Selby and Goole	As title
71	Selby and Market Weighton	As title
72	Blank	Blank
73	South Durham and Lancashire Union	Barnard Castle and Tebay (LNWR)
74	Stockton and Darlington	Shildon and Eaglescliffe
75	Stockton and Hartlepool	Stockton and West Hartlepool
76	Stockton and Sunderland (via Wellfield)	As title
77	Sunderland and Seaham	As title
78	Swinton and Knottingley Joint line	Swinton (MR)/Mexboro' (GCR) and Ferrybridge
79	Tees Valley branch	Barnard Castle and Middleton-in-Teesdale
80	Thirsk and Malton	Pilmoor and Malton
81	Tynemouth branch	Heaton and Tynemouth
82	Victoria Dock branch (Hull)	Hull (Paragon) and Wilmington
83	Wear Valley Railway	Wear Valley Junction and Wearhead
84	Whitby branch	Rillington and Whitby
85	Withernsea branch	Sculcoates and Withernsea
86	York and Newcastle (Main Line)	As title

No	Line/branch	Between
87	York and Doncaster	York and Arksey (GNR)
88	York and Harrogate	As title
89	York and Market Weighton	As title
90	York and North Midland	York and Normanton (Joint)
91	York and Scarborough	As title

NOTE: In 1905 the NER listed 30 'Passenger branches on which there is no station': these were mainly connecting loops and curves, although there were some quite lengthy stretches of line, such as Church Fenton to Micklefield, known as the Mickfield branch.

At the same time there were 113 'Goods and Mineral Lines'. (The list of lines and branches has been extracted from a North Eastern Railway publication intended for internal use titled 'Index of North Eastern Railway Acts 1854–1904. Part I – Works'.)

ACKLINGTON: L/B 86; LO 1847; PS 2259; TI 13696; G Timber 253, hay/clover 211, barley 133; L 1072; CP—; CG 5–9–1966.

AINDERBY: L/B 33; LO 1848; PS 656; TI 8480; G Gravel & sand 2532; L 18; CP 26–4–1954; CG 1–11–1965.

AIRMYN & RAWCLIFFE: L/B 70A; LO 1910; SO 1912; PS 2339; TI—; G Timber, round 489, Potatoes 480; L 2; R AIRMYN 12–6–1961; CP 15–6–1964; CG 6–1–1964. REM Converted to single line May 1935 and down platform abandoned.

AKELD: L/B 3; LO 1887; PS 426; TI 4078; G Barley 787; L 140; CP 22–9–1930; CG 29–3–1965.

ALDIN GRANGE FOR BEARPARK: L/B 42; LO 1862; SO 1883; PS 1966; TI 41864; G NF; L—; R BEARPARK 1–5–1927; CP 1–5–1939; CG—. REM New station authorised 16–11–1882 £491; new stationmaster's house auth. 6–1903.

ALLENDALE: L/B 35; LO 1868; SO 1869; PS 1530; TI 10691; G—; L 236; R From CATTON ROAD 1–5–1898; CP 22–9–1930; CG 20–11–1950.

ALLERTON: L/B 88; LO 1848; PS 457; TI 5901; G Barley 421, potatoes 367; L 41; R To HOPPERTON 1–10–1925; CP 15–9–1958; CG 5–11–1962.

ALNE: L/B 86; LO 1841; PS 825; TI 18779; G Potatoes 1425, hay/clover 605; L 78; CP 5–5–1958; CG 10–8–1964. REM New station buildings on down side 1933, demolished 1959. Easingwold Railway used bay platform at north end (up side) until closure 28–12–1957.

ALNMOUTH: L/B 52; LO 1847; SO 1850; PS 1765; TI 49041; G Flour/bran 520; L 273; R From BILTON 2–5–1892; CP—; CG 7–6–1965. Goods facilities (Public Delivery Siding) reopened to replace Alnwick 7–10–1968.

ALNWICK: L/B 4; LO 1850; PS 8117; TI 77771; G Building stone 2304, grain 1754; L 1380; CP 29–1–1968; CG 7–10–1968. REM New station auth. 3–9–1885, opened 5–9–1887 £10,445.

ALSTON: L/B 5; LO 1852; PS 2706; TI 12349; G Ores 15393, lime 4103, roadstone 2966, manure 291; L 241; CP 3–5–1976; CG 6–9–1965. Station now used by South Tynedale Railway Preservation Society for narrow gauge train service.

AMBLE: L/B 6; LO 1849; SO 1879; PS 6673; TI 31806; G Timber 1813; L 38; CP 7–7–1930; CG 14–12–1964. REM New station auth. 22–11–1877 £722.

AMOTHERBY: L/B 80; LO 1853; PS 1047; TI 4711; G Barley 621; L 15; CP 1–1–1931; CG 17–10–1964.

AMPLEFORTH: L/B 80; LO 1853; PS 877; TI 3300; G Potatoes 465; L 51; CP 5–6–1950; CG 5–6–1950.

ANNFIELD PLAIN: L/B 1; LO 1893; SO 1894; PS 17798; TI 99907; G Gravel/sand 3620, bricks 1105; L 10; CP 23–5–1955; CG 10–8–1964.

ANNITSFORD: L/B 52; LO 1847; SO 1878; PS 6719; TI 49132; G Bricks 1221; L 6; CP 15–9–1958; CG 11–11–1963. REM New station authorised 15–2–1877 to replace Dudley Colliery; opened 8–7–1878.

APPLEBY: L/B 26; LO 1862; PS 2759; TI 18419; G Timber 100; L 453; R APPLEBY EAST 1–9–1952; CP 22–1–1962; CG 2–11–1964 (except coal).

ARRAM: L/B 38; LO 1846; SO 1855; PS 397; TI 4804; G Wheat 246; L 78; CP—; CG 4–5–1964. REM New station auth. 7–11–1862 £159.

ARTHINGTON: L/B 44; LO 1849; PS 1078; TI 28535; G—; L 22; R From POOL 1852; CP 22–3–1965; CG 27–4–1964. REM New station auth. (on new site) 8–4–1875 £1425; rebuilding auth. 19–12–1895 £729; REM closed goods on opening of Pool (on Otley line) 1866.

ASHINGTON: L/B 14; LO 1872; SO 1878; PS 21297; TI 257883; G Bricks 1509, hay/clover 746; L 2; R From HIRST FOR ASHINGTON 1–10–1889; CP 2–11–1964; CG 3–2–1964. REM Additions to station auth. 25–7–1895 £2917; further additions 1913 £448.

ASKRIGG: L/B 33; LO 1878; PS 1338; TI 16566; G—; L 270; CP 26–4–1954; CG 27–4–1964.

AYCLIFFE: L/B 86; LO 1844; PS 1142; TI 10635; G Limestone 8599, lime 5363; L 15; CP 2–3–1953; CG 2–3–1953.

AYSGARTH: L/B 33; LO 1878; PS 1467; TI 14877; G Flour/bran 287; L 273; CP 26–4–1954; CG 27–4–1964.

BACKWORTH: L/B 12; LO 1864; PS 9114; TI 164927; G NF; L—; R FROM HOTSPUR 1865; CP 13–6–1977; CG—.

BAINTON: L/B 48A; LO 1890; PS 824; TI 5426; G Wheat 655; L 25; CP 20–9–1954; CG 27–1–1964.

BALDERSBY: L/B 50; LO 1848; PS 676; TI 5206; G Potatoes 1031, barley 533; L 60; R From BALDERSBY GATE 1863; CP 14–9–1959; CG 14–9–1959.

BALNE: L/B 87; LO 1871; PS 523; TI 4253; G Potatoes 333, vegetables 258; L 196; CP 15–9–1958; CG 6–7–1964.

BARDON MILL: L/B 53; LO 1838; PS 1097; TI 17745; G Sanitary tubes 864; L 313; CP—; CG 26–4–1965.

BARDSEY: L/B 46; LO 1876; PS 864; TI 13906; G Potatoes 193; L 14; CP 6–1–1964; CG 6–1–1964.

BARLOW: L/B 70A; LO 1910; SO 1912; PS 378; TI—; G Potatoes 1035, vegetables in bulk 433, hay/clover 548; L—; CP 15–6–1964; CG 7–12–1964.

BARNARD CASTLE: L/B 20; LO 1856; SO 1861; PS 7177; TI 66714; G Building stone 233; L 1196; CP 30–11–1964; CG 5–4–1965. REM Replaced 1856 station but on new site in connection with South Durham & Lancashire Union Railway.

BARRAS: L/B 73; LO 1861; PS 454; TI 3677; G Roadstone 1187; L 42; CP 22–1–1962; CG 1–12–1952. REM Name derived from Bar House.

BARTON HILL: L/B 91; LO 1845; PS 922; TI 7274; G Hay/clover 748, barley 454, timber, round 400; L 59; R From BARTON 1853; CP 22–9–1930; CG 10–8–1964.

BARTON-LE-STREET: L/B 80; LO 1853; PS 457; TI 2876; G Barley 294; L 31; CP 1–1–1931; CG 10–8–1964.

BATTERSBY: L/B 56; LO 1858; SO 1867; PS 416; TI 6217; G—; L—; R From INGLEBY JUNCTION to BATTERSBY JUNCTION 30–9–1878 and from BATTERSBY JUNCTION to BATTERSBY 1–5–1893; CP—; CG 6–1–1964.

BEAL: L/B 52; LO 1847; PS 2143; TI 10683; G Roadstone 1166, barley 598; L 485; CP 29–1–1968; CG 26–4–1965. REM Demolished 1979.

BEAMISH: L/B 1; LO 1893; SO 1894; PS 2734; TI 59378; G Roadstone 725, building stone 407; L—; CP 21–9–1953; CG 2–8–1960.

BEBSIDE: L/B 13; LO 1857; SO 1858; PS 58; TI 57324; G—; L—; R From COWPEN LANE 1860; CP 2–11–1964; CG 9–12–1963.

BEDALE: L/B 33; LO 1855; PS 2846; TI 26400; G Barley 476; L 53; CP 26–4–1954; CG 4–9–1967.

BEDLINGTON: L/B 13; LO 1857; SO 1858; PS 14755; TI 227121; G Bricks 12489; L 7; CP 2–11–1964; CG 7–6–1965.

BEECHBURN: L/B 10; LO 1843; SO 1869; PS 2135; TI 43950; G NF; L—; R From HOWDEN 16–4–1869; CP 8–3–1965; CG 10–2–1964.

BELFORD: L/B 52; LO 1847; PS 1760; TI 12461; G Roadstone 2239; L 761; CP 29–1–1968; CG 7–6–1965.

BEMPTON: L/B 38; LO 1847; PS 461; TI 9584; G—; L 70; CP—; CG 10–8–1964.

BENINGBROUGH: L/B 86; LO 1841; PS 1202; TI 9416; G Hay/clover 927, timber 578; L 24; R From SHIPTON 1898; CP 15–9–1958; CG 5–7–1965. REM Demolished 5–1961.

BENSHAM: L/B 86; LO 1868; SO 1892; PS ???; TI 69998; G NF; L—; CP 5–4–1954; CG—. REM Cost of station £6830; opened 1–11–1892.

BENTON: L/B 12; LO 1864; SO 1871; PS 8172; TI 177003; G Scrap 126; L—; CP 23–1–1978 (reopened by Metro 11–8–1980); CG 14–8–1967. REM Replaced Forest Hall and Long Benton 1–3–1871.

BEVERLEY: L/B 38; LO 1846; PS 18587; TI 167616; G Cement 5360, oil cake 3684, grain 2631, manure 2170; L 1119; CP—; CG—. REM G. T. Andrews roof replaced 1908.

BILLINGHAM: L/B 75; LO 1833; PS 1776; TI 23262; G Hay/clover 394; L 31; R BILLINGHAM-on-TEES 1926 and BILLINGHAM 1973; CP—; CG 6–11–1978; REM New station on new site opened 7–11–1966.

BIRSTWITH: L/B 55; LO 1862; PS 1060; TI 14069; G Flour/bran 461; L 59; CP 2–4–1951; CG 31–10–1964.

BIRTLEY: L/B 86; LO 1868; PS 11726; TI 139188; G Bricks 48786, iron & steel 5570; L 1; CP 5–12–1955; CG—.

BISHOP AUCKLAND: L/B 24; LO 1843; PS 27998; TI 447315; G Scrap iron & steel 3460, flour/bran 3239, timber 1562; L 48; CP—; CG 27–9–1971. REM Tender for Joint station 15–8–1856 £2329 and new station 1889 £12035. Triangular station with two platforms on East to North line but only one on East to West and West to North lines. Now largely demolished with only service to Darlington remaining.

BLACKHALL ROCKS: L/B 25; LO 1905; SO 1912; PS—; TI—; G NF; L—; CP 4–1–1960; CG 7–12–1964. REM Originally open only Saturdays and Wednesdays in summer from 1912; open fully 1919. Intended as BLACK-HALLS but changed prior to opening. Goods facilities added by LNER.

BLACKHILL: L/B 42; LO 1867; PS 12478; TI 134405; G Flour/bran 8027, roadstone 7578, building stone 1358; L 173; R From CONSETT & BLACKHILL 1896; CP 23–5–1955; CG June 1982. REM Bay platform for trains to Darlington originally had overall roof. Originally intended as BLACKHILL but opened as BENFIELDSIDE.

BLAYDON: L/B 53; LO 1837; PS 16038; TI 261705; G Creosote & tar 18938, gravel & sand 11527, clay & gannister 9758; L 29; CP—; CG—. REM New station 1911 but largely demolished due vandalism.

BLYTH: L/B 12; LO 1847; PS 32807; TI 348623; G Timber 28564, fish 6091, gravel & sand 5270; L 7; CP 2–11–1964; CG 23–9–1963. REM Original Blyth & Tyne station of 1847 replaced on new site 1867, and latter station rebuilt and enlarged by NER 1894–6. Demolished 1972.

BOLTON PERCY: L/B 90; LO 1839; PS 786; TI 9300; G Hay & clover 357; L 62; CP 13–9–1965; CG 27–4–1964. REM New station on widened lines 1904, old station converted to houses 1905 £166. Coach service from Bolton Percy to Tadcaster and Harrogate prior to opening of Church Fenton–Harrogate line.

BOOSBECK: L/B 31; LO 1865; SO 1878; PS 4399; TI 50304; G Barley 114; L 14; CP 2–5–1960; CG 14–9–1964.

BOROUGHBRIDGE: L/B 16; LO 1847; PS 3549; TI 22089; G Sanitary tubes 4079, bricks 2847, potatoes 1460; L 981; CP 25–9–1950; CG 5–10–1964. REM New station opened 1–4–1875. Part of old station converted to two cottages auth. 7–6–1877 £150.

BOTANIC GARDENS: L/B 82; LO 1853; PS—; TI 44915; G LF; L—; R Open 6–1853 to 11–1854 as CEMETERY; reopened as CEMETERY GATES 1866 and renamed BOTANIC GARDENS 1–11–1881; CP 19–10–1964; CG 6–9–1965. REM 1866 station authorised 17–3–1865 £179.

BOWES: L/B 73; LO 1861; PS 769; TI 6169; G Roadstone 1754; L 102; CP 22–1–1962; CG 22–1–1962. REM Course of line used for by-pass road 2–12–1982.

BRADBURY: L/B 86; LO 1844; PS 610; TI 6324; G Hay/clover 329; L 63; CP 2–1–1950; CG 2–1–1950.

BRAFFERTON: L/B 16; LO 1847; PS 1218; TI 7684; G Potatoes 963; L 170; CP 25–9–1950; CG 5–10–1964. REM Only three stationmasters between opening and 1929 (1847 to 1885, 1885 to 1901, and 1901 to 1929). In 1929 placed under stationmaster Boroughbridge.

BRAMPTON JUNCTION: L/B 53; LO 1838; PS 3894; TI 27876; G Manure 1049; L 455; R Originally MILTON (until 1–9–1870); to BRAMPTON (CUMBERLAND) March 1971, to BRAMPTON (CUMBRIA) August 1975. CP—; CG 5–7–1965. REM Rear of up platform converted to accommodate Brampton Town service 1913.

BRAMPTON TOWN: L/B 16A; LO 1836; SO 1–8–1913; PS 2392; TI—; G—; L—; CP 1–3–1917, reopened 1–3–1920, closed 29–10–1923; CG 1–1–1924.

BRANCEPETH: L/B 24; LO 1857; PS 716; TI 16371; G—; L 73; CP 4–5–1964; CG 10–8–1964.

BRANDON COLLIERY: L/B 24; LO 1857; SO 1878; PS 6263; TI 69856; G Sanitary tubes 2823, creosote/tar 1928, bricks 219; L—; R From BRANDON 1–7–1896; CP 4–5–1964; CG 10–8–1964. REM New station auth. 7–10–1875 £1879.

BRIDLINGTON: L/B 38; LO 1846; PS 16083; TI 124951; G Wheat 1463, barley 1191, gas water 1040, fish 310; L 251; CP—; CG—. REM Additional platforms (Nos. 5 and 6) authorised 21–9–1911; opened 20–5–1912. In 1983 platforms 1, 2 and 3 abandoned and platform 4 converted to down platform.

BROCKLEY WHINS: L/B 60; LO 1839; PS 4295; TI 63708; G Ashes/cinders 669; L 3; R To BOLDON COLLIERY 1–3–1925; CP—; CG 9–3–1964. REM Station opened 1844 to serve Brandling Junction line and curve from Stanhope & Tyne to Brandling Junction line.

BROMPTON: L/B 45; LO 1852; PS 1206; TI 8104; G Hay/clover 311; L—; CP 6–9–1965; CG 6–9–1965.

BROOMFLEET: L/B 39; LO 1840; SO 1896; PS 924; TI 3449; G—; L—; CP—; CG 4–5–1964. REM Open Market Day only to 1–10–1907, then AS REQUIRED to 12–7–1920, then full service.

BROOMHILL: L/B 6; LO 1849; SO 1878; PS 3800; TI 27746; G Scrap 285; L—; CP 7–7–1930; CG 4–5–1964. REM Station auth. 22–11–1877 £263.

BROTTON: L/B 68; LO 1865; SO 1875; PS 5286; TI 41111; G Iron ore 89730, scrap iron/steel 321; L 10; CP 2–5–1960; CG 3–4–1967 (except coal).

BROUGH: L/B 39; LO 1840; PS 2289; TI 32403; G Gravel/sand 4173, barley 329, timber, round 234; L 50; CP—; CG 5–1–1970. REM On widening to four tracks in 1904 new station provided having two island platforms (four faces).

BUBWITH: L/B 71; LO 1848; PS 561; TI 6054; G Potatoes 478, hay/clover 228, timber, round 150; L 104; CP 20–9–1954; CG 27–1–1964.

BURDALE: L/B 47; LO 1853; PS 328; TI 2894; G Barley 855, oats 117; L 74; CP 5–6–1950; CG 20–10–1958.

BURNHILL: L/B 10; LO 1859; PS 275; TI 4896; G NF; L—; R From BURNHILL JUNCTION 1–5–1893; CP 1–5–1939; CG—.

BURTON AGNES: L/B 38; LO 1846; PS 1486; TI 11399; G Wheat 2281, barley 2143, oats 391; L 414; CP 5–1–1970; CG 2–11–1964.

BURTON SALMON: L/B 90; LO 1840; PS 1598; TI 13637; G Vegetables in bulk 521, potatoes 391, vegetables 386; L 48; CP 14–9–1959; CG 3–6–1968. REM New station auth. 1902 £2248. Platforms removed Nov. 1960.

BYERS GREEN: L/B 11; LO 1885; PS 3672; TI 51797; G Bricks 8267, clay/gannister 115, scrap 101; L—; CP 4–12–1939; CG 2–6–1958, but station yard subsequently used by J. G. Potts Ltd, timber merchant.

BYKER: L/B 67; LO 1879; PS 48709; TI 28741; G NF; L—; CP 5–4–1954; CG—. REM Originally opened 1884 for the use of workmen and remained Workmen Only until 1–3–1901.

CALLERTON: L/B 63; LO 1905; PS 813; TI 14657; G Potatoes 230, hay/clover 192; L 3; CP 17–6–1929; CG 6–12–1965; REM Station buildings destroyed by fire 21–3–1915.

CARGO FLEET: L/B 21; LO 1846; PS 682; TI 55070; G NF; L—; R From CLEVELAND PORT Aug. 1867; CP—; CG—. REM New station opened 8–11–1885.

CARHAM: L/B 40; LO 1849; PS 682; TI 3268; G Barley 316; L 39; CP 4–7–1955; CG 18–5–1964.

CARLTON: L/B 29; LO 1833; SO 1885; PS 694; TI 13133; G Creosote/tar 17409, gas water 777, hay/clover 407; L 35; R REDMARSHALL 1–7–1923; CP 31–3–1952; CG 15–9–1958. REM Station authorised 10–1–1884 £526 'to be similar to that at Stillington'.

CARNABY: L/B 38; LO 1846; PS 607; TI 6712; G Wheat 447, barley 174; L 141; CP 5–1–1970; CG 4–5–1964.

CARVILLE: L/B 67; LO 1879; SO 1–8–1891; PS—; TI 29780; G NF; L—; CP 23–3–1973; CG—. REM Goods station renamed Wallsend 1–12–1913.

CASTLE EDEN: L/B 28; LO 1835; SO 1866; PS 1889; TI 36947; G Grain 681, timber 132; L 162; CP 9–6–1952; CG 1–6–1964. REM Station auth. 15–9–1865 £455; station additions auth. 1883 £440 and stationmaster's house £303.

CASTLEFORD: L/B 90; LO 1840; PS 30715; TI 228312; G Glass inc. bottles 19285, bricks 19188, chemicals/acid 8423, manure 6572; L 1; R to CASTLEFORD CENTRAL 15–9–1952; to CASTLEFORD 20–2–1969; CP—; CG 5–10–1970. REM New station auth. 17–12–1869 £888 on new site.

CASTLE HOWARD: L/B 91; LO 1845; PS 830; TI 6061; G barley 480, hay/clover 272; L 7; CP 22–9–1930; CG 2–11–1959. REM Platforms removed Feb. 1961. From October 1865 members of Castle Howard family and visitors allowed to stop all York–Scarborough trains (except 2.30pm ex York).

CASTLETON: L/B 66; LO 1861; PS 728; TI 11463; G Clay/gannister 15741, bricks 2064, sanitary tubes 2136; L 186; R to CASTLETON MOOR 1965; CP—; CG 7–6–1982. REM Station authorised 13–4–1860 £883.

CATTAL: L/B 88; LO 1848; PS 2276; TI 15169; G Potatoes 1137, barley 813, hay/clover 631; L 134; CP—; CG 3–5–1965.

CATTERICK BRIDGE: L/B 66; LO 1846; PS 1726; TI 16215; G Timber, round 880, barley 499, hay/clover 368; L 387; CP 3–3–1969; CG 9–2–1970. REM Buildings damaged by explosion 4–2–1944.

CAWOOD: L/B 17; LO 1897; SO 1898; PS 1195; TI 6173; G Potatoes 2590, vegetables 1274, hay/clover 555; L 18; CP 1–1–1930; CG 2–5–1960. REM demolished 13–1–1980.

CAYTON: L/B 38; LO 1846; PS 511; TI 5273; G NF; L—; CP 5–5–1952; CG—. REM Closed temp. in World War I.

CHATHILL: L/B 52; LO 1847; PS 1075; TI 15335; G Barley 304, fish 185, timber, round 170; L 395; CP—; CG 7–6–1965. REM North Sunderland Railway used bay platform at north end (up side); closed 28–10–1951.

CHERRY BURTON: L/B 48; LO 1865; PS 1154; TI 8027; G Barley 720, wheat 510; L 144; CP 5–1–1959; CG 27–1–1964.

CHESTER-LE-STREET: L/B 86; LO 1868; PS 15405; TI 139568; G Creosote/tar 158; L 86; CP—; CG 4–10–1965.

CHEVINGTON: L/B 52; LO 1847; PS 888; TI 8584; G—; L 185; CP 15–9–1958; CG 10–8–1964. REM Bay platform at north end (down side) used by Amble branch trains.

CHOPPINGTON: L/B 13; LO 1857; SO 1858; PS 6680; TI 115642; G Bricks 14913; L—; CP 3–4–1950; CG 9–3–1964.

CHRISTON BANK: L/B 52; LO 1847; PS 1002; TI 8185; G Roadstone 31375, building stone 2407, hay/clover 202; L 276; CP 15–9–1958; CG 7–6–1965.

CHURCH FENTON: L/B 90; LO 1839; SO 1847; PS 1304; TI 21052; G Potatoes 1022, vegetables 1037, barley 556; L 152; CP—; CG 3–10–1966. REM first station opened 10–8–1847 with branch to Harrogate; new station auth. 23–7–1903 £7348 and opened Sept. 1904.

CLIBURN: L/B 26; LO 1862; PS 877; TI 5325; G Potatoes 167; L 33; CP 17–9–1956; CG 17–9–1956.

CLIFF COMMON: L/B 71; LO 1848; PS 505; TI 7494; G Potatoes 1197, hay/clover 665, vegetables in bulk 399; L 57; R From CLIFF COMMON GATE Oct. 1864; CP 20–9–1954; CG 27–1–1964. REM DVLR traffic potatoes 4151, hay/clover 1121, barley 409; L 52. Separate platform for DVLR passengers (CP 1–9–1926).

CLIFTON: L/B 26; LO 1863; PS 1084; TI 5291; G Potatoes 164; L 20; R to CLIFTON MOOR 1–9–1927; CP 22–1–1962; CG 6–7–1964 (by LMR).

CLOUGHTON: L/B 69; LO 1885; PS 866; TI 14279; G Barley 133, timber 126; L 18; CP 8–3–1965; CG 4–5–1964.

COANWOOD: L/B 5; LO 1852; PS 304; TI 7317; G—; L 6; R from SHAFTHILL 1–3–1885; CP 3–5–1976; CG 19–9–1955. REM New station auth. 3–6–1875 £670.

COCKFIELD: L/B 9; LO 1863; PS 6619; TI 38261; G NF; L—; R to COCKFIELD FELL 1–7–1923; CP 15–9–1958; CG—. REM Doubling of line authorised 14–9–1899 involved provision of second platform.

COLDSTREAM: L/B 40; LO 1849; PS 3259; TI 22341; G Barley 2285, potatoes 697, oats 418; L 1090; R from CORNHILL 1–10–1873; CP 15–6–1964; CG 29–3–1965.

COLLINGHAM BRIDGE: L/B 46; LO 1876; PS 1137; TI 18156; G Timber, round 586, barley 464, potatoes 407; L 92; CP 6–1–1964; CG 6–1–1964. REM Lord Leconfield allowed to stop all trains under Agreement of 29–12–1871.

COMMONDALE: L/B 56; LO 1861; SO 1891; PS 389; TI 5520; G NF; L—; R from COMMONDALE SIDING Dec. 1891. CP— (unstaffed halt from 16–1–1950); CG—.

CONSETT: L/B 1; LO 1834; PS 5604; TI 72746; G Clay/gannister 7108, roadstone 2798, timber 156; L 1; CP 23–5–1955; CG—. REM New station opened 17–8–1896 on new site.

CONSTABLE BURTON: L/B 33; LO 1855; SO 1856; PS 524; TI 4527; G Timber, round 185; L 234; CP 26–4–1954; CG 14–10–1957.

COPGROVE: L/B 16; LO 1875; PS 463; TI 9568; G Barley 225; L—; R from COPGROVE AND STAVELEY 1–11–1881; CP 25–9–1950; CG 5–10–1964.

COPMANTHORPE: L/B 90; LO 1839; PS 1216; TI 10438; G Potatoes 547, barley 498, hay/clover 438; L 37; CP 5–1–1959; CG 4–5–1964. REM New station auth. 4–6–1903 £3530. Redundant station converted to house for stationmaster 1905 £283.

CORBRIDGE: L/B 53; LO 1838; PS 3648; TI 66897; G Sanitary tubes 1563, clay/gannister 1103, timber 580; L 636; CP—; CG 26–4–1965.

COTHERSTONE: L/B 79; LO 1868; PS 644; TI 14716; G—; L 4; CP 30–11–1964; CG 5–4–1954. REM Also known as COTHERSTON 1906–1914.

COTTINGHAM: L/B 38; LO 1846; PS 4944; TI 114909; G Barley 200, wheat 193, vegetables 123; L 46; CP—; CG 5–1–1970.

COUNDON: L/B 11; LO 1885; PS 5740; TI 45586; G Timber, round 117; L—; CP 4–12–1939; CG 6–9–1956.

COWTON: L/B 86; LO 1841; PS 940; TI 8435; G Hay/clover 545, barley 213, potatoes 129; L 64; CP 15–9–1958; CG 1–6–1964.

COXGREEN: L/B 61; LO 1853; PS 839; TI 25641; G NF; L—; CP 4–5–1964; CG—. REM Name also rendered as COX GREEN.

COXHOE BRIDGE: L/B 28; LO 1839; SO 1846; PS 4240; TI 26328; G NF; L—; CP 9–6–1952; CG 19–9–1955. REM Mineral and goods traffic handled at Coxhoe WH:Limestone 114519, bricks 13739, lime 2990, gravel/sand 2008. Coxhoe Bridge and Coxhoe WH 1 mile apart and on different lines. Coxhoe WH = Coxhoe (West Hartlepool).

COXLODGE: L/B 63; LO 1905; PS—; TI 5355; G Roadstone 4581; L—; CP 17–6–1929; CG 6–12–1965. REM Now on Metro line to Bank Foot opened 10–5–1981.

COXWOLD: L/B 80; LO 1853; PS 1214; TI 6961; G Hay/clover, 343; L 108; CP 2–2–1953; CG 10–8–1964. REM Passing place to be provided, present platform to be lengthened and new platform provided; cost £1850 and authorised 11–5–1900.

CRAKEHALL: L/B 33; LO 1855; SO 1856; PS 526; TI 4004; G NF; L—; CP 26–4–1954; CG—. REM Closed temp. in World War I.

CRAMLINGTON: L/B 52; LO 1847; PS 5659; TI 32042; G Hay/clover 163; L 95; CP—; CG 4–7–1966.

CROFT SPA: L/B 86; LO 1841; PS 2454; TI 60966; G NF; L—; CP 3–3–1969; CG—. REM Goods traffic handled at Croft Depot: gravel/sand 529; L 12. From 15–9–1958 served only by Richmond branch trains (until 3–3–1969).

CROOK: L/B 10; LO 1843; PS 12792; TI 108592; G Bricks 59536, clay/gannister 15241, creosote/tar 13601, manure 3862; L 21; CP 8–3–1965; CG 5–7–1965. REM Goods facilities retained at original station after closure 1845.

CROSS GATES: L/B 44; LO 1834; PS 6403; TI 138421; G Iron ore 269; L 6; CP—; CG 1–6–1964. REM New station auth. 11–2–1870 £807; replaced on widening to four tracks c1902.

CROXDALE: L/B 86; LO 1872; SO 1877; PS 5287; TI 43306; G Clay/gannister 173; L—; CP 26–9–1938; CG 26–9–1938. REM Station auth. 1876 £1684.

CULLERCOATS: L/B 15; LO 1882; PS—; TI 271939; G—; L 9; CP 10–9–1979 but reopened Metro 11–8–1980; CG 10–2–1964.

DACRE: L/B 55; LO 1862; PS 1221; TI 15781; G Timber 1211; L 129; R from DACRE BANKS June 1866; CP 2–4–1951; CG 31–10–1964.

DANBY: L/B 56; LO 1865; PS 1357; TI 10171; G Potatoes 293; L 128; CP—; CG 2–8–1965.

DANBY WISKE: L/B 86; LO 1841; SO 1884; PS 431; TI 4774; G Hay/clover 403; L 15; CP 15–9–1958; CG 15–9–1958. REM Station auth. 5–6–1884 £381 and opened 1–12–1884. Demolished 1959.

DARLEY: L/B 55; LO 1862; SO 1864; PS 1095; TI 8262; G Cement 108; L—; CP 2–4–1951; CG 2–10–1953.

DARLINGTON: L/B 86; LO 1829; SO (present) 1887; PS 60468; TI 420519; G Bricks 874; L 2472. (Handled at Hopetown: Iron & steel 53204; Bars, joists & girders 34042; Scrap iron & steel 25314; Creosote, tar & pitch 22470; cinder 17347; Rails, iron & steel 12338; L 1747.) CP—; CG—. REM New station authorised 5–3–1885 £84691; opened 1–7–1887. Stand for No 1 engine authorised 2–4–1891 £98 and later joined by S&DR *Derwent*. Both locomotives removed 1975.

DARRAS HALL: L/B 21A; LO 1913; PS—; TI—; G—; L—; CP 17–6–1929; CG 2–8–1954. REM Name originally suggested LITTLE CALLERTON. Station buildings used as church in 1960s.

DINSDALE: L/B 21; LO 1887; PS 2614; TI 44456; G NF; L—; CP—; CG—. REM On new line opened 1–7–1887 replacing FIGHTING COCKS on original line opened 27–9–1825, where goods facilities retained until 9–3–1964.

DRAX HALES: L/B 70A; LO 1910; SO 1912; PS 830; TI—; G Hay/clover 534; L 34; R To DRAX 12–6–1961; CP 15–6–1964; CG 15–6–1964. REM Converted to single line May 1935 and down platform abandoned.

DRIFFIELD: L/B 38; LO 1846; PS 7871; TI 89416; G Oil cake 9034, barley 3164, wheat 1085; L 1681; CP—; CG—. REM Station roof removed 1949.

DUNSTON ON TYNE: L/B 65; LO 1907; SO 1909; PS 6050; TI 44780; G Flour/bran 61959, creosote/tar 17207, timber 11399; L—; CP 4–5–1926; CG 5–7–1965. REM Closed temp. World War I; station and warehouse auth. 1904 £2752. Station reopened 1–10–1984.

DURHAM: L/B 86; LO 1857; PS 35090; TI 442744; G NF; L 9; CP—; CG—. REM Original station auth. 14–9–1855 £2610; roofing auth. 10–10–1856 £1264; present station auth. 16–12–1870 £11330 and opened 1872. (Goods traffic handled at Durham Gilesgate: G Gravel/sand 6602, iron/steel 1066).

DURHAM ELVET: L/B 51; LO 1893; PS—; TI 57552; G Gravel/sand 1526; L—; CP 1–1–1931; CG 11–1–1954. REM used for annual Durham Miners' Gala traffic until 18–7–1953. Demolished 1964.

EAGLESCLIFFE: L/B 21; LO 1825; SO 1852; PS 1702; TI 75358; G Roadstone 32624, sulphuric acid 13865, iron ore 12115, clay/gannister 2328; L—; R EAGLESCLIFFE to PRESTON JUNCTION Dec. 1853; PRESTON JUNCTION to EAGLESCLIFFE 1–2–1878; CP—; CG 6–7–1964. REM Station extensions auth. 5–1–1893 £13553 but reductions in facilities carried out in 1969.

EARSWICK: L/B 89; LO 1847; PS 1461; TI 7867; G Bricks 517; L 10; R from HUNTINGTON 1–11–1874; CP 29–11–1965; CG 7–6–1965. REM Final station not on site of original station, which still exists as a private residence.

EASINGTON: L/B 25; LO 1905; SO 1–7–1913; PS—; TI—; G Ashes/ cinders 279; L—; CP 4–5–1964; CG 6–1–1964. REM Station cost £2494.

EAST BOLDON: L/B 60; LO 1839; PS 4559; TI 184172; G Bricks 6914, scrap iron and steel 4943, roadstone 2669; L 6; R from CLEADON LANE 1–10–1898; CP—; CG 1–1–1966 (except coal).

EASTGATE: L/B 83; LO 1895; PS 856; TI 7819; G Roadstone 35400; L 77; CP 29–6–1953; CG 14–9–1980. REM Cement traffic from nearby works continues.

EBBERSTON: L/B 62; LO 1882; PS 674; TI 5728; G Barley 554; L 50; R From WILTON 1–4–1903; CP 5–6–1950; CG 5–6–1950.

EBCHESTER: L/B 19; LO 1867; PS 2857; TI 32996; G Bricks 2200; L 28; CP 21–9–1953; CG 21–9–1953.

EDLINGHAM: L/B 3; LO 1887; PS 576; TI 1819; G—; L 6; R To EDLINGHAM HALT 20–9–1925; later EDLINGHAM SIDING 1938; CP 22–9–1930; CG 2–3–1953.

EGTON: L/B 56; LO 1865; PS 513; TI 12862; G—; L 48; CP—; CG 2–8–1965. REM Also known as EGTON BRIDGE.

ELLERBY: L/B 36; LO 1864; PS 493; TI 7291; G Barley 513; L 124; R MARTON to BURTON CONSTABLE Aug. 1864; BURTON CONSTABLE to ELLERBY 1–1–1922; CP 19–10–1964; CG 11–11–1963.

ELRINGTON: L/B 35; LO 1868; SO 1869; PS 92; TI 927; G Roadstone 3422; L 14; R To ELRINGTON HALT 1–9–1926; CP 22–9–1930; CG 20–11–1950.

ELSWICK: L/B 53; LO 1839; SO (present) 1889; PS—; TI 133780; G NF; L—; CP 2–1–1967; CG—. REM New station auth. 12–7–1888 £3755, opened 2–9–1889.

ENTHORPE: L/B 48A; LO 1890; PS 109; TI 1354; G Barley 380; L 59; CP 20–9–1954; CG 14–9–1959.

ESCRICK: L/B 87; LO 1871; PS 1649; TI 8050; G Potatoes 1332; L 30; CP 8–6–1953; CG 11–9–1961.

ESTON: L/B 27; LO 1902; PS 28095; TI 46732; G Bricks 6416; L 7; CP 11–3–1929; CG 3–10–1966. REM Station opened 1–1–1902 £563, but not on site of earlier ESTON (closed 22–11–1885).

ETHERLEY: L/B 10; LO 1843; PS 3282; TI 66204; G Roadstone 19474; L—; CP 8–3–1965; CG 1–11–1965. REM Also known as ETHERLEY AND WITTON PARK. Trains in both directions used the single platform.

EVENWOOD: L/B 9; LO 1863; PS 4488; TI 32174; G Creosote/tar 5008, clay/gannister 2115, manure 1543; L—; CP 14–10–1957; CG 14–10–1957. REM New station opened 2–6–1884 with no G facilities. G traffic handled at pre-1884 station. Doubling of line authorised 14–9–1899 included provision of second platform at 1884 station.

EVERINGHAM: L/B 71; LO 1848; PS 407; TI 3118; G Potatoes 494; L 99; R From HARSWELL GATE 1–9–1874; CP 20–9–1954; CG 2–8–1965.

FANGFOSS: L/B 89; LO 1847; PS 1024; TI 6789; G Potatoes 1783; L 110; CP 5–1–1959; CG 7–6–1965.

FEATHERSTONE PARK: L/B 5; LO 1852; PS 472; TI 15094; G—; L 27; R From FEATHERSTONE 1–1–1902; to FEATHERSTONE PARK HALT 1933; to FEATHERSTONE PARK 1937; CP 3–5–1976; CG 23–8–1954.

FELLING: L/B 54; LO 1839; SO (present) 1896; PS—; TI 284026; G Bricks 6599, building stone 3403, ashes/cinders 1555; L—; CP 5–11–1979 but reopened by Metro 15–11–1981; CG 2–8–1965. REM New station opened 18–11–1896; previous (Brandling Junction) station remains on north side of line but not in railway use.

FENCEHOUSES: L/B 54; LO 1838; PS 20485; TI 141237; G Creosote/tar 428; L 89; CP 4–5–1964; CG 1–6–1964. REM Also known as FENCE HOUSES.

FERRIBY: L/B 39; LO 1840; PS 1276; TI 29569; G Bricks 1058; L 15; CP—; CG 3–5–1965. REM Part of station buildings used as art gallery; new station 1904 on widening to four tracks but tracks now reduced to three and down platform widened to suit.

FERRYHILL: L/B 86; LO 1837; PS 18188; TI 160790; G Roadstone 72340, gravel/sand 16432, scrap 1964; L 216; CP 6–3–1967; CG—. REM New station authorised 3–7–1876, opened 17–6–1877. Cost £13,612. Demolished after closure and site cleared.

FILEY: L/B 38; LO 1846; PS 3641; TI 55514; G Fish 164; L 15; CP—; CG 10–8–1964.

FINGHALL LANE: L/B 33; LO 1855; PS 371; TI 4045; G—; L—; CP 26–4–1954; CG 26–4–1954.

FLAMBOROUGH: L/B 38; LO 1847; PS 369; TI 10618; G Fish 386; L 57; R from MARTON 1–7–1884; CP 5–1–1970; CG 10–8–1964.

FLAXTON: L/B 91; LO 1845; PS 1588; TI 13181; G Hay/clover 1999, barley 878; L 61; CP 22–9–1930; CG 10–8–1964.

FOGGATHORPE: L/B 71; LO 1848; PS 612; TI 4755; G Hay/clover 1119; L 183; R from FOGGATHORPE GATE Oct. 1864; CP 20–9–1954; CG 27–1–1964.

FOREST HALL: L/B 52; LO 1847; PS 2043; TI 40491; G NF; L—; R from BENTON 1–12–1874; CP 15–9–1958; CG—.

FORGE VALLEY: L/B 62; LO 1882; PS 1111; TI 19518; G Timber 458; L 25; CP 5–6–1950; CG 5–6–1950. REM Station buildings and yard now used by North Yorkshire County Council Highways Department.

FOURSTONES: L/B 53; LO 1838; PS 2011; TI 22042; G Lime 15726, barytes 7900, clay/gannister 4714; L 300; CP 2–1–1967; CG 26–4–1965. REM New station auth. 31–7–1879 £880; old station converted to station-master's house 1880 £69.

FROSTERLEY: L/B 83; LO 1847; PS 1400; TI 23372; G Limestone 15110, clay/gannister 11075, roadstone 4294; L—; CP 29–6–1953; CG 3–3–1969.

FYLING HALL: L/B 69; LO 1885; PS 196; TI 5744; G—; L 12; CP 8–3–1965; CG 4–5–1964. REM Closed temp. in World War I.

GAINFORD: L/B 20; LO 1856; PS 1959; TI 18203; G Barley 186; L 169; CP 30–11–1964; CG 5–4–1965.

GAISGILL: L/B 73; LO 1861; PS 423; TI 4092; G—; L 49; CP 1–12–1952; CG 1–12–1952.

GANTON: L/B 91; LO 1845; PS 1068; TI 9370; G Barley 674; L 203; CP 22–9–1930; CG 10–8–1964.

GARFORTH: L/B 44; LO 1834; PS 7040; TI 86924; G Gravel/sand 7486, ashes/cinders 5459, timber, round 1631; L 130; CP—; CG—.

Some joint stations: (*above*) Maltby on the South Yorkshire Joint Railway, which was open for passengers for only 19 years from 1910 to 1929 (*Lens of Sutton*); (*below*) Haxey Junction on the Axholme Joint Railway, closed to passengers in 1933. (*W.A. Camwell*)

Light railways in the North East: (*above*) Seahouses terminus on the North Sunderland Railway photographed just after Nationalisation in 1948; the engine shed is in the background and the train is formed of an NER 0–4–0T, a Great Eastern six-wheel third, and a North Eastern four-wheel saloon. (*W.A. Camwell*); (*below*) The Pateley Bridge terminus of the Nidd Valley Light Railway, which was completely separate from the North Eastern station. Coaches were from the Metropolitan District Railway in London. (*Lens of Sutton*)

GARTON: L/B 47; LO 1853; PS 535; TI 2065; G Barley 329; L 39; CP 5–6–1950; CG 20–10–1958.

GATESHEAD EAST: L/B 54; LO 1849; PS 122967; TI (inc. Gateshead West) 491920; G Scrap 36212, cement 27965, alkali 14314, iron/steel 11532; L—; R GATESHEAD EAST to GATESHEAD March 1971; CP 22–11–1981; CG—. REM New station auth. 7–8–1884 £20416; separate goods station.

GATESHEAD WEST: L/B 86; LO 1868; PS 122967; TI (inc. Gateshead East) 491920; G NF; L—; CP 1–11–1965; CG—.

GILLING: L/B 80; LO 1853; PS 762; TI 8010; G Timber, round 538; L 113; CP 2–2–1953; CG 10–8–1964.

GILSLAND: L/B 53; LO 1838; PS 610; TI 17965; G—; L 259; R from ROSEHILL 1–5–1869; CP 2–1–1967; CG 5–4–1965.

GLAISDALE: L/B 56; LO 1865; PS 926; TI 11816; G Building stone 357; L 79; CP—; CG 2–8–1965.

GLANTON: L/B 3; LO 1887; PS 696; TI 4479; G—; L 56; CP 22–9–1930; CG 2–3–1953.

GOATHLAND: L/B 84; LO 1865; PS 519; TI 13216; G Roadstone 5745; L 5; R from GOATHLAND MILL 1–11–1891; CP 8–3–1965; CG 27–4–1964. REM Reopened by NYMR 22–4–1973.

GOLDSBOROUGH: L/B 88; LO 1848; PS 374; TI 4405; G Barley 251; L—; CP 15–9–1958; CG 3–5–1965.

GOOLE: L/B 37; LO 1869; PS 23514; TI 141675; G Flour/bran 13889, manure 6138, hay/clover 4635; L 208; R GOOLE TOWN to GOOLE 12–6–1961; CP—; CG—. REM Station also used by Lancashire & Yorkshire trains from opening in 1869.

GOSWICK: L/B 52; LO 1847; SO 1–6–1885; PS 277; TI 4612; G Barley 142; L 167; R from WINDMILL HILL 1–1–1898; CP 15–9–1958; CG 10–8–1964.

GRANGETOWN: L/B 21; LO 1846; PS—; TI 82385; G NF; L—; R from ESTON GRANGE (on opening of ESTON) 1–1–1902; CP—; CG—. REM New station opened 22–11–1885 £4185.

GREAT AYTON: L/B 2; LO 1864; SO 1870; PS 2423; TI 25364; G Roadstone 17061; L 3; CP—; CG 6–9–1965. REM New station authorised 22–5–1868 £99; also accounted for iron ore traffic from local mines 77301 tons.

GREATHAM: L/B 75; LO 1840; SO 1841; PS 1039; TI 21475; G Bricks 19124, clay/gannister 10816; L 23; CP—; CG 5–4–1965.

GREENHEAD: L/B 53; LO 1838; PS 1000; TI 13610; G Roadstone 6094, building stone 4258; L 100; CP 2–1–1967; CG 5–4–1965.

GRINKLE: L/B 68; LO 1883; PS 853; TI 7158; G—; L—; R from EASINGTON 1–4–1904; CP 11–9–1939; CG 11–9–1939. REM demolished Aug. 1952. Line closed May 1958 but reopened May 1974 for Boulby Potash Mine traffic.

GRISTHORPE: L/B 38; LO 1846; PS 336; TI 7158; G Barley 112; L—; CP 16–2–1959; CG 16–2–1959. REM New station 1897 cost £506.

GROSMONT: L/B 84; LO 1835; PS 754; TI 24428; G Roadstone 46866, bricks 2299; L 122; CP—; CG 2–8–1965. REM Platform 1 used by BR Esk Valley trains; platforms 2 and 3 by NYMR Pickering trains.

GUISBOROUGH: L/B 30; LO 1853; SO 1854; PS 7453; TI 72722; G Timber, round 1059, iron/steel 745; L 34; CP 2–3–1964; CG 31–8–1964. REM Demolished 1967.

HALTWHISTLE: L/B 53; LO 1838; PS 4648; TI 59795; G Roadstone 11145, building stone 2432; L 817; CP—; CG—.

HAMBLETON: L/B 44; LO 1834; PS 715; TI 9748; G Potatoes 2085; L 42; CP 14–9–1959; CG 7–9–1964. REM Subsequently used by Selby passengers when main line trains diverted via Gascoigne Wood.

HAMMERTON: L/B 88; LO 1848; PS 731; TI 10653; G Hay/clover 715; L—; CP—; CG 3–5–1965.

HAMPSTHWAITE: L/B 55; LO 1862; SO 1866; PS 791; TI 7846; G NF; L—; CP 2–1–1950; CG—. REM Station authorised 9–8–1864, opened 1–7–1866.

HARPERLEY: L/B 83; LO 1847; SO 1892; PS 407; TI 3276; G Timber 1529; L—; CP 29–6–1953; CG 1–10–1955. REM Opened 1–11–1892.

HARROGATE: L/B 18; LO 1862; PS 34513; TI 510247; G Scrap 282; L 4; CP—; CG—. REM Station authorised 13–9–1861 £7592; improvements authorised 24–1–1873 £1319; alterations and additions auth. 30–4–1896 £12434. Station rebuilt and modernised 1966 in conjunction with development company, Copthall Holdings.

HART: L/B 28; LO 1835; PS 297; TI 13787; G NF; L—; CP 31–8–1953; CG—. REM Closed temp. World War II.

HARTLEPOOL: L/B 28; LO 1835; PS 18643; TI 316919; G—; L—; CP 16–6–1947; CG 30–9–1963. REM New station auth. 10–5–1877 £5043; opened 16–11–1878 cost £7339. Old station conv. to warehouse 1880 £837. Station continued in use after closure for school traffic until 23–3–1964.

HARTLEY: L/B 12; LO 1847; PS 2217; TI 46999; G Gravel/sand 2357; L—; CP 2–11–1964; CG 9–12–1963.

HASWELL: L/B 76; LO 1835; PS 5752; TI 78365; G Bricks 14905, clay/gannister 1839; L 488; CP 9–6–1952; CG 5–12–1966.

HAVERTON HILL: L/B 64; LO 1833; PS 1725; TI 67766; G Salt 80547, cement 38181, iron/steel 4366; L—; CP 1–3–1954 (but continued in use for workmen until 6–11–1961); CG—. REM New station auth. 1887 £2321.

HAWSKER: L/B 69; LO 1885; PS 406; TI 8982; G—; L 9; CP 8–3–1965; CG 4–5–1964.

HAXBY: L/B 91; LO 1845; PS 1903; TI 21026; G Hay/clover 460; L 10; CP 22–9–1930; CG 10–8–1964.

HAYBURN WYKE: L/B 69; LO 1885; PS 54; TI 4256; G NF; L—; CP 8–3–1965; CG—. REM Closed temp. in World War I.

HAYDON BRIDGE: L/B 53; LO 1838; PS 1907; TI 27597; G Roadstone 14504; L 484; CP—; CG 26–4–1965. REM New station and warehouse auth. 1877 £2291.

HEADINGLEY: L/B 45; LO 1849; PS—; TI 28889; G Ale and ale empties 1810; L 12; CP—; CG 30–9–1963.

HEADS NOOK: L/B 53; LO 1838; PS 961; TI 17979; G Potatoes 436; L—; CP 2–1–1967; CG 5–4–1965.

HEATON: L/B 52; LO 1839; PS—; TI 519350; G NF; L—; CP 11–8–1980; CG—. REM New station authorised 24–5–1861 £665; new station £10617 opened 1–4–1887 after widening; HEATON FOR BYKER on station name board until 1887.

HEBBURN: L/B 59; LO 1872; PS 21763; TI 415656; G Iron ore 57215, sulphuric acid 9504, alkali 9135, scrap iron & steel 5954; L 6; CP 1–6–1981; CG 4–10–1965.

HECK: L/B 87; LO 1871; PS 654; TI 3646; G Potatoes 299, gravel/sand 239; L 124; CP 15–9–1958; CG 29–4–1963.

HEDDON-ON-THE-WALL: L/B 70; LO 1876; SO 1881; PS 1691; TI 14124; G Clay/gannister 5294; L—; CP 15–9–1958; CG 15–9–1958.

HEDGELEY: L/B 3; LO 5–9–1887; PS 590; TI 4014; G Timber 158; L 208; CP 22–9–1930; CG 2–3–1953.

HEDON: L/B 85; LO 1854; PS 4448; TI 40545; G Barley 1137; L 333; CP 19–10–1964; CG 3–6–1968.

HEIGHINGTON: L/B 74; LO 1825; PS 1137; TI 12163; G Hay/clover 436; L 29; R From AYCLIFFE AND HEIGHINGTON 1–9–1874; CP—; CG 2–3–1970. REM Originally known as AYCLIFFE LANE, where *LOCOMOTION No 1* was put on rails in 1825 after journey by road from Newcastle. Now inn and restaurant.

HELMSLEY: L/B 34; LO 1871; PS 2926; TI 14934; G Timber, round 2591, barley 1211; L 238; CP 2–2–1953; CG 10–8–1964.

HEMINGBROUGH: L/B 39; LO 1840; PS 1689; TI 19621; G Potatoes 2130; L 38; R from CLIFFE 1874; CP 6–11–1967; CG 4–5–1964.

HEPSCOTT: L/B 13; LO 1857; SO 1858; PS 344; TI 13961; G Vegetables 216; L—; CP 3–4–1950; CG 9–3–1964.

HESLEDEN: L/B 28; LO 1835; PS 2093; TI 52098; G Hay/clover 416; L 12; R from CASTLE EDEN COLLIERY 1891; CP 9–6–1952; CG 30–9–1963. REM Tender for new station 5–10–1882 £440.

HESLERTON: L/B 91; LO 1845; PS 612; TI 6360; G Barley 786; L 167; CP 22–9–1930; CG 10–8–1964.

HESSAY: L/B 88; LO 1848; PS 368; TI 3292; G LF; L—; CP 15–9–1958; CG 4–5–1964. REM Closed temp. World War I.

HESSLE: L/B 39; LO 1840; PS 5319; TI 69716; G Chalk 38358; L 13; CP—; CG 4–12–1967. REM New station on widening to four tracks 1904, subsequently reduced to two and platforms widened accordingly.

HETTON: L/B 51; LO 1836; PS 11283; TI 109593; G Bricks 4352, clay/gannister 1877; L—; CP 5–1–1953; CG 11–11–1963.

HEXHAM: L/B 53; LO 1838; PS 11405; TI 121314; G Timber 2324, flour/bran 1873; L 2050; CP—; CG—.

HIGH FIELD: L/B 71; LO 1848; PS 798; TI 5898; G Potatoes 1962, hay/clover 1562; L 131; R from BUBWITH HIGH FIELD 1–12–1873; CP 20-9-1954; CG 27–1–1964.

HIGH SHIELDS: L/B 59; LO 1879; PS—; TI 301687; G NF; L—; CP 1–6–1981 (for Metro); CG—.

170

HIGH WESTWOOD: L/B 19; LO 1867; SO 1–7–1909; PS 6511; TI 83240; G NF; L—; CP 4–5–1942; CG—. REM WESTWOOD in timetable 1–7–1909 but as HIGH WESTWOOD in opening notice. Station £965; stationmaster's house and three cottages £954.

HINDERWELL: L/B 68; LO 1883; PS 1317; TI 26090; G Timber 182; L 32; CP 5–5–1958; CG 5–5–1958.

HOLME: L/B 71; LO 1848; PS 1716; TI 6259; G Potatoes 873; L 159; R To HOLME MOOR 1–7–1923; CP 20–9–1954; CG 2–8–1965.

HOLTBY: L/B 89; LO 1847; SO 1848; PS 1015; TI 4813; G Potatoes 650; L—; R from GATE HELMSLEY 1–2–1872; CP 11–9–1939; CG 1–1–1951.

HORDEN: L/B 25; LO 1905; PS 6280; TI 89204; G Scrap iron/steel 1085, gravel/sand 990; L—; CP 4–5–1964; CG 6–9–1965. REM Station opened 1–9–1905.

HORNSEA: L/B 36; LO 1864; PS 4892; TI 32518; G NF; L—; R to HORNSEA TOWN 1950; CP 19–10–1964; CG—.

HORNSEA BRIDGE: L/B 36; LO 1864; PS—; TI 12411; G Gravel/sand 4614; L 353; CP 19–10–1964; CG 3–5–1965.

HORSFORTH: L/B 45; LO 1849; PS 13537; TI 43879; G Gravel/sand 22118, roadstone 5984, building stone 4766; L 29; CP—; CG 3–5–1965. REM New station and goods warehouse auth. 24–1–1884 £2221.

HOVINGHAM SPA: L/B 80; LO 1853; PS 1163; TI 8073; G Barley 675; L 143; R from HOVINGHAM 1–10–1896; CP 1–1–1931; CG 10–8–1964.

HOWDON-ON-TYNE: L/B 81; LO 1839; PS—; TI 116204; G Bricks 3328; L 2; R from HOWDON 1–12–1875; CP 11–8–1980 (to Metro); CG 7–7–1964.

HOW MILL: L/B 53; LO 1838; PS 1151; TI 11917; G Potatoes 509; L 102; CP 5–1–1959; CG 5–1–1959.

HULL PARAGON: 2L/B 39; LO 1848; PS 277991; TI 860515; G Hull Goods: Fish 86910; Maize 61203, Timber 57949, Potatoes 42240, Wheat 38552, Barley 38528. Hull Drypool: Timber 250432, Flour & bran 85998, Oats 10430. Hull Stepney: Oil cake 24392, Manure & Gas lime 9087, Oils 9408. Hull Wilmington: Cement 75557, Flour & bran 62440, Oil cake 44945, Manure & Gas lime 8838. The subsequent opening of King George Dock, Saltend Jetty and Stoneferry provided the following traffic in 1923: King George Dock: Timber 23498, Fruit 19953, Wheat 11104, Maize 6149, Barley 6877, Wool 6964. Saltend Jetty: Oils 112257. Stoneferry: Cement 31530, Oil cake 5688, oils 3972. (NOTE: Hull Goods accounted for the traffic passing through the various docks on the west side of the River Hull). REM The 1848 station buildings designed by G. T. Andrews still remain, but the operational part of the station consists of the 1904 rebuilding; tender for extensions and alterations accepted 4–12–1902 £75098.

HULL RIVERSIDE QUAY: L/B 39A. LO 1907. REM Used only by passengers on L&YR/NER Joint steamship service to the Continent.

HUNMANBY: L/B 38; LO 1847; PS 2389; TI 19602; G Bricks 5655, barley 1667, wheat 1220; L 221; CP—; CG 10–8–1964.

HUNWICK: L/B 24; LO 1857; PS 3143; TI 40082; G Bricks 14030, clay/gannister 11366, sanitary tubes 4847; L—; CP 4–5–1964; CG 15–9–1958.

HURWORTH BURN: L/B 76; LO 1877; SO 1880; PS 504; TI 2759; G Hay/clover 583; L 94; CP 2–11–1931; CG 2–4–1951.

HUSTHWAITE GATE: L/B 80; LO 1853; PS 856; TI 5250; G Hay/clover 532; L—; CP 2–2–1953; CG 10–8–1964.

HUTTON CRANSWICK: L/B 38; LO 1846; PS 1210; TI 16513; G Wheat 631; L 202; CP—; CG 10–8–1964.

HUTTON GATE: L/B 30; LO 1854; PS 354; TI 10410; G NF; L—; CP 2–3–1964; CG—. REM closed 1–10–1903 to 1–1–1904 on failure of Pease's Bank.

HUTTONS AMBO: L/B 91; LO 1845; PS 533; TI 8937; G Hay/clover 192; L 11; R from HUTTON 1–2–1885; CP 22–9–1930; CG 10–8–1964.

HYLTON: L/B 61; LO 1853; PS 5629; TI 99017; G Paper 3610, iron/steel 1897, cinders 1512; L 28; CP 4–5–1964; CG 4–10–1965.

ILDERTON: L/B 3; LO 1887; PS 1252; TI 4279; G Barley 394; L 112; CP 22–9–1930; CG 2–3–1953.

INGLEBY: L/B 56; LO 1858; PS 538; TI 3888; G Hay/clover 184; L 15; CP 14–6–1954; CG 14–6–1954. REM Tender for new station buildings 11–7–1873 £809.

JARROW: L/B 59; LO 1872; PS 34381; TI 625200; G Pig iron 43849, bars/joists/girders 42639, iron ore 41599; L 1; CP 1–6–1981 (for Metro); CG—. REM Tender accepted for goods warehouse, stables, and house for stationmaster £2443 5–6–1879.

JERVAULX: L/B 33; LO 1856; PS 797; TI 8295; G Barley 459; L 263; R from NEWTON-LE-WILLOWS 1–12–1877; CP 26–4–1954; CG 11–11–1963. REM Used after closure by adjacent public school pupils.

JESMOND: L/B 12; LO 1864; PS—; TI 144158; G NF; L—; CP 23–1–1978; CG—. REM Station displaced by Metro. Converted to restaurant using ex Great North saloon 397 placed on length of track on platform.

KENTON: L/B 63; LO 1905; PS 599; TI 10146; G Potatoes 105; L—; R to KENTON BANK 1–7–1923; CP 17–6–1929; CG 3–1–1966. REM Present terminus of Metro system opened 10–5–1981.

KETTLENESS: L/B 68; LO 1883; PS 54; TI 6574; G Iron ore 2595; L 26; CP 5–5–1958; CG 5–5–1958.

KEYINGHAM: L/B 85; LO 1854; PS 547; TI 8332; G Wheat 607; L 148; CP 19–10–1964; CG 3–5–1965.

KILDALE: L/B 56; LO 1858; PS 198; TI 4285; G—; L 45; CP—; CG 11–6–1956.

KILLINGWORTH: L/B 52; LO 1847; PS 3300; TI 34429; G Bricks 4206; L 70; CP 15–9–1958; CG 7–6–1965. REM Remained open for race specials and excursions.

KIPLING COTES: L/B 48; LO 1865; PS 127; TI 3011; G Barley 591; L 103; CP 29–11–1965; CG 27–1–1964.

KIPPAX: L/B 43; LO 1878; PS 5444; TI 44421; G Gravel/sand 956; L—; CP 22–1–1951; CG 30–9–1963.

KIRBY MOORSIDE: L/B 34; LO 1874; PS 3538; TI 19265; G Barley 732; L 244; CP 2–2–1953; CG 10–8–1964. REM Also rendered as KIRBYMOOR-SIDE. Station and yard now used by agricultural machinery engineers.

KIRKBY STEPHEN: L/B 73; LO 1861; PS 2495; TI 24436; G—; L 828; R to KIRKBY STEPHEN EAST announced 1950 but not implemented in timetable until 15–6–1959; CP 22–1–1962; CG 4–9–1971. Station lighting, luggage lift and engine shed machinery operated electrically by power from turbine driven by adjacent River Eden. Installed c1902.

KIRKBY THORE: L/B 26; LO 1862; PS 762; TI 7603; G Limestone 2282; L 126; CP 7–12–1953; CG 7–12–1953.

KIRKHAM ABBEY: L/B 91; LO 1845; PS 806; TI 6132; G Gravel/sand 3025; L 1; R from KIRKHAM 1875; CP 22–9–1930; CG 10–8–1964.

KIRKNEWTON: L/B 3; LO 1887; PS 304; TI 3213; G Barley 133; L 81; CP 22–9–1930; CG 30–3–1953.

KNAPTON: L/B 91; LO 1845; PS 450; TI 4572; G Barley 693; L 84; CP 22–9–1930; CG 8–10–1979.

KNARESBOROUGH: L/B 88; LO 1851; PS 7014; TI 191752; G Gaswater 244; L 463; CP—; CG 3–5–1965. REM New station auth. 3–3–1865 £1738.

KNITSLEY: L/B 42; LO 1862; PS 881; TI 5782; G Timber 423; L 28; CP 1–5–1939; CG 9–3–1964. REM Closed temp. World War I.

LAMBLEY: L/B 5; LO 1852; PS 318; TI 6976; G—; L 38; CP 3–5–1976; CG 12–9–1960.

LAMESLEY: L/B 86; LO 1868; PS 4777; TI 17752; G—; L—; CP 4–6–1945; CG 14–9–1959. REM Demolished 1961 and site occupied by Tyne Yard.

LANCHESTER: L/B 42; LO 1862; PS 4948; TI 37464; G Creosote 2809, manure 1064; L 297; CP 1–5–1939; CG 5–7–1965.

LANGLEY: L/B 35; LO 1869; PS 299; TI 2976; G Sanitary tubes 1189; L 6; R to LANGLEY-ON-TYNE 29–7–1936; CP 22–9–1930; CG 20–11–1950.

LARTINGTON: L/B 73; LO 1861; PS 193; TI 4030; G Timber, round 1012; L 48; CP 22–1–1962; CG 2–2–1953.

LEADGATE: L/B 1; LO 1896; PS 5549; TI 65490; G—; L—; CP 23–5–1955; CG 10–8–1964.

LEALHOLM: L/B 56; LO 1865; PS 322; TI 9061; G Clay/gannister 2977; L 245; CP—; CG 2–8–1965. REM Also rendered as Lealholm Bridge and Lealholme.

LEAMSIDE: L/B 54; LO 1844; PS 6005; TI 61571; G Bricks 11228; L 21; CP 5–10–1953; CG 5–10–1953.

LEDSTON: L/B 43; LO 1878; PS 2584; TI 15208; G Ashes/cinders 27377; L—; R from LEDSTONE 1–7–1915; CP 22–1–1951; CG 30–9–1963.

LEEDS-MARSH LANE: L/B 44; LO 1834; PS—; TI—; G Manure and gas lime 22600, ale & ale empties 4406, bricks 2506; L 43; CP 15–9–1958; CG 15–12–1980. REM New station auth. 28–8–1868 £1329. Population and traffic figs. included under Leeds New (Joint) station.

LEEMING BAR: L/B 33; LO 1848; PS 1210; TI 16338; G Ale and ale empties 3363; L 179; R from LEEMING LANE 1–7–1902. CP 26–4–1954; CG 1–11–1965.

LEMINGTON: L/B 70; LO 1876; PS 4414; TI 78465; G Bricks 6384; L—; CP 15–9–1958; CG 4–1–1960 (but reopened for coal traffic 17–6–1963 to 7–7–1964).

LEVISHAM: L/B 84; LO 1836; PS 419; TI 5837; G—; L 57; CP 8–3–1965; CG 27–4–1964. Reopened by NYMR 22–4–1973.

LEYBURN: L/B 33; LO 1856; PS 2900; TI 23950; G Roadstone 1542; L 1017; CP 26–4–1954; CG 31–5–1982.

LINTZ GREEN: L/B 19; LO 1867; PS 3192; TI 30044; G Clay/gannister 9723; L—; CP 2–11–1953; CG 2–11–1953. REM In October 1911 the stationmaster was shot and killed outside his own front door; the assailant was never traced.

LITTLE MILL: L/B 52; LO 1847; PS 1010; TI 6898; G Roadstone 12678, building stone 8443, manure 2074; L 300; CP 15–9–1958; CG 7–6–1965.

LOCKINGTON: L/B 38; LO 1846; PS 986; TI 9131; G Wheat 390; L 220; CP 13–6–1960; CG 13–6–1960.

LOFTUS: L/B 68; LO 1867; SO 1875; PS 6137; TI 58513; G Iron ore 228096, bars/joists/girders 26422, pig iron 4884; L 24; R from LOFT-HOUSE (S&D) 1–11–1874; CP 2–5–1960; CG 12–8–1963. REM Station and warehouse auth. 11–12–1872 and opened 1–4–1875. Originally a terminus but converted to a through station to accommodate the Whitby, Redcar & Middlesbrough Union Railway opened in December 1883.

LONDESBOROUGH: L/B 89; LO 1847; PS 504; TI 5460; G Vegetables in bulk 262; L 28; R from SHIPTON (Y&NM) Jan. 1867; CP 29–11–1965; CG 4–5–1964.

LONGHIRST: L/B 52; LO 1847; PS 1022; TI 11083; G Barley 101; L 185; CP 29–10–1951; CG 10–8–1964.

LONGHOUGHTON: L/B 52; LO 1847; PS 796; TI 6107; G Roadstone 26249, building stone 3875; L 143; CP 18–6–1962; CG 18–6–1962.

LOW FELL: L/B 86; LO 1868; PS—; TI 26703; G NF; L—; CP 7–4–1952; CG—.

LOW ROW: L/B 53; LO 1838; PS 546; TI 6482; G—; L 197; CP 5–1–1959; CG 5–4–1965.

LOWTHORPE: L/B 38; LO 1846; PS 1693; TI 9633; G Wheat 641; L 297; CP 5–1–1970; CG 2–11–1964.

LUCKER: L/B 52; LO 1847; PS 734; TI 5567; G Barley 414; L 392; CP 2–2–1953; CG 7–6–1965. REM Demolished July 1960.

MALTON: L/B 91; LO 1845; PS 10463; TI 99533; G Manure 4971, flour/bran 3218, ale & ale empties 2243; L 3232; CP—; CG—. REM Up platform abandoned 10am 22–5–1966 but station retains overall roof. Plans to convert part of station for use as supermarket turned down.

MARFLEET: L/B 85; LO 1854; PS—; TI 3946; G—; L—; CP 19–10–1964; CG 1–5–1972.

MARISHES ROAD: L/B 84; LO 1845; PS 244; TI 2519; G Barley 277; L 8; R from HIGH MARISHES pre-1848; CP 8–3–1965; CG 10–8–1964.

MARKET WEIGHTON: L/B 89; LO 1847; PS 3379; TI 29911; G Barley 1639; L 622; CP 29–11–1965; CG 1–11–1965. REM Station site now occupied by housing estate.

MARSKE: L/B 21; LO 1861; PS 3101; TI 84308; G Barley 172; L 6; CP—; CG 5–4–1965.

MARSTON MOOR: L/B 88; LO 1848; PS 984; TI 6234; G Hay/clover 444; L 46; R from MARSTON 1–10–1896; CP 15–9–1958; CG 3–5–1965.

MASHAM: L/B 49; LO 1875; PS 3642; TI 15141; G Timber, round 255; L 279; CP 1–1–1931; CG 11–11–1963.

MELMERBY: L/B 45; LO 1848; PS 939; TI 14300; G Potatoes 866; L 111; CP 6–3–1967; CG 27–4–1964. REM New station auth. 25–5–1876 £751. Passenger service to Masham withdrawn 1–1–1931; to Thirsk 14–9–1959.

MENTHORPE GATE: L/B 71; LO 1848; PS 266; TI 2634; G Potatoes 1500; L—; CP 7–12–1953; CG 27–1–1964.

MICKLEFIELD: L/B 44; LO 1834; PS 2114; TI 32283; G Limestone 12163, lime 8649, manure 1215; L 46; CP—; CG 10–2–1964. REM New station auth. 31–7–1879 £550.

MICKLETON: L/B 79; LO 1868; PS 271; TI 9582; G Timber 378; L—; CP 30–11–1964; CG 7–6–1954.

MIDDLESBROUGH: L/B 21; LO 1830; SO 3–12–1877; PS 104767; TI 996148; G Pig iron 249900, bars/joists/girders 220099, iron ore 184325, roadstone 146863; L 9. REM Tender for station £47530 and ironwork

£21852. Roof badly damaged by bombing 3–8–1942 and subsequently demolished. Zetland House office block straddling station approach road opened 1960.

MIDDLETON-IN-TEESDALE: L/B 79; LO 1868; PS 3111; TI 19871; G Roadstone 91847, building stone 6886, barytes 1985; L 258; R from MIDDLETON June 1894; CP 30–11–1964; CG 5–4–1965. REM New station authorised 1–3–1888 £1420.

MIDDLETON-ON-THE-WOLDS: L/B 48A; LO 1890; PS 1204; TI 87469; G Cement 3155, barley 1554; L 499; CP 20–9–1954; CG 27–1–1964.

MILLFIELD: L/B 61; LO 1853; PS—; TI 87469; G Flour/bran 17067, ale & ale empties 5484, glass 3282; L—; CP 2–5–1955; CG—. REM New station 1890 £4187.

MINDRUM: L/B 3; LO 1887; PS 584; TI 4234; G Barley 747; L 224; CP 22–9–1930; CG 29–3–1965.

MONK FRYSTON: L/B 90; LO 1840; SO 1904; PS 960; TI 15057; G Grain 3178, vegetables in bulk 1076; L 47; CP 14–9–1959; CG 4–5–1964. REM Opened 1–10–1904 to replace Milford Junction. Cost £639.

MONKSEATON: L/B 15; LO 1864; PS 2971; TI 241313; G—; L—; R from WHITLEY 3–7–1882; CP 10–9–1979 (to Metro); CG 2–3–1959. REM New station on new site 25–7–1915.

MONKWEARMOUTH: L/B 60; LO 1848; PS 21767; TI 163294; G—; L—; CP 6–3–1967; CG 30–3–1981. (Goods traffic included with Sunderland).

MORPETH: L/B 52; LO 1847; PS 10133; TI 170713; G Iron & steel 1163; L 2201; CP—; CG—. REM Extensive alterations auth. 17–7–1878 cost £2925. Roof to be fitted from Fawcett Street station, Sunderland, auth. 11–8–1881 £251; trains from Blyth & Tyne section to use main line station May 1880; old B&T station to two cottages 1881 £227.

MOSS: L/B 87; LO 1871; PS 715; TI 5515; G timber 303; L 109; CP 8–6–1953; CG 8–6–1953.

MOULTON: L/B 66; LO 1846; PS 377; TI 6258; G Hay/clover 266; L 40; CP 3–3–1969; CG 1–10–1956.

MURTON: L/B 76; LO 1836; PS 7159; TI 69107; G—; L 9; CP 5–1–1953; CG 13–6–1960.

MUSGRAVE: L/B 26; LO 1862; PS 634; TI 5678; G—; L—; CP 3–11–1952; CG 3–11–1952.

NABURN: L/B 87; LO 1871; PS 652; TI 7105; G Potatoes 4218; L 7; CP 8–6–1953; CG 6–7–1964.

NAFFERTON: L/B 38; LO 1846; PS 1679; TI 20177; G Flour/bran 7299; L 184; CP—; CG 5–7–1976.

NAWORTH: L/B 53; LO 1838; PS 449; TI 3389; G Lime 3185; manure 1242; L—; CP 5–5–1952; CG ???. REM Originally private station, first in timetable 1–6–1871. General goods traffic not handled.

NAWTON: L/B 34; LO 1874; PS 1108; TI 8382; G Barley 428; L 88; CP 2–2–1953; CG 10–8–1964.

NEWBIGGIN: L/B 14; LO 1872; PS 3736; TI 165927; G Potatoes 229; L 7; CP 2–11–1964; CG 3–2–1964.

NEWBURN: L/B 70; LO 1876; PS 8872; TI 106798; G Gravel/sand 39588, plates, iron & steel 22964, scrap 8486; L—; CP 15–9–1958; CG 26–4–1965.

NEWBY WISKE: L/B 45; LO 1852; PS 265; TI 1985; G Barley 263; L 1; CP 11–9–1939; CG 11–11–1963. REM closed temp. World War I.

NEWCASTLE: L/B 86; LO 1850; PS 266603; TI 3054004; G Handled at Forth Goods: Flour & bran 36559, Manure & Gas lime 14149, Ale and Ale empties 10517; L 16832; Handled at New Bridge Street Goods: Manure & Gas lime 22366, Flour & Bran 13173, Potatoes 8854; Handled at Newcastle Quay: Oats 21832, Maize 7078, Potatoes 5271, vegetables 4937. Totals from all Newcastle Goods Stations: Flour & Bran 52594; Manure & Gas lime 39,226, Oats 26678. The 986 tons of fish despatched by rail in 1913 had risen to 5,600 tons in 1924, but the number of wagons of livestock had decreased from 16832 in 1913 to 4929 in 1924. REM 13–9–1861 Tender accepted for extensions £7777, 21–11–1862 Tender accepted for portico £5428, 20–9–1888 Tender accepted for alterations and extensions £37472, 20–9–1888 Tender accepted for hotel alterations £51000. Platforms renumbered January 1894. Electric service to Tynemouth commenced 1–7–1904 and to South Shields 14–3–1938; withdrawn 18–6–1967 and 7–1–1963 respectively.

NEWHAM: L/B 52; LO 1847; PS 315; TI 2453; G—; L—; CP 25–9–1950; CG 25–9–1950.

NEWSHAM: L/B 12; LO 1847; PS 2943; TI 133659; G Roadstone 227; L—; CP 2–11–1964; CG 7–6–1965.

NEWTON KYME: L/B 18; LO 1847; PS 591; TI 8972; G Barley 159; L 95; CP 6–1–1964; CG 6–7–1964.

NIDD BRIDGE: L/B 45; LO 1848; PS 468; TI 10134; G Timber, round

105; L 46; R from RIPLEY 1–6–1862; CP 18–6–1962; CG 10–8–1964. REM New station auth. Feb. 1870 £411.

NORHAM: L/B 40; LO 1849; PS 2200; TI 14277; G Barley 1407; L 485; CP 15–6–1964; CG 29–3–1965. REM Now maintained as private railway museum by redundant railwayman living on the premises.

NORTHALLERTON: L/B 86; LO 1841; PS 6627; TI 81323; G Timber 987; L 3151; CP—; CG—. REM World War II emergency platforms used in 1950s during main line Sunday diversions. Original station buildings remain on up side but other parts of station demolished.

NORTH GRIMSTON: L/B 47; LO 1853; PS 564; TI 3789; G Barley 447; L 56; CP 5–6–1950; CG 20–10–1958. REM Plans for waiting room, etc, on raised platform dated 1893: this building now a private residence.

NORTH HOWDEN: L/B 39; LO 1840; PS 2287; TI 12549; G Manure 2970; L 191; R from HOWDEN 1–7–1922; to HOWDEN 12–6–1961; CP—; CG 3–5–1965. REM Despatched 1307 tons of 'Locos on own wheels' in 1923.

NORTH ROAD: L/B 74; LO 1825; PS—; TI 82045; G NF; L—; R from DARLINGTON (NORTH ROAD) Oct. 1868; CP—; CG—. REM Goods traffic handled at Darlington (HOPETOWN). Part of 1842 station buildings occupied by Darlington North Road Station Museum opened 27–9–1975.

NORTH SEATON: L/B 14; LO 1859; PS 7734; TI 100192; G Roadstone 984; L—; CP 2–11–1964; CG 9–12–1963.

NORTH SHIELDS: L/B 81; LO 1839; PS 631; TI 1107300; G Creosote 2974, bricks 2531, ashes/cinders 1189; L 10; R from SHIELDS Nov.1874; CP 11–8–1980 to Metro; CG 8–10–1979. REM New station auth. Sept.1889 £10674: this was the third station.

NORTH SKELTON: L/B 68; LO 1872; SO 1902; PS 3043; TI 24079; G iron ore 323101; L—; CP 1–2–1952; CG 21–1–1964. REM Opened 1–7–1902 £1447.

NORTH WYLAM: L/B 70; LO 1876; PS 1352; TI 27488; G Rails, iron and steel 361; L—; CP 11–3–1968; CG 2–1–1961.

NORTON-ON-TEES: L/B 75; LO 1833; PS 1527; TI 16585; G Roadstone 17096, gravel/sand 5043, building stone 4261; L—; R from NORTON 1–10–1901; CP 7–3–1960; CG 10–8–1964. REM New station on new site July 1870.

NUNBURNHOLME: L/B 89; LO 1847; PS 869; TI 5338; G Barley 590; L 104; R from BURNBY 1–1–1873; CP 1–4–1951; CG 1–4–1951.

NUNNINGTON: L/B 34; LO 1871; PS 444; TI 3637; G Barley 494; L 59; CP 2–2–1953; CG 10–8–1964. REM Now Ryedale Lodge Restaurant.

NUNTHORPE: L/B 30; LO 1853; SO 1854; PS 567; TI 20799; G Barley 241; L 34; CP—; CG 10–8–1964.

ORMESBY: L/B 30; LO 1853; PS 1375; TI 31962; G Barley 241; L—; R to MARTON 17–5–1982; CP—; CG 10–8–1964.

OTTERINGTON: L/B 86; LO 1841; PS 943; TI 9204; G Barley 437; L—; CP 15–9–1958; CG 10–8–1964.

OTTRINGHAM: L/B 85; LO 1854; PS 1297; TI 10726; G Wheat 1174; L 359; CP 19–10–1964; CG 3–5–1965.

PALLION: L/B 61; LO 1852; PS—; TI 32661; G—; CP 4–5–1964; CG 5–7–1965. REM Station buildings (inc. house) authorised 17–3–1898 £9391.

PANNAL: L/B 45; LO 1848; PS 2599; TI 32425; G Grain 550; L 675; CP—; CG 3–5–1965. REM Station house auth. 1862 £540. Now in use as a restaurant and inn.

PATELEY BRIDGE: L/B 55; LO 1862; PS 4101; TI 22199; G Building stone 5146, roadstone 1086; L 247; CP 2–4–1951; CG 31–10–1964.

PATRINGTON: L/B 85; LO 1854; PS 2631; TI 23277; G Wheat 1457; L 647; CP 19–10–1964; CG 3–5–1965.

PEGSWOOD: L/B 52; LO 1847; SO 1–1–1903?; PS 2737; TI 34262; G Bricks 11245, clay/gannister 7239; L—; CP—; CG 10–8–1964.

PELAW: L/B 54; LO 1839; PS 25026; TI 207536; G Bricks 24454; L—; R from PELAW MAIN Jan.1886; CP 5–11–1979 for Metro; CG 4–10–1965. REM New station opened 18–11–1896.

PELTON: L/B 1; LO 1894; PS 10183; TI 73002; G Bricks 5577; L—; CP 7–12–1953; CG 7–12–1953.

PENSHAW: L/B 54; LO 1838; PS 16833; TI 134243; G Bricks 19406, creosote/tar/pitch 2474, building stone 1198; L 12; R from PENSHER 1–7–1881; CP 4–5–1964; CG 30–4–1981. REM Station rebuilt 1913 after fire £1970.

PERCY MAIN: L/B 81; LO 1839; PS—; TI 228273; G—; L 1; CP 11–8–1980 to Metro; CG 29–4–1968.

PICKERING: L/B 84; LO 1836; PS 5699; TI 44432; G Manure 1624, barley

1179, roadstone 1080; L 523; CP 8–3–1965; CG 4–7–1966. REM Reopened by North York Moors Railway 24–5–1976. Station buildings designed by G. T. Andrews remain in use, but overall roof removed 1952.

PICKHILL: L/B 45; LO 1852; PS—; TI—; G NF; L—; CP 14–9–1959; CG—. REM Mineral traffic handled at Pickhill Siding, ¼-mile north of station; siding closed 11–11–1963.

PICTON: L/B 45; LO 1852; PS 522; TI 11212; G hay/clover 813; L 73; CP 4–1–1960; CG 7–9–1964.

PIERCEBRIDGE: L/B 20; LO 1856; PS 3001; TI 15311; G Barley 764; L 101; CP 30–11–1964; CG 5–4–1965.

PILMOOR: L/B 86; LO 1841; SO 1847; PS 134; TI 3505; G Potatoes 239; L—; CP 5–5–1958; CG 14–9–1959.

PINCHINTHORPE: L/B 30; LO 1853; SO 1854; PS 287; TI 7531; G—; L—; R from PINCHINGTHORPE 1–4–1920; CP 29–10–1951; CG 29–10–1951. REM New station authorised 21–12–1876 when adjacent level crossing replaced by road bridge over line.

PITTINGTON: L/B 51; LO 1836; PS 2053; TI 28248; G—; L—; CP 5–1–1953; CG 4–1–1960. REM New station auth. 17–6–1875 £383; platform extended 1904.

PLAWSWORTH: L/B 86; LO 1868; PS 5927; TI 41220; G Scrap 110; L—; CP 7–4–1952; CG 30–9–1963.

PLESSEY: L/B 52; LO 1847; PS 394; TI 6342; G—; L 22; R from PLESSAY 1864; CP 15–9–1958; CG 2–4–1962.

POCKLINGTON: L/B 89; LO 1847; PS 5124; TI 32294; G Vegetables in bulk 3300, potatoes 2302, barley 1591; L 744; CP 29–11–1965; CG 1–11–1965. REM Train shed, with ends filled in, now forms gymnasium for Pocklington School.

POINT PLEASANT: L/B 67; LO 1879; PS—; TI 24934; G NF; L—; CP 23–7–1973; CG—. REM Prior to 1–1–1902 was Workmen's platform.

PONTELAND: L/B 63; LO 1905; PS 3586; TI 32084; G Hay/clover 263; L 194; CP 17–6–1929; CG 14–8–1967. REM Station opened to passengers 1–6–1905.

POOL: L/B 57; LO 1865; PS 889; TI 19046; G Gravel/sand 4302, building stone 3919; L 7; R to POOL-IN-WHARFEDALE 1–7–1927; CP 22–3–1965; CG 5–7–1965. REM New station and stationmaster's house auth.

16–2–1866 £1079. Replaced Arthington for goods and mineral traffic. Site now occupied by small housing estate.

POPPLETON: L/B 88; LO 1848; PS 874; TI 17041; G Barley 389; L—; CP—; CG 4–5–1964.

PORT CLARENCE: L/B 64; LO 1833; PS 2713; TI 83203; G Rails, iron & steel 71000, blooms 66742, roadstone 30477, scrap 26508; L—; CP 11–9–1939; CG 2–11–1964. REM New station auth. 4–5–1882 £1561. Platforms extended April 1929.

POTTO: L/B 56; LO 1857; PS 1645; TI 12133; G hay/clover 435; L 58; CP 14–6–1954; CG 1–12–1958.

PRUDHOE: L/B 53; LO 1838; PS 8072; TI 70221; G Sanitary tubes 2517; L 344; R to PRUDHOE FOR OVINGHAM 3–5–1937; to PRUDHOE March 1971; CP—; CG 26–4–1965.

RASKELF: L/B 86; LO 1841; PS 531; TI 5137; G Potatoes 1656; L 108; CP 5–5–1958; CG 10–8–1964. REM New buildings on up platform 1933 due widening; demolished 1959.

RAVENSCAR: L/B 69; LO 1885; PS 230; TI 4860; G Bricks 4888; L—; R from PEAK 1–10–1897; CP 8–3–1965; CG 4–5–1964. REM Closed 6–3–1895 to 1–4–1896 due to NER complaint that no house available for stationmaster.

RAVENSTONEDALE: L/B 73; LO 1861; PS 1353; TI 7535; G—; L 49; R from NEWBIGGEN 1–1–1877; CP 1–12–1952, CG 22–1–1962.

REDCAR: L/B 21; LO 1861; PS 11140; TI 353939; G Gravel/sand 20348; L 42; R REDCAR CENTRAL 1951; CP—; CG 6–10–1980. REM Replaced original station of 1846 but on different site; up platform opened 1935 but reverted to single (down) platform 1–11–1970.

REDMIRE: L/B 33; LO 1878; PS 364; TI 8288; G Timber, round 212; L 124; CP 26–4–1954; CG 3–8–1970.

RICCALL: L/B 87; LO 1871; PS 804; TI 10848; G Potatoes 3543; L 31; CP 15–9–1958; CG 6–7–1964.

RICHMOND: L/B 66; LO 1846; PS 6823; TI 33996; G Minerals 1167; L 348; CP 3–3–1969; CG 2–10–1967. REM Train shed now in use as Garden Centre. Engine shed and gasworks derelict. Swimming baths on site of goods sheds. Stationmaster's house on opposite side of main road. Note bridge over River Swale constructed by railway company to give access to station.

RIDING MILL: L/B 53; LO 1838; PS 1697; TI 24775; G Timber 929; L 204; CP—; CG 26–4–1965.

Light railways in the North East: (*above*) Easingwold station. The wooden building on the platform was completely destroyed by a fierce fire one night in 1967 and the site of the station is now difficult to locate as it is covered with houses. However, the nearby Station Hotel still proclaims its identity. (*Author's collection*); (*below*) Sand Hutton Central station on the Sand Hutton Light Railway, which terminated at Warthill on the NER line from York to Market Weighton. The line was a private venture of Sir Robert Walker but its closure followed his death in 1930 at the early age of 39. (*H.G.W. Household*)

LNER architecture: (*above*) Otterington, between Thirsk and Northallerton, required new buildings when the main line was widened in 1933. (*K. Hoole*); (*below*) Widening also took place at the same time at Alne, further south, necessitating new buildings on the down side only, leaving the Alne & Easingwold bay untouched. This view shows the new booking office and signalbox. (*British Rail*)

RILLINGTON: L/B 91; LO 1845; PS 1164; TI 12796; G Barley 647; L 28; CP 22–9–1930; CG 10–8–1964. REM roof removed 1955.

RIPLEY VALLEY: L/B 55; LO 1862; PS 1397; TI 13842; G Gravel/sand 425; L—; R from KILLINGHALL to RIPLEY 1–6–1862 and from RIPLEY to RIPLEY VALLEY 1–4–1875. CP 2–4–1951; CG 6–11–1961.

RIPON: L/B 45; LO 1848; PS 11920; TI 83070; G Timber, round 1181; L 1502; CP 6–3–1967; CG 5–9–1969. REM New station auth. 1–9–1854 £3850.

ROBIN HOOD'S BAY: L/B 69; LO 1885; PS 1242; TI 27336; G Gravel/sand 151; L 70; CP 8–3–1965; CG 10–8–1964. REM Due to delay in traffic arriving at Scarborough for Robin Hood's Bay the last freight train ran one week later than intended, namely on 14–8–1964.

ROMALDKIRK: L/B 79; LO 1868; PS 950; TI 10697; G clay/gannister 2792; L 59; CP 30–11–1964; CG 5–4–1965.

ROWLANDS GILL: L/B 19; LO 1867; PS 17502; TI 112149; G clay/gannister 26245, bricks 11578, pig iron 2644; L 24; CP 1–2–1954; CG 11–11–1963.

ROWLEY: L/B 10; LO 1834; SO 1846; PS 996; TI 9737; G clay/gannister 10111; L 9; R from COLD ROWLEY 1868; CP 1–5–1939; CG 6–6–1966. REM Station buildings demolished and re-erected at Beamish Open Air Museum 1976.

RUSWARP: L/B 84; LO 1835; PS 869; TI 42907; G Flour/bran 781; L 191; CP—; CG 2–8–1965.

RYEHILL: L/B 85; LO 1854; PS 942; TI 11205; G Wheat 971; L 191; R from BURSTWICK AND RYEHILL 1–7–1881; to RYEHILL AND BURSTWICK 23–9–1929; CP 19–10–1964; CG 3–5–1965.

RYHOPE: L/B 76; LO 1836; PS 11236; TI 138568; G Scrap iron/steel 1476; L 27; CP 5–1–1953; CG 7–3–1960. REM New station auth. 2–11–1893 £1080. Public Delivery Siding continued in use but known as Ryhope East from 7–3–1960 to closure 1–6–1964.

RYHOPE EAST: L/B 77; LO 1854; SO 1900; Details as for Ryhope. G NF; L—; CP 7–3–1960; CG 1–6–1964 (PDS formerly known as Ryhope).

RYTON: L/B 53; LO 1838; PS 11236; TI 138568; G NF; L—; CP 5–7–1964; CG—.

ST ANTHONYS: L/B 67; LO 1879; PS—; TI 11283; G—; L—; CP 12–9–1960; CG 12–9–1960.

ST JOHNS CHAPEL: L/B 83; LO 1845; PS—; TI 23404; G Clay/gannister 6974; L 30; CP 29–6–1953; CG 1–11–1965.

ST PETERS: L/B 67; LO 1879; PS—; TI 37111; G Manure 13073, roadstone 9850, timber 3557; L—; CP 23–7–1973; CG 31–10–1966.

SALTBURN: L/B 21; LO 1861; PS 4754; TI 144236; G—; L 12; CP—; CG 3–4–1967 (but remained open for coal).

SALTMARSHE: L/B 37; LO 1869; PS 1225; TI 11593; G Hay/clover 1329, manure 1123, potatoes 1098; L 137; CP—; CG 4–5–1964.

SANDSEND: L/B 68; LO 1883; PS 956; TI 42960; G Gravel/sand 275; L—; CP 5–5–1958; CG 5–5–1958. REM Coal traffic was handled at station but general goods facilities were provided from a goods shed at East Row, ½-mile nearer Whitby, which still exists as a boat repair yard.

SAWDON: L/B 62; LO 1882; PS 590; TI 7761; G Barley 260; L 25; CP 5–6–1950; CG 5–6–1950. REM Sawdon station actually at Brompton-by-Sawdon. Sawdon village 2 miles away to the north.

SCALBY: L/B 69; LO 1885; PS 1578; TI 40972; G—; L 10; CP 2–3–1953; CG 4–5–1964. REM Site cleared and now occupied by old people's homes.

SCARBOROUGH: L/B 91; LO 1845; PS 37674; TI 306791; G Fish 7791, bricks 3481, ale & ale empties 1305, manure 1113; L 69; (NOTE: the goods traffic was handled at a goods station at Gallows Close). CP—; CG 6–4–1981. REM All the G. T. Andrews station buildings dating from 1845 remain in use, retaining the train shed roof, but the portico was demolished c1883 to make way for the clock tower. Former Andrews-designed goods shed incorporated into passenger station in 1903, housing Platform 8, with Platform 9 along the exterior of the south wall.

SCARBOROUGH (WASHBECK EXCURSION STATION): L/B 91; LO 1845; SO 1908; Details as for Scarborough; R to LONDESBOROUGH ROAD 17–7–1933; CP 4–7–1966; CG—. REM Last used 24–8–1963. Station auth. 1907 £7635. Station normally used Saturdays, Sundays and Bank Holidays only.

SCHOLES: L/B 46; LO 1876; PS 1340; TI 16893; G Barley 215; L 29; CP 6–1–1964; CG 27–4–1964.

SCORTON: L/B 66; LO 1846; PS 1725; TI 10311; G Hay/clover 472, barley 333; L 152; CP 3–3–1969; CG 2–8–1965.

SCOTBY: L/B 53; LO 1838; PS 532; TI 24792; G Spent bark 270; L 1; CP 2–11–1959; CG 2–11–1959.

SCOTSWOOD: L/B 53; LO 1839; PS 3216; TI 117431; G Blooms 5545, ashes/cinders 3710, iron & steel 2795, scrap iron and steel 2416; L 10; CP 1–5–1967; CG 26–4–1965. REM SN&W portion of station destroyed by fire 17–7–1879; new Scotswood station and goods warehouse auth. 15–4–1884 £1412.

SCREMERSTON: L/B 52; LO 1847; PS 538; TI 4225; G Bricks 518; L 6; CP 8–7–1951; CG 8–7–1951.

SCRUTON: L/B 33; LO 1848; PS 564; TI 6948; G Flour/bran 208; L 39; CP 26–4–1954; CG 7–5–1956. REM Also known as Scruton Lane.

SEAHAM: L/B 77; LO 1854; PS 23014; TI 247794; G Limestone 11484, glass 4423, timber 4420, bricks 4004; L—; R to SEAHAM HARBOUR 1–3–1925; CP 11–9–1939; CG 4–10–1965.

SEAHAM COLLIERY: L/B 77; LO 1905; PS—; TI 156308; G NF; L—; R to SEAHAM 1925; CP—; CG—. REM House for stationmaster 1903.

SEAMER: L/B 91; LO 1845; PS 1130; TI 25168; G Barley 668; L 571; CP—; CG—. REM Additional down platform auth. Dec.1911; platform demolished and track removed Nov.1964. Goods shed demolished by burning Dec.1980.

SEATON: L/B 76; LO 1836; PS 1460; TI 27030; G Barley 111; L—; CP 1–9–1952; CG 14–9–1959.

SEATON CAREW: L/B 75; LO 1840; PS 2294; TI 20019; G Gravel/sand 8887; L 24; R from SEATON 1–5–1875; CP—; CG 6–12–1965. REM New station auth. 1883 £2135.

SEATON DELAVAL: L/B 12; LO 1847; PS 7573; TI 77375; G Bricks 282; L 21; R from SEATON DELAVAL COLLIERY Aug.1864; CP 2–11–1964; CG 9–12–1963. REM New station auth. April 1884 £1205.

SEDGEFIELD: L/B 29; LO 1834; PS 3185; TI 15293; G Gravel/sand 1106, hay/clover 1078, timber 1035; L 12; CP 31–3–1952; CG 10–2–1964.

SEGHILL: L/B 12; LO 1847; PS 2049; TI 39020; G Bricks 7466, clay/gannister 3698; L—; CP 2–11–1964; CG 9–12–1963. Single platform used by trains in both directions although running lines were double track.

SELBY: L/B 87; LO 1834; PS 10465; TI 125804; G Oilcake 50841, flour/bran 15051, oils 11697, creosote, tar & pitch 7533; L 1024; CP—; CG—; Diversion requiring new bridge over River Ouse, with additions and alterations to station auth. 6–7–1888 and 25–7–1889 £30102. Station enlarged 1898/9.

SESSAY: L/B 86; LO 1841; PS 762; TI 4759; G Potatoes 860; L 117; CP 15–9–1958; CG 10–8–1964. New station buildings and platforms on widening 1942. Buildings demolished (but not house) May 1961.

SETTRINGTON: L/B 47; LO 1853; PS 549; TI 5076; G Barley 383; L—; CP 5–6–1950; CG 20–10–1958.

SEXHOW: L/B 56; LO 1857; PS 452; TI 4352; G Building stone 414; L 12; CP 14–6–1954; CG 1–12–1958.

SHERBURN COLLIERY: L/B 54; LO 1844; PS 3060; TI 25326; G Barley 178; L 29; R from SHERBURN (YN&B) 1–4–1874; CP 28–7–1941; CG 14–9–1959.

SHERBURN HOUSE: L/B 51; LO 1893; SO 1893; PS 3429; TI 47216; G Bricks 8473; L—; CP 1–1–1931; CG 11–1–1954. REM Replaced earlier station (opened 6–11–1837 on adjacent site on Shincliffe Town line) which had been renamed SHERBURN (D&S) to SHERBURN HOUSE 1–11–1874.

SHERBURN-IN-ELMET: L/B 90; LO 1839; PS 533; TI 8285; G Vegetables in bulk 483; L 47; R from SHERBURN (Y&NM) 1–7–1903; CP 13–9–1965; CG 1–5–1967.

SHIELD ROW: L/B 1; LO 1893; SO 1894; PS 31561; TI 157011; G Building stone 182; L 1; R to WEST STANLEY 1–2–1934; CP 23–5–1955; CG 11–9–1961.

SHILDON: L/B 11A; LO 1842; PS 14916; TI 136879; G Creosote/tar/pitch 15777, scrap 5911, manure 4558, oils 3664; L 48; CP—; CG—.

SHINCLIFFE: L/B 54; LO 1844; PS 3690; TI 17394; G Potatoes 187; L 34; CP 28–7–1941; CG 11–11–1963.

SHOTLEY BRIDGE: L/B 19; LO 1867; PS 4825; TI 28962; G NF; L—; CP 21–9–1953; CG—.

SHOTTON BRIDGE: L/B 76; LO 1835; SO 1877; PS 6280; TI 63328; G NF; L—; CP 9–6–1952; CG—. REM New station and stationmaster's house auth. 23–9–1875 £1142. Opened 1–9–1877.

SIGGLESTHORNE: L/B 36; LO 1864; PS 342; TI 4597; G Wheat 469; L 283; R from HATFIELD 1–10–1874; CP 19–10–1964; CG 11–11–1963.

SINDERBY: L/B 45; LO 1852; PS 963; TI 6040; G Barley 797; L 218; CP 1–1–1962; CG 11–11–1963.

SINNINGTON: L/B 34; LO 1875; PS 784; TI 8258; G Barley 491; L 70; CP 2–2–1953; CG 2–2–1953.

SKINNINGROVE: L/B 68; LO 1875; PS 2871; TI 56241; G NF; L—; R from CARLIN HOW 1–10–1903; CP 5–5–1958; CG—. REM Workmen only from 4–2–1952. Buildings demolished Aug.1952, leaving only platform.

SKIRLAUGH: L/B 36; LO 1864; PS 858; TI 8645; G Wheat 605; L 151; CP 6–5–1957; CG 11–11–1963.

SLAGGYFORD: L/B 5; LO 1852; PS 428; TI 5940; G—; L 119; CP 3–5–1976; CG 12–9–1960.

SLEDMERE & FIMBER: L/B 47; LO 1853; PS 1108; TI 6546; G Barley 1937, timber 1105; wheat 600; L 271; CP 5–6–1950; CG 20–10–1958. REM Also referred to as FIMBER.

SLEIGHTS: L/B 84; LO 1835; PS 1364; TI 50598; G—; L 51; CP—; CG 5–6–1967 (coal excepted): coal 2–5–1983.

SLINGSBY: L/B 80; LO 1853; PS 698; TI 6879; G Barley 421; L 75; CP 1–1–1931; CG 10–8–1964.

SMARDALE: L/B 73; LO 1861; PS 325; TI 2091; G—; L 48; CP 1–12–1952; CG 1–12–1952. REM Closed temp. in World War I.

SMEAFIELD: L/B 52; LO 1847; PS 35; TI 369; G NF; L—; CP 1–5–1930; CG—. REM Originally private station (see text).

SNAINTON: L/B 62; LO 1882; PS 976; TI 8591; G Barley 386; L 47; CP 5–6–1950; CG 5–6–1950.

SOUTH BANK: L/B 21; LO 1846; PS—; TI 370690; G Pig iron 348634, rails, iron & steel 149110, bars/joists/girders 90087, roadstone 85493; L—; R from SOUTHBANK Nov.1891. CP—; CG 2–10–1972. REM New station, goods warehouse and 3 cottages auth. 1880 £7703. Opened 1–5–1882, replacing previous SOUTH BANK (originally ESTON) which reverted to ESTON from this date.

SOUTHBURN: L/B 48A; LO 1890; PS 326; TI 3562; G Barley 503, wheat 488, oats 144; L 104; CP 20–9–1954; CG 27–1–1964.

SOUTHCOATES: L/B 85; LO 1854; PS—; TI 51275; G NF; L—; CP 19–10–1964; CG—. REM New station auth. 2–9–1883 £1801.

SOUTH EASTRINGTON: L/B 39; LO 1840; PS 825; TI 3581; G Hay/clover 1037, potatoes 284, wheat 255; L 44; R from EASTRINGTON 10–7–1922; to EASTRINGTON 12–6–1961; CP—; CG 4–5–1964.

SOUTH GOSFORTH: L/B 12; LO 1864; PS 16193; TI 210455; G Building stone 716, roadstone 338; L—; R from GOSFORTH 1–3–1905; CP 23–1–1978 (for Metro); CG 14–8–1967. REM Reopened by Metro 11–8–1980.

SOUTH HETTON: L/B 76; LO 1836; PS 7260; TI 76710; G NF; L—; CP 9–6–1952; CG—. REM New station auth. 11–4–1878 £1179.

SOUTH MILFORD: L/B 44; LO 1834; PS 2429; TI 26051; G Vegetables in bulk 474; L 32; R from MILFORD 1867; CP—; CG 30–9–1963.

SOUTH SHIELDS: L/B 59; LO 1879; PS 108647; TI 649785; G Manure/gas lime 21243, iron & steel 4735, scrap iron & steel 4718, creosote/tar/pitch 3059; L 5; CP 1–6–1981 (for Metro); CG 31–3–1970. Station opened 2–6–1879 £10496.

SPEETON: L/B 38; LO 1847; PS 411; TI 3089; G Barley 202; L 75; CP 5–1–1970; CG 4–5–1964.

SPENNITHORNE: L/B 33; LO 1856; PS 478; TI 2492; G NF; L—; CP 26–4–1954; CG—. REM Closed temp. World War I.

SPENNYMOOR: L/B 11; LO 1837; PS 16408; TI 125680; G Creosote/tar/pitch 44206, pig iron 41162, bricks 20273, clay/gannister 12217; L 6; CP 31–3–1952; CG 2–5–1966. REM New station auth. 6–5–1875 £1357.

SPOFFORTH: L/B 18; LO 1847; PS 1534; TI 13898; G Barley 224; L 2; CP 6–1–1964; CG 6–1–1964.

SPROUSTON: L/B 40; LO 1849; PS 876; TI 4722; G Barley 361; L 51; CP 4–7–1955; CG 25–1–1965.

STADDLETHORPE: L/B 39; LO 1840; PS 981; TI 15397; G Timber 10393, hay/clover 2083; L 200; R to GILBERDYKE 1–2–1974; CP—; CG 3–5–1965. REM New station auth. 1903 £2606 on widening to four tracks. 1974 renaming delayed due non-arrival of new station nameboards!

STAINTONDALE: L/B 69; LO 1885; PS 247; TI 5687; G—; L 41; R to STAINTON DALE 1937; CP 8–3–1965; CG 4–5–1964.

STAITHES: L/B 68; LO 1883; PS 1718; TI 24888; G Fish 203, oil cake 130; L—; CP 5–5–1958; CG 5–5–1958.

STAMFORD BRIDGE: L/B 89; LO 1847; PS 1866; TI 12468; G Potatoes 849, barley 715, hay/clover 698; L 145; CP 29–11–1965; CG 7–6–1965.

STANHOPE: L/B 83; LO 1862; PS 2567; TI 27771; G Limestone 100660, ores 12521; L 88; CP 29–6–1953; CG 1–11–1965. REM New station on new site auth. 1894; opened 21–10–1895, 1862 station remained in used as goods station.

STANNINGTON: L/B 52; LO 1847; PS 800; TI 14968; G sanitary tubes 215, hay/clover 206; L 50; R from NETHERTON 1–1–1892; CP 15–9–1958; CG 10–8–1964.

STARBECK: L/B 45; LO 1851; PS 217; TI 124217; G Gaswater 3347, bricks 1588, grain 1484; L 321; CP—; CG 5–10–1970. REM Station rebuilt 1897/8. Subway authorised 9–10–1902 £4056.

STAWARD: L/B 35; LO 1869; PS 720; TI 4547; G timber 344; L 320; CP 22–9–1930; CG 20–11–1950. REM To STAWARD HALT 1–4–1939. Let as Holiday Cottage by BR.

STEPNEY: L/B 82; LO 1853; PS—; TI 45569; G NF; L—; CP 19–10–1964; CG—. REM Disused wooden station waiting room destroyed by fire 24–2–1959.

STILLINGTON: L/B 29; LO 1833; PS 1435; TI 27949; G Pig iron 80738, roadstone 4296, creosote/tar/pitch 3027; L 18; R from CARLTON IRON WORKS 1–11–1879; CP 31–3–1952; CG 5–7–1965. REM New station auth. 31–5–1880 £1367.

STOCKSFIELD: L/B 53; LO 1838; PS 3187; TI 40540; G Building stone 681; L 326; CP—; CG 26–4–1965.

STOCKTON: L/B 45; LO 1852; PS 47567; TI 255961; G NF; L—; R from NORTH STOCKTON 1–11–1892; CP—; CG—. REM New station auth. 16–10–1890 £24013, opened 1893. Train shed roof removed 1978. (NOTE: Goods traffic handled at North Shore, where the main traffic was Plates, iron & steel 149293 tons, and at Stockton South – pig iron 175705 tons.)

STOKESLEY: L/B 56; LO 1857; PS 2716; TI 16514; G Hay/clover 482; L 674; CP 14–6–1954; CG 2–8–1965.

STRENSALL: L/B 91; LO 1845; PS 950; TI 30691; G Bricks 1037, hay/clover 872, spent bark 480; L 30; CP 22–9–1930; CG 10–8–1964. REM Station used for military traffic in World War II.

SUNDERLAND: L/B 61; LO 1879; PS 151159; TI 1207968; G NF; L—; G Handled at Millfield, Monkwearmouth, Pallion, Southwick and Wearmouth Docks. Totals (all goods stations), iron ore 142935, timber 79751, oil 37016, wheat 30686; L 66; CP—; CG—. REM New station opened 4–8–1879 £13387; alterations 1895 £746; bombed 1943 and rebuilt 1953; rebuilt and remodelled 1965.

SUNILAWS: L/B 40; LO 1849; SO 1851; PS 228; TI 2680; G Barley 560, potatoes 203; L 114; R from WARK 1–10–1871; CP 4–7–1955; CG 29–3–1965.

SUTTON-ON-HULL: L/B 36; LO 1864; PS 2103; TI 23775; G Barley 219; L 28; R from SUTTON 1–12–1874; CP 19–10–1964; CG 3–5–1965.

SWALWELL: L/B 19; LO 1867; PS 4583; TI 65213; G Bricks 3031, scrap iron & steel 406, paper making mill 230; L—; CP 2–11–1953; CG 7–3–1960.

SWINE: L/B 36; LO 1864; PS 727; TI 6156; G Wheat 135, barley 130; L 119; CP 19–10–1964; CG 11–11–1963.

TADCASTER: L/B 18; LO 1847; PS 4546; TI 30151; G Ale & ale empties 55530, grain 5456; L 512; CP 6–1–1964; CG 30–11–1966.

TANFIELD: L/B 44; LO 1875; PS 1274; TI 7494; G Manure 612; L 80; CP 1–1–1931; CG 11–11–1963.

TEMPLE HIRST: L/B 87; LO 1871; PS 743; TI 4820; G Potatoes 3598, hay/clover 1134; L 63; CP 6–3–1961; CG 6–7–1964.

TEMPLE SOWERBY: L/B 26; LO 1862; PS 509; TI 5033; G Sanitary tubes 235; L 61; CP 7–12–1953; CG 22–1–1962.

THIRSK: L/B 86; LO 1841; PS 8652; TI 51799; G Potatoes 1921, hay/clover 1602, barley 1182; L 1210; CP—; CG 3–10–1966. REM New station auth. 1–3–1861 £5416.

THORNABY: L/B 21; LO 1830; PS 29412; TI 245768; G NF; L—; R from SOUTH STOCKTON 1–11–1892; CP—; CG—. REM New station auth. 1881, estimate £8211 but actual cost £11482. Opened 1–10–1882.

THORNE: L/B 37; LO 1869; PS 5991; TI 32450; G Hay/clover 9833, bricks 2896, oil cake 1404, potatoes 1355; L 26; R to THORNE NORTH 1–7–1923; CP—; CG 5–4–1965.

THORNER: L/B 46; LO 1876; PS 2889; TI 21617; G Barley 327, potatoes 124; L 36; R from THORNER AND SCARCROFT 1–5–1901; CP 6–1–1964; CG 6–1–1964. REM Also known as SCARCROFT (in 1885).

THORNLEY: L/B 76; LO 1835; PS 3042; TI 43306; G NF; L—; CP 9–6–1952; CG—. REM New station, stationmaster's house and 3 cottages auth. 1910 £1654.

THORNTON DALE: L/B 62; LO 1882; PS 1246; TI 11103; G Barley 228, hay/clover 146; L 16; CP 5–6–1950; CG 10–8–1964.

THORP ARCH (FOR BOSTON SPA): L/B 18; LO 1847; PS 3303; TI 20610; G Barley 186, potatoes 111; L 2; R to THORP ARCH 12–6–1961; CP 6–1–1964; CG 10–8–1964.

THORPE THEWLES: L/B 76; LO 1880; PS 214; TI 2026; G Hay/clover 236; L 92; CP 2–11–1931; CG 2–4–1951.

TOLLERTON: L/B 86; LO 1841; PS 1296; TI 10740; G Hay/clover 1173, potatoes 843, barley 491; L 110; CP 1–11–1965; CG 6–9–1965. REM New station, stationmaster's house and cottage 1899 £1839.

TOPCLIFFE: L/B 50; LO 1848; PS 729; TI 2634; G Barley 253, potatoes 237; L 4; CP 14–9–1959; CG 14–9–1959. REM Also known as TOPCLIFFE GATE.

TOW LAW: L/B 10; LO 1867; SO 1868; PS 5295; TI 40292; G Clay/gannister 8261; L 580; CP 11–6–1956; CG 5–7–1965.

TRENHOLME BAR: L/B 56; LO 1857; PS 1141; TI 7157; G Hay/clover 388, barley 169; L 42; CP 14–6–1954; CG 1–12–1958; REM New station auth. 22–4–1870 £401.

TRIMDON: L/B 28; LO 1839; SO 1846; PS 8407; TI 73604; G Creosote/tar/pitch 1040, manure 301; L 3; CP 9–6–1952; CG 1–1–1962. REM New station and goods warehouse auth. 5–7–1877 £1855.

TWEEDMOUTH: L/B 52; LO 1847; PS 3631; TI 29125; G Manure 5852, timber 5138, oil cake 3603, grain 2563; L 1029; CP 15–6–1964; CG—. REM Tender for roof renewal 20–9–1906 £964, when overall roof was replaced.

TWIZELL: L/B 40; LO 1849; SO Aug. 1861; PS 186; TI 3614; G Barley 265, oats 109; L 57; CP 4–7–1955; CG 5–3–1962.

TYNE DOCK: L/B 59; LO 1834; PS 2064; TI 384137; G Iron ore 399211; timber 174507; paper making materials 35006; oats 13601; L—; R from JARROW DOCK c1859; CP 1–6–1981 (for Metro); CG ???. REM New station auth. 10–2–1881 £21732.

TYNEMOUTH: L/B 81; LO 1882; PS 58816; TI 356302; G Fish 22674, manure & gas lime 19640; L 4; CP 11–8–1980 (for Metro); reopened Metro 11–8–1980; CG 2–3–1959. REM Goods traffic handled at former Newcastle & Berwick Tynemouth station.

ULLESKELF: L/B 90; LO 1839; PS 636; TI 9356; G Potatoes 677, vegetables in bulk 379, barley 251; L 23; CP—; CG 27–4–1964.

USHAW MOOR: L/B 22; LO 1877; PS 5064; TI 98424; G—; L—; CP

29–10–1951; CG 28–12–1964. REM Station authorised 20–12–1883 £398, opened 1–9–1884.

USWORTH: L/B 54; LO 1850; PS 9946; TI 65093; G Bricks 333, potatoes 199, gravel/sand 183; L 15; CP 9–9–1963; CG 14–9–1959.

VELVET HALL: L/B 40; LO 1849; PS 899; TI 9582; G Barley 597, potatoes 206, oats 112; L 248; CP 4–7–1955; CG 29–3–1965.

WALKER: L/B 67; LO 1879; PS—; TI 37247; G Scrap iron & steel 6306, iron & steel 903, locos and tenders on own wheels 302; L—; R from LOW WALKER 13–5–1889; CP 23–7–1973; CG 14–8–1967.

WALKER GATE: L/B 81; LO 1839; PS—; TI 56278; G Scrap iron & steel 2022, wagons on own wheels 874, iron & steel 131; L—; R from WALKER 1–4–1889. CP 11–8–1980 (for Metro); CG 14–8–1967. REM New station 1908 £708.

WALLSEND: L/B 81; LO 1839; PS 41461; TI 322763; G NF (goods traffic handled at Carville, on Riverside branch); L 1; CP 11–8–1980 (for Metro); CG—. REM 13–1–1879 tender accepted for additions and improvements – subway, stationmaster's house and goods warehouse £1725; new station authorised 18–8–1884 £2111.

WARCOP: L/B 26; LO 1862; PS 1300; TI 9107; G Barytes 3976, manure 285; L 133; CP 22–1–1962; CG 18–10–1971.

WARKWORTH: L/B 52; LO 1847; PS 1287; TI 17682; G Hay/clover 221, barley 210; L 164; CP 15–9–1958; CG 2–4–1962.

WARTHILL: L/B 89; LO 1847; PS 819; TI 6476; G Potatoes 532, hay/clover 378, barley 342; L 40; R from STOCKTON-ON-FOREST 1–2–1872; CP 5–1–1959; CG 7–6–1965. REM Interchange sidings with Sand Hutton Light Railway.

WASHINGTON: L/B 54; LO 1834; PS 7297; TI 60760; G Bricks 25547, iron & steel 2074, composition 1861; L 10; CP 9–9–1963; CG 7–12–1964.

WASSAND: L/B 36; LO 1864; PS 62; TI 59; G Wheat 138; L—; R from GOXHILL 1–10–1904; CP 21–9–1953; CG 31–10–1960. REM Market day station open Tuesdays Only from 1–4–1865 and Mondays Only from 1936.

WATERHOUSES: L/B 22; LO 1877; PS 9983; TI 76133; G Bricks 17009, clay/gannister 11624, creosote/tar/pitch 9204, barytes 4877; L 4; CP 29–10–1951; CG 28–12–1964.

WEARHEAD: L/B 83; LO 1895; PS 2143; TI 22721; G Roadstone 34915, ores 6253, clay/gannister 5256; L 83; CP 29–6–1953; CG 2–1–1961.

WEAR VALLEY JUNCTION: L/B 10; LO 1843; PS 1184; TI 16283; G NF; L—; R from WITTON JUNCTION 1872; CP 8–7–1935; CG—.

WEAVERTHORPE: L/B 91; LO 1845; PS 1452; TI 11035; G Barley 1244, wheat 386, oats 227; L 233; R from SHERBURN (Y&S) to WYKEHAM 1–4–1874 and from WYKEHAM to WEAVERTHORPE 1–5–1882; CP 22–9–1930; CG 3–8–1981. REM Renamed Weaverthorpe on opening of Wykeham on Seamer-Pickering line.

WEETON: L/B 45; LO 1848; PS 1218; TI 20244; G—; L 44; CP—; CG 3–5–1965.

WELBURY: L/B 45; LO 1852; PS 1100; TI 10097; G Hay/clover 519, barley 320; L 62; CP 20–9–1954; CG 30–9–1963.

WELLFIELD: L/B 76; LO 1835; SO 1882; PS 3975; TI 37551; G NF; L—; CP 9–6–1952; CG—. REM New station auth. 1890 £4155.

WENSLEY: L/B 33; LO 1878; PS 862; TI 6695; G Timber, round 417; CP 26–4–1954; CG 3–7–1967.

WEST AUCKLAND: L/B 9; LO 1825; PS 6346; TI 51061; G Bricks 6316, creosote, tar & pitch 3591, manure 953; L—; R from ST HELENS 1–3–1878; CP 18–6–1962; CG 15–9–1958.

WEST CORNFORTH: L/B 28; LO 1839; PS 6000; TI 44448; G Creosote/tar/pitch 1585, manure 329, clay/gannister 306; L—; R from THRISLINGTON 1–7–1891; CP 9–6–1952; CG 30–9–1963. REM Station first in timetable July 1866.

WESTGATE-IN-WEARDALE: L/B 83; LO 1895; PS 778; TI 23225; G Ores 4295, clay/gannister 2671, roadstone 1390; L 75; CP 29–6–1953; CG 1–7–1968.

WEST GOSFORTH: L/B 63; LO 1905; PS 280; TI 22599; G—; L—; CP 17–6–1929; CG 14–8–1967. REM Now on Metro line to Bank Foot, opened 10–5–1981.

WEST HARTLEPOOL: L/B 32; LO 1841; PS 65110; TI 552408; G Iron ore 534054, timber 532494, plate iron & steel 136778, pig iron 91254; L 70; R to HARTLEPOOL 20–4–1967; CP—; CG 4–12–1967. REM New station auth. 10–5–1877 £8425, opened 3–5–1880; new platforms opened 18–12–1904. Renaming to HARTLEPOOL also quoted as 1–5–1967.

WEST JESMOND: L/B 12; LO 1864; SO 1900; PS—; TI 112440; G—; L—; CP 23–1–1978 (for Metro), reopened 11–8–1980; CG 14–8–1967. REM New station auth. £5244 and opened 1–12–1900.

WEST ROUNTON GATES: L/B 45; LO 1852; PS—; TI—; G NF; L—; CP 13–9–1939; CG—. REM Open Wednesdays Only.

WETHERAL: L/B 53; LO 1838; PS 2890; TI 41053; G Potatoes 161, timber, round 149; L 54; CP 2–1–1967 but reopened 5–10–1981; CG 1–4–1955.

WETHERBY: L/B 46; LO 1876; PS 3086; TI 46804; G Barley 663, timber, round 558, potatoes 229; L 775; CP 6–1–1964; CG 4–4–1966. REM New station on new site 1–7–1902 £2124. Goods traffic continued to be handled at pre-1902 station.

WETWANG: L/B 47; LO 1853; PS 956; TI 6219; G Barley 1007, wheat 637, oats 193; L 156; CP 5–6–1950; CG 20–10–1958.

WHARRAM: L/B 47; LO 1853; PS 877; TI 4438; G Barley 1630, wheat 438, oats 268; L 131; CP 5–6–1950; CG 20–10–1958.

WHITBY: L/B 84; LO 1835; SO 1847; PS 10762; TI 152062; G Timber 518, manure & gaslime 513, gravel & sand 487, fish 182; L 27; R to WHITBY TOWN 30–9–1951, to WHITBY 5–9–1966; CP—; CG 2–5–1983. REM Goods shed partially destroyed by bombing in September 1940. G. T. Andrews station of 1847 remains in use but train shed roof removed 1953.

WHITBY WEST CLIFF: L/B 68; LO 1883; PS—; TI 69104; G—; L 10; CP 12–6–1961; CG 12–6–1961. REM Now in use as Water Board offices and stores.

WHITEDALE: L/B 36; LO 1864; PS 1280; TI 6558; G Wheat 766, barley 515; L 333; CP 19–10–1964; CG 3–5–1965.

WHITLEY BAY: L/B 15; LO 1882; PS 11436; TI 509974; G NF; L—; R from WHITLEY 1–7–1899; CP 10–9–1979 (for Metro), reopened 11–8–1980; CG—. REM New station opened 9–10–1911, cost station £6175 and platform roofing £5344.

WHITTINGHAM: L/B 3; LO 1887; PS 862; TI 6942; G Timber 511, barley 164; L 462; CP 22–9–1930; CG 2–3–1953.

WIDDRINGTON: L/B 52; LO 1847; PS 1765; TI 15156; G—; L 239; CP—; CG 28–12–1964.

WILLINGTON: L/B 24; LO 1857; PS 12756; TI 125433; G Creosote, tar & pitch 23779, bricks 13800, manure 5989, clay/gannister 4096; L 4; CP 4–5–1964; CG 10–8–1964.

WILLINGTON QUAY: L/B 67; LO 1879; PS—; TI 30684; G Gravel/sand

6966, scrap iron & steel 5282, creosote, tar & pitch 1324, alkali 1134; L—; CP 23–7–1973; CG 2–10–1967.

WILMINGTON: L/B 82; LO 1853; PS—; TI 17459; G—; L—; CP 19–10–1964; CG 3–3–1969. REM New station on new site 9–6–1912.

WILSTROP SIDING: L/B 88; LO 1848; CP 1–5–1931; CG 4–5–1964. REM Passenger service on Saturdays Only.

WINGATE: L/B 28; LO 1846; PS 7662; TI 62644; G—; L—; CP 9–6–1952; CG 1–6–1964. REM New station 1899 £988.

WINSTON: L/B 20; LO 1856; PS 2073; TI 16025; G Barley 376, timber, round 214, building stone 113; L 272; CP 30–11–1964; CG 5–4–1965.

WISTOW: L/B 17; LO 1898; PS 650; TI 5223; G Potatoes 2597, timber, round 967, hay/clover 570; L 26; CP 1–1–1930; CG 2–5–1960.

WITHERNSEA: L/B 85; LO 1854; PS 3055; TI 41610; G Wheat 621, barley 311, gaswater 167; L 147; CP 19–10–1964; CG 3–5–1965.

WITTON GILBERT: L/B 42; LO 1862; PS 3055; TI 41610; G Creosote/tar & pitch 1138, scrap iron & steel 372, manure 344; L 30; CP 1–5–1939; CG 30–9–1963.

WITTON-LE-WEAR: L/B 83; LO 1847; PS 2354; TI 17670; G Clay/gannister 26431, bricks 18127, sanitary tubes 3802, timber 1640; L 43; CP 29–6–1953; CG 1–11–1965. REM New station on new site 15–11–1888 £567.

WOLSINGHAM: L/B 83; LO 1847; PS 3414; TI 29921; G Clay/gannister 21431, iron & steel 3098, timber 548; L 146; CP 29–6–1953; CG 6–9–1982.

WOOLER: L/B 3; LO 1887; PS 1940; TI 13199; G Building stone 3328, barley 508, potatoes 293; L 1354; CP 22–9–1930; CG 29–3–1965.

WOOPERTON: L/B 3; LO 1887; PS 482; TI 2613; G Barley 155; L 128; CP 22–9–1930; CG 2–3–1953.

WORMALD GREEN: L/B 45; LO 1848; PS 1826; TI 14944; G Barley 359, manure 332; L 113; CP 18–6–1962; CG 31–8–1964.REM New station auth. 12–5–1865 £456.

WRESSLE: L/B 39; LO 1840; PS 642; TI 4949; G Hay/clover 676, potatoes 546, vegetables in bulk 238; L 132; CP—; CG 11–5–1964. REM Also rendered as WRESSEL.

WYKEHAM: L/B 62; LO 1882; PS 531; TI 7266; G Gravel & sand 206, timber 183, barley 175; L—; CP 5–6–1950; CG 5–6–1950. Now used as Estate Office for Wykeham Abbey.

WYLAM: L/B 53; LO 1838; PS 2467; TI 45184; G Bricks 440, gravel & sand 200, scrap iron & steel 115; L 348; CP—; CG 26–4–1965. REM Closed temp. 2–9–1966 to 1–5–1967 for bridge repairs.

WYNYARD: L/B 76; LO 1880; PS 277; TI 4064; G Hay/clover 922; L 199; CP 2–11–1931; CG 2–4–1951.

YARM: L/B 45; LO 1852; PS 2715; TI 55615; G Gravel & sand 3626, hay/clover 906, spent bark 605; L 203; CP 4–1–1960; CG 21–9–1964.

YORK: L/B 90; LO 1839; SO 1877; PS 91608; TI 647264; G Flour 101863, scrap iron & steel 13215, timber 6856, wagons on own wheels 5940, manure & gas lime 5263, potatoes 4231; L(at Foss Islands) 7122; CP—; CG (Leeman Road) 3–4–1972. REM Station opened 25–6–1877 with 13 platforms; No 14 added 1900 and Nos. 15 and 16 added 1938. Footbridge erected 1900 and extended to serve Platforms 15 and 16 in 1938. Station buildings damaged by bombing 29–4–1942. Electric signalling installation commenced prior to World War II but not completed until 1951. Platforms renumbered 1938. In 1975 platforms 8S, 8N, 9S and 9N became 8A, 8B, 9A and 9B respectively.

SECTION TWO
JOINT STATIONS

Joint stations and lines were usually provided to cut out wasteful duplication and competition and many formal agreements covering such arrangements go back to the early days of railways. For instance, the joint operation of Normanton station was instituted by an Agreement dated 23 January 1844 between the North Midland (later Midland), Manchester & Leeds (later Lancashire & Yorkshire) and the York & North Midland (later North Eastern). The LNWR was included at its own request from 6 March 1860 but withdrew in 1890. Tebay station was operated under a LNWR/South Durham & Lancashire Union Railway Agreement of 9 July 1860, and Penrith under a LNWR/Stockton & Darlington Agreement of 10 May 1862. As a result of the LNWR/NER Agreement of 24 February 1866 Leeds New station was built.

The operation of joint stations or lines was shared in different ways. In some examples one company would work the line for a certain period and then the other company would work it for a similar period, or one company worked the trains, and maintained the track and signalling, both companies sharing the expense. Items such as buildings and furniture were supplied by one company with the approval of the other, again the two companies sharing the cost. However, the station staff was usually employed by the Joint Committee, with distinctive uniforms or insignia so that the travelling public realised that the station did not belong to either company but was shared. The stationmasters were usually appointed from either company depending on qualifications. The accounts were invariably kept entirely separate and not included in those of either partner.

The companies went to great lengths to ensure that there was no preference given to either partner and there was one classic example where the station notepaper had to be headed 'Midland and North Eastern Joint' and 'North Eastern and Midland Joint' in alternate periods!

However, by some means the Midland did seem to have the edge over the North Eastern, and at Tebay and Penrith, where the North Eastern connected with the LNWR, the NER appeared to be the poor relation, tucked away virtually out of sight of the LNWR main line expresses!

The following Joint Stations and Joint Lines appeared in the 1922 NER timetable:

JOINT STATIONS

Station	Joint Owners	Class of Traffic
Hawes	MR and NER	All
Holbeck	MR and NER	Coaching
Leeds (New)	LNWR and NE	Coaching
Normanton	L&YR, MR and NER	All
Penrith	CK&P, LNWR and NER	All
Tebay	LNWR and NER	All

JOINT LINES

Line	Joint Owners	Controlled by	Passenger Stations
Axholme Joint	L&YR and NER	Joint Committee	9
Otley & Ilkley Joint	MR and NER	Joint Committee	4
South Yorkshire Joint	GCR, GNR, L&YR, MR and NER	Joint Committee	3
Swinton & Knottingley Joint	MR and NER	Joint Committee	6

(NOTE: The Methley Joint line passenger services did not appear in the NER Timetable for 1922. Stations were opened in 1869 at Lofthouse & Outwood, Methley and Stanley; these were closed Lofthouse & Outwood 17–6–1957; Methley South 13–6–1960; Stanley 2–11–1964.)

The largest station in which the North Eastern had a share was Leeds New, opened in 1869, but by the time it became part of Leeds City station in 1938 it was anything but new! Nevertheless, except for a renumbering of the platforms, it continued in use in the same form until extensive rebuilding took place in the 1960s, culminating in the opening of the new Leeds City station by the Lord Mayor of Leeds on 17 May 1967.

In its New Station form the station had three through platforms and seven bays and as altered to handle all the Leeds services at one station it had five through platforms and still seven bays. The centre portion of the 1869 station was covered by three Mansard roof spans, with the centre span smaller than the two outer spans. However, over the years additional protection from the weather had been provided by additional roofing at both ends, but not to the same design.

The Joint Committee set up by the two partners first met on 21 January 1866 and George Leeman, MP, of the NER was appointed

Chairman; one of the first decisions recorded was that the 'connection from Marsh Lane to the LNWR to be pressed on with all speed'.

Before the opening of the station on 1 April 1869 (and yet the Board of Trade did not give permission until 13 April according to NER records) the Joint Committee decided that the station should be in charge of a Superintendent, assisted by three Inspectors at £1 10s, £1 7s 6d and £1 5s per week, with 20 porters (on two shifts), two policemen on day duty and one on night duty, lampmen, waiting room attendant, excess luggage porter etc, with three clerks in the Parcels Office. The name suggested for the station was Neville or Neville Street but it was known as New Station from the outset; this appears to have been taken from the title of the Joint Committee which met to plan a new station rather than the New Station.

JOINT STATIONS
HAWES: LO 1878; PS 2357; TI 10325; G Building stone 778; L 362; CP 26–4–1954 (to Northallerton) and 16–3–1959 (to Garsdale); CG 16–3–1959 (to Garsdale) and 27–4–1964 (to Northallerton).

HOLBECK: LO 1846; PS—; TI 26090; G NF; CP 7–7–1958; CG—. REM New joint station opened 6–6–1862; MR added platform 1873; Joint staff provided from Nov.1898; Tickets issued 1901 49579.

LEEDS NEW: LO 1869; PS 449591; TI (including Marsh Lane) 1047658; G NF; CP—; CG—. REM Became part of Leeds City station 2–5–1938.

NORMANTON: LO 1840; PS 27766; TI (NE only) 20455; G—; L—; CP—; CG—.

PENRITH: LO (L&C) 1846, (NER 1863); PS 9519; TI 21125(NE only); G—; CP (to Darlington) 22–1–1962; CG 4–1–1971.

TEBAY: LO (L&C) 1846, (S&DR 1861); PS 1389; TI 7838; G—; L 37; CP (to Kirkby Stephen) 1–12–1952; CG 2–3–1964.

JOINT LINES
Axholme Joint
BELTON: LO 1904; SO 1905; PS 2154; TI 3575; G—; L—; CP 17–7–1933; CG 5–4–1965.

CROWLE: LO 1903; PS 2853; TI 6952; G—; L—; CP 17–7–1933; CG 5–4–1965.

EASTOFT: LO 1903; PS 486; TI 2633; G—; L—; CP 17–7–1933; CG 5–4–1965.

EPWORTH: LO 1904; SO 1905; PS 1836; TI 6050; G—; L—; CP 17–7–1933; CG 5–4–1965.

FOCKERBY: LO 1903; SO 1904; PS 785; TI 3296; G—; L—; CP 17–7–1933; CG 5–4–1965.

HAXEY TOWN: LO 1904; SO 1905; PS 3194; TI 8253; G—; L—; CP 17–7–1933; CG 1–2–1956.

HAXEY JUNCTION: LO 1904; SO 1905; Population and Tickets Issued included under Haxey Town; G—; L—; CP 17–7–1933; CG 1–2–1956.

LUDDINGTON: LO 1903; PS 632; TI 3036; G—; L—; CP 17–7–1933; CG 5–4–1965.

REEDNESS JUNCTION: LO 1900; SO 1903; PS 164; TI 1851; G—; L—; CP 17–7–1933; CG 5–4–1965.

Otley and Ilkley Joint
BEN RHYDDING: LO 1865; SO 1866; PS 1579; TI 11339; G—; L 34; CP—; CG 5–7–1965. REM Station originally proposed as WHEATLEY.

BURLEY-IN-WHARFEDALE: LO 1865; PS 3966; TI 19337; G—; L 5; R from BURLEY 2–10–1922TT; CP—; CG 27–4–1964.

ILKLEY: LO 1865; PS 7004; TI 54231; G Ale and ale empties 623; L 97; CP—; CG 7–8–1967.

OTLEY: LO 1865; PS 10826; TI 103335; G Scrap iron and steel 619; L 442; CP 22–3–1965; CG 5–7–1965.

South Yorkshire Joint
DINNINGTON & LAUGHTON: LO 1909; SO 1910; No P or G details; CP 2–12–1929; CG 3–5–1965.

MALTBY: LO 1909; SO 1910; No P or G details; CP 2–12–1929; CG 14–6–1965.

TICKHILL & WADWORTH: LO 1909; SO 1910; No P or G details; CP 8–7–1929; CG 2–11–1964.

(NOTE: At closure there was only one train in each direction daily between Worksop, Dinnington & Laughton and Maltby.)

Swinton & Knottingley Joint

ACKWORTH: LO 1879; PS 4876; TI 31888; G—; L—; CP 2–7–1951; CG 1–8–1955.

BOLTON-ON-DEARNE: LO 1879; PS 26027; TI 38164; G—; L—; R Opened as HICKLETON and renamed BOLTON-UPON-DEARNE 1–11–1879; further renamed BOLTON-ON-DEARNE c1900, BOLTON-ON-DEARNE for GOLDTHORPE 14–7–1924TT and finally BOLTON-ON-DEARNE 12–6–1961. CP—; CG 5–9–1966. REM NER note 'All the civil parishes under Bolton-on-Dearne are also served by other companies'.

FERRYBRIDGE FOR KNOTTINGLEY: LO 1879; SO 1882; PS 7549; TI 32076; G—; L—; R from FERRYBRIDGE 1–6–1901; CP 13–9–1965; CG 27–4–1964. REM Station opened 1–5–1882 £2834.

FRICKLEY: LO 1879; PS 4686; TI 8502; G—; L—; R from CLAYTON 1–11–1892; CP 8–6–1953; CG 30–9–1963.

MOORTHORPE and SOUTH KIRKBY: LO 1879; PS 25945; TI 92084; CP—; CG—; R from MOORTHORPE 1–7–1902; to MOORTHORPE 12–6–1961; CP—; CG 10–2–1964.

PONTEFRACT: LO 1879; PS 17023; TI 92084; G—; L—; R to PONTE-FRACT BAGHILL 9–7–1923TT; CP—; CG 2–11–1964.

APPENDICES

1 STATIONS CLOSED IN WORLD WAR I

Station	Closed to Passengers	Reopened to Passengers	
Benton Square	20–9–1915	NEVER	
Brampton Town	1–3–1917	1–3–1920	
Cayton	20–9–1915	2–5–1921	
Crakehall	1–3–1917	6–2–1922TT	
Dunston-on-Tyne	1–5–1918	1–10–1919	
Fyling Hall	20–9–1915	18–9–1920	
Hayburn Wyke	1–3–1917	2–5–1921	
Hessay	20–9–1915	12–7–1920TT	
Knitsley	1–2–1916	30–3–1925	
Newby Wiske	20–9–1915	1–3–1920	
Newport	8–8–1915	NEVER	(Except for excursions)
Smardale	20–9–1915	1–11–1918	
Spennithorne	1–3–1917	18–9–1920	

TT=date of timetable in which first reappeared.

NOTE: The timetable which should have been in force from 1 January 1917 showed the following stations as closed: Arram, Bempton, Botanic Gardens, Carnaby, Enthorpe, Finghall Lane, Londesborough, Marfleet, Settrington, Sexhow and Stepney but this timetable was not implemented and in the next issue, dated 1 March 1917, the stations remained open.

2 STATIONS CLOSED IN WORLD WAR II

Station	Closed to Passengers	Reopened to Passengers
Christon Bank	5–5–1941	7–10–1946
Goswick	5–5–1941	7–10–1946
Grinkle	11–9–1939	NEVER
Hart	28–7–1941	7–10–1946
Little Mill	5–5–1941	7–10–1946
Longhoughton	5–5–1941	7–10–1946
Lucker	5–5–1941	7–10–1946
Newby Wiske	11–9–1939	NEVER
Newham	5–5–1941	7–10–1946
Scremerston	5–5–1941	7–10–1946
Seaham Harbour	11–9–1939	NEVER

3 STATIONS AND HALTS OPENED BY THE LNER (NORTH EASTERN AREA)

Station	Opened	Closed	Remarks
Belasis Lane Halt	8–7–1929TT	6–11–1961	Not advertised after 14–6–1954. Belasis Lane from 3–5–1937TT
Blackhall Colliery	24–7–1936	4–5–1964	
Bowers Halt	15–12–1934	22–1–1951	Bowers from 3–5–1937TT
Broomielaw	9–6–1942	30–11–1964	Converted from private station
Filey Holiday Camp	10–5–1947	26–11–1977	Closure announced 26–10–1977. Last trains ran 17–9–1977
Longbenton	14–7–1947	23–1–1978	For Metro. Reopened 11–8–1980
Osmondthorpe Halt	29–9–1930	7–3–1960	Osmondthorpe from 3–5–1937TT. Used by excursions after closure
Penda's Way	5–6–1939	6–1–1964	
Redcar East Halt	18–5–1929	—	Redcar East from 3–5–1937TT
Seaburn	3–5–1937	—	
Springhead Halt	8–4–1929	1–8–1955	
Strensall Halt	17–9–1926TT	22–9–1930	Served only by local rail-bus to and from York
Tyne Commission Quay	15–6–1928	4–5–1970	Actually owned by Tyne Improvement Commission. Closed 1939–1945. Used only by boat trains.
West Monkseaton	2–3–1933	10–9–1979	For Metro. Reopened 11–8–1980.

TT=date of timetable in which first appeared

4 STATIONS AND HALTS OPENED BY BRITISH RAILWAYS (NORTH EASTERN AND EASTERN REGIONS)

Station	Opened	Closed	Remarks
Boothferry Park	6–1–1951	—	For Hull City Football Club's ground
British Steel, Redcar	19–6–1978	—	Replaced Warrenby (workmen only)
Gypsy Lane	3–5–1976	—	
Hedon Halt	14–8–1948	c10–49	For Hull Motor Cycle Speedway
Newton Aycliffe	1–1–1978	—	
Teesside Airport	3–10–1971	—	

5 THE EFFECT OF THE TYNESIDE METRO

The greatest changes, as distinct from closures, have occurred in the Tyneside area where many of the former North Eastern lines and stations have been taken over by the Tyne & Wear Passenger Transport Executive, which operates the modern electric trains on the Metro network on both sides of the Tyne. Except in the centre of Newcastle and Gateshead the Metro uses former NER tracks, those on the north bank of the river first electrified in 1904, and those south of the river in 1938, although both were de-electrified in the 1960s by BR and the services taken over by diesel multiple-units.

Most of the NER station locations have been retained, many with their old buildings replaced by Metro structures, but some have disappeared from the network for good, such as Manors North, Heaton, Jesmond and Backworth north of the river, and Gateshead East and Pelaw south of the river, the latter replaced by a Metro/BR/Bus interchange at Heworth, a short distance to the west. Backworth has been replaced by Shiremoor, while Jesmond has survived as a restaurant, with the added attraction of accommodation in an old Great Northern coach standing on what was the platform. In addition the Metro now runs to Bank Foot, on the former Ponteland branch, originally intended to be electrified when opened in 1905, but the expected housing development did not take place at that time and the branch lost its steam worked service in 1929.

In the course of constructing the Metro system it was necessary to pass below Newcastle Central Station and in 1977 it was found that the tunnelling work was affecting the east end of the station portico dating from 1863. This had to be closed in May 1977 and in the following month work commenced on dismantling this part of the structure. After completion of the Metro tunnel the portico was rebuilt and reopened in 1979. The line also passed under Gateshead Diesel Traction Depot and here it was constructed on the cut-and-cover method.

The smaller stations on the North Tyneside circle have been modernised as economically as possible; mostly the old NER buildings have been removed and simple prefabricated structures erected on the refaced and resurfaced platforms. Typical examples are Walkergate, Wallsend and Percy Main. Some of the stations on the coast are little changed and still recognisable as former North Eastern stations; Cullercoats, Whitley Bay and Monkseaton are good examples. Tynemouth is also little changed except that the Metro utilises only two platforms, leaving six bay platforms and the station buildings empty and unused because of pressure to preserve the station. North Shields has gained a bay platform at the west end for the daytime service to and from St James, and because of an open level crossing at Howdon the platforms have been staggered, with the new platform on the east side of the level crossing and on the site of a loading dock. A number of new stations have been inserted on the surface lines, such as Hadrian Road (between Wallsend and Howdon), Smith's Park (between Percy Main and North Shields), Shiremoor (between West Monkseaton and Benton, replacing Backworth), Ilford Road (between South Gosforth and West Jesmond) and others.

South Gosforth is a mixture of old and new and it is now the operational control centre for the whole system, supervising train running, power supplies and station working from three control positions in the control room, each with its own display panel. This new building occupies most of the former down platform and also accommodates the trainmen's facilities as most crew changing takes place at South Gosforth, where there is also a staff canteen. The 'something old' is the metal footbridge retained to give access between platforms and, surprisingly painted a bright red and looking unfinished, as though it has been left in a red lead primer!

The underground stations are spacious, clean and bright, utilising modern materials; at Monument, the hub of the system, there is a circular wall enclosing the foundations of the Grey monument directly above. At Central Station there is direct access from the Metro system into the concourse at the BR station and this, from my experience, satisfies a long-standing need as in pre-Metro days many of the local road transport services could not be conveniently reached from Central Station. During the day there is a three-minute service between Heworth and South Gosforth, with a ten-minute service on the coastal circle.

As completed, the Heworth–South Shields section was the last to open early in 1984, and it has since been announced that a new station is to be built on the site of the former BR station at Pelaw. The Metro serves 41 stations and covers 34 route miles.

6 SIDINGS DIAGRAMS

Around the turn of the century the NER issued a diagram of the track and buildings layout at every station and siding including sidings not situated at a station. By Grouping in 1923 the diagrams had reached a total of almost 1400, ranging from a small sheet with a single siding for a farmer, to numerous large folded sheets for the large installations at Hull, York, Middlesbrough, Newcastle, etc.

The drawings were prepared by the Civil Engineer's Department, and although not to scale they were roughly in proportion. In the Civil Engineer's Department they were known as Sidings Diagrams, but in all other Departments as White Prints, even though some were printed in white on blue paper.

Their main purpose was to give a record of the amount of wagon standage available at each station or depot, taking the average length of a wagon as 21ft, and they were also used to produce the annual track mileage statement for the Ministry of Transport. The Civil Engineer's copy used to record the relevant drawing numbers of switch and crossing renewals, and were kept up to date with details of track alterations and abandonments.

All sidings were numbered and listed in tables giving the total length of the siding and its standage capacity, with the clearance point generally taken as 6ft between gauge faces, although many NER sidings did not reach this figure anywhere along their length! Some diagrams also numbered and tabulated the running lines using the prefix T for through lines and R for running lines. Some private sidings were numbered and tabulated where the maintenance was carried out by the NER under an agreement with the trader.

The North point was always shown but other information was variable; for instance bridge numbers, platform lengths and the location of water cranes were not always given, and it was sometimes difficult to tell from the diagram whether roads crossed the line on the level or by an underbridge. Distances, where quoted, could be to the branch end, to the next station or junction, or to the next major station.

A selection of 12 diagrams is given. The first two are 'as issued' but the remainder have been specially redrawn for this work by J. F. Addyman. They cover

As issued	Ferriby	1926
	Ferrybridge	1925
Redrawn	Coldstream	1909
	Chathill	No date
	Christon Bank	1926
	Broomhill	1921
	Pelaw	1920
	Chester-le-Street	1927
	Etherley	1928
	Brompton	1923
	Masham	1930
	Burton Agnes	1908

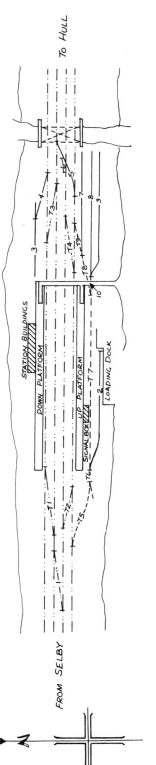

FERRIBY

TO HULL

FROM SELBY

STATION BUILDINGS

DOWN PLATFORM

UP PLATFORM

SIGNAL BOX

LOADING DOCK

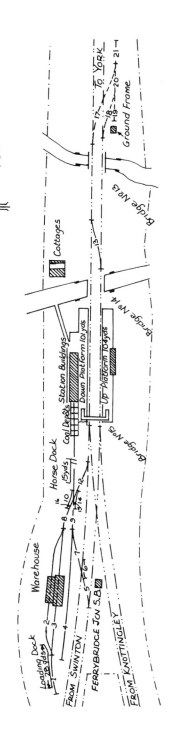

FERRYBRIDGE JUNCTION

TO YORK

Ground Frame

Bridge Nº 13

Cottages

Bridge Nº 14

Station Buildings

Coal Depôts

Down Platform 101 yds

Up Platform 104 yds

Bridge Nº 15

Horse Dock

Warehouse

15 yds

Loading Dock 28 yds

FROM SWINTON

FERRYBRIDGE JCN S.B.

FROM KNOTTINGLEY

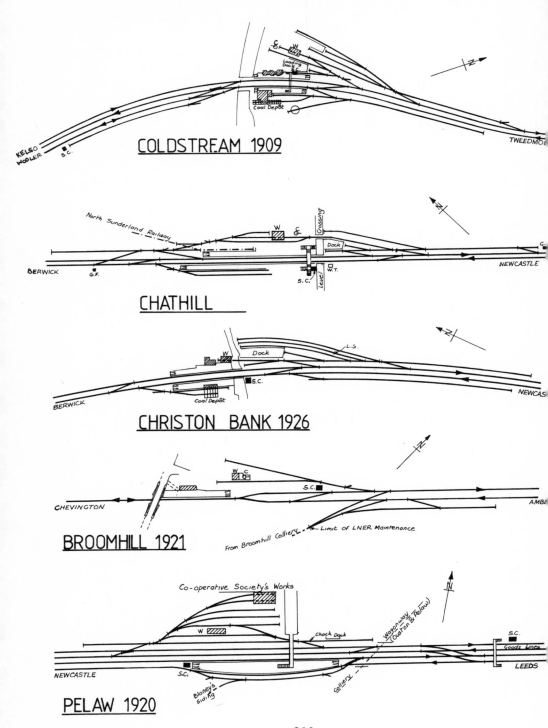

COLDSTREAM 1909

KELSO
WOOLER
S.C.

TWEEDMO

CHATHILL

North Sunderland Railway

BERWICK
G.F.
NEWCASTLE
W
C
Crossing
Dock
Level
W.T.
S.C.
G.

CHRISTON BANK 1926

BERWICK
W
Dock
L.S.
S.C.
Coal Depôt
NEWCAS

BROOMHILL 1921

CHEVINGTON
W C
S.C.
AMBL
From Broomhill Colliery — Limit of LNER Maintenance

PELAW 1920

Co-operative Society's Works
W
Chock Dock
Wagonway (Ouston & Pelaw)
S.C.
Goods Lines
NEWCASTLE
S.C.
Blaney's Siding
Colliery
LEEDS

210

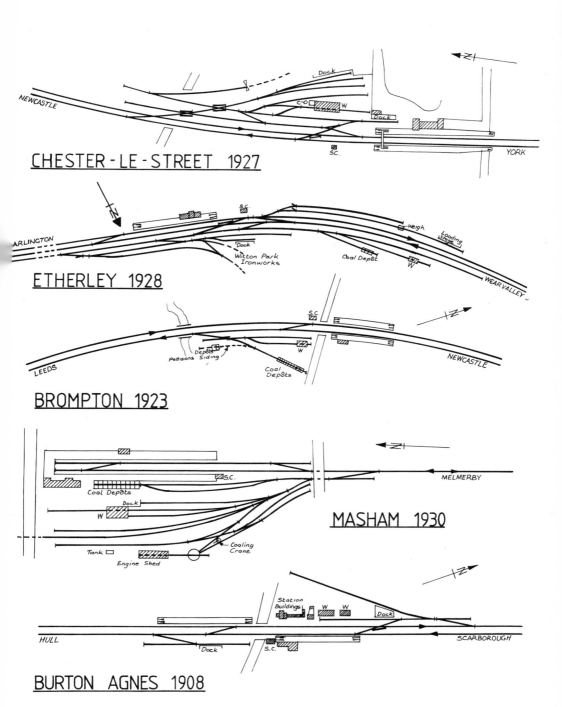

CHESTER-LE-STREET 1927

ETHERLEY 1928

BROMPTON 1923

MASHAM 1930

BURTON AGNES 1908

211

INDEX

213